Introduction to Media and Politics

Introduction to Media and Politics

Sarah Oates

Los Angeles • London • New Delhi • Singapore

First published 2008

Apart from any fair dealing for the purposes of research
or private study, or criticism or review, as permitted under
the Copyright, Designs and Patents Act, 1988, this
publication may be reproduced, stored or transmitted
in any form, or by any means, only with the prior
permission in writing of the publishers, or in the case of
reprographic reproduction, in accordance with the terms
of licences issued by the Copyright Licensing Agency.
Enquiries concerning reproduction outside those terms
should be sent to the publishers.

SAGE Publications Ltd
1 Oliver's Yard
55 City Road
London EC1Y 1SP

SAGE Publications Inc.
2455 Teller Road
Thousand Oaks, California 91320

SAGE Publications India Pvt Ltd
B 1/I 1 Mohan Cooperative Industrial Area
Mathura Road
New Delhi 110 044

SAGE Publications Asia-Pacific Pte Ltd
33 Pekin Street #02-01
Far East Square
Singapore 048763

British Library Cataloguing in Publication data

A catalogue record for this book is available from the
British Library

ISBN 978-1-4129-0261-8
ISBN 978-1-4129-0262-5

Library of Congress Control Number: 2007930355

Typeset by C&M Digitals (P) Ltd., Chennai, India
Printed in Great Britain by The Cromwell Press, Trowbridge, Wiltshire
Printed on paper from sustainable resources

Contents

Preface

Whenever I prepare a lecture on media and politics, I agonize over how much I feel I have left out. When I teach the students, I can see them agonizing over how much I have put in. This book represents an attempt to get that balance right – to inform and elucidate without alienating the reader with too much analysis at once. As a result, this book offers what I hope is enough analysis to provide the questions and sufficient information in the three case studies of the U.S., the U.K., and Russia for people to start to answer critical questions on media and politics in their own way.

It is not until you are an American teaching the politics of the Russian media to a roomful of British students that you realize how much we are all bounded by our own understanding of what is "good" media practice. We rather blindly accept things in our own countries – naked women on page 3 of the *Sun* newspaper in Britain, mindless local news announcers on local U.S. television, bold-faced bias on the Russian news – that just wouldn't "fly" in another place. This is what has fascinated and intrigued me perhaps most of all – bits of the media that I find abhorrent, other people find not only acceptable, but even praiseworthy. I am assured by my students that paying an annual license fee for television is an important part of democracy, although I find it strange that I have to pay both my cable bill and the BBC license. Back in the U.S. and bombarded by advertising, Americans assure me that commercial television is the only option (never having peacefully enjoyed a commercial-free film on the BBC). In Russia, the notion of objectivity is laughable and, anyway, news *is* politics and you're fooling yourself if you think differently. All of these people have a point, none of them is wrong, and none of them is necessarily right. But what does it all mean?

One of the central points to this book is that it is really hard to reach an understanding of the value of what your media offer until you get a good look at what others have in different places. That is why the book uses the U.S., the U.K., and Russia to contrast and compare media systems in ways to get people thinking about the generally unseen relationship between democracy and free media. In the U.S., there is grave concern that we are so hooked on entertainment that citizens refuse to pay attention to serious issues – which means that news programs now refuse to cover them. In Britain, the growth of commercial television as well as the visible power struggle between the government and the BBC raise some real questions about the future of public service news values. Scandals, wars, terrorism coverage, mud-slinging election campaigns, and the rise of an online world that seems to change overnight, all appear to contribute to an atomized media that parallels a fragmented society. But when these problems are contrasted with those of the Russian media sphere, the dilemmas of American and British news values seem quite trivial in comparison. Once media freedom falls below a critical point – as it has done in Russia – there is little to stop one political faction from seizing and maintaining power indefinitely. The media wield great political power. It is often just very hard to see that until it disappears and the citizens no longer have a voice – even a distant, distorted, unequal voice.

I stumbled upon a way to spend my life comparing the media and politics of all three countries. Fresh out of college in the U.S. in the 1980s, I suffered from the delusion that I wanted to be a journalist. I was lucky, for I had experience as a stringer for *The New York Times* and as editor-in-chief of *The Yale Daily News*. I was an intern at *The Washington Post*, *The Wall Street Journal*, *The Miami Herald,* and *Los Angeles Times* Washington bureau before landing a full-time job at the *Orlando Sentinel* in Florida for six years. If you had told me during those years that I was engaged in grounded fieldwork for my academic career, I would have laughed. Most days I was just trying to make deadlines, avoid getting a really boring assignment from my editor, and trying to get time for lunch (or dinner as well if I was stuck at my desk). There is no question, however, that my experience as a reporter and editor has informed my research in media and politics. In particular, I felt that journalists in and of themselves had little power. As a result, I wanted to study the entire machinery of media and politics.

I quit journalism in 1992 to get a PhD from Emory University in political science, writing a dissertation about the burgeoning Russian political parties, election campaigns, and how they were covered on television. Fieldwork took me to Russia in 1995, where I watched parties try – and mostly fail – to market their messages to the voters via television. I started my first research job at the University of Glasgow in 1996, working with scholars to further understanding of the Russian political system. Meanwhile, I was fascinated by the differences in British television and news culture. Did people really talk that way? For my first undergraduate seminar at the University of Glasgow, I thought I would try out an idea of teaching about media and politics in comparative perspective, surmising that a class on Russian political parties probably would not attract the minimum numbers. I expected 20 students to enrole; 72 showed up and my first media and politics class was under way with standing room only.

Since then, I have taught at least one class in media and politics every year. In 2006, the Department of Politics at the University of Glasgow launched a post-graduate program in political communication, which I founded and now co-direct. Every year, my students continue to challenge and amaze me. Their comments, essays, and exam answers prove to me that the analysis of media and politics provides one of the most interesting interpretations of political life. There have been many times in class when my students have made the intuitive leap. Are terrorists politicians or criminals? Why is war coverage almost always shown from the point of view of the soldier, and not from the point of view of the citizen? How can a system call itself democratic if only rich people can afford political advertising? Last year I asked a question on the exam about whether terrorism can be considered "armed propaganda", which I thought would have students reflecting on Northern Irish leader Gerry Adams' comments about terrorism. Instead, most students interpreted this as a way to theorize about how governments – not terrorist groups – use their military might to impose their political views on other cultures. Once again, they were way ahead of me.

This book is written in the hope it can spark the same sorts of discussion and ideas in other classrooms. Funding for research that is cited throughout this book came from three grants from the British Economic and Social Research Council (R223250028, R228250048, R000223133) as well as from the Leverhulme Foundation for a research fellowship in 2003–4. Aside from my graduate and undergraduate students, there have been many people who have been very helpful in writing this book. In particular, I would like to thank my three co-lecturers on media and politics over the years – Mike Berry, Will Dinan, and Ana I. Langer. They know a lot more about British media and politics than I do. I also would like to thank people with whom I have worked on Internet research, especially Rachel K. Gibson and Paul Reilly. In addition, research partners on projects stretching from Missouri to Moscow have been very helpful in educating me about comparative media and politics. I would especially like to thank Lynda Lee Kaid, Gillian McCormack, and Laura Roselle for their help and insight. Participants in the 2006 Media Literacy program at Kyiv-Mohyla Academy in Ukraine provided amazing academic and personal insights from their first-hand experience with media in emerging democracies. Murray Leith and Kate Smith have helped me to become more informed about British (and especially Scottish) mass media and politics. Lucy Robinson and David Mainwaring at SAGE have been helpful, understanding, and most of all patient beyond measure. David, Laura, and Emma Cross provided their usual support on the home front. All errors and omissions are, of course, my own. If you would like to keep up with the trials and tribulations of teaching and learning media and politics, please visit my website: www.media-politics.com.

Sarah Oates
August 2007

Introduction

⌐1

Overview

1.1 As individuals, we tend to remember important events in modern history through their media coverage. Every generation in contemporary society has a set of images and words associated with defining political moments, from the assassination of John F. Kennedy in 1963, to the images of the planes hitting the World Trade Center on 9/11, to the sight of Western soldiers on the streets of Baghdad. As societies, we communicate, share, and attempt to come to terms with political events through the mass media. At the same time, most people are aware that there is a range of filters in place that shape this relationship between politics and the mass media. In some countries, the mass media focus more on light news and entertainment at the expense of serious political analysis. In other places, state-run or public media dictate a greater emphasis on the needs of society rather than the demands of commercialism. Much of the time, viewers, listeners, and readers are fairly complacent about what they learn from the mass media. Yet, at times of change and crisis – ranging from elections, acts of terrorism, war, to the collapse of a regime – citizens find themselves in great need of comfort, information, and even direction from their mass media.

How can we understand the dynamics between modern mass media and the political sphere? It is a complicated yet fascinating relationship that has engaged scholars and analysts for decades. This scholarship, which has provided a range of useful insights into the relationship among politics, media, and citizens, spans different disciplines and subject areas. Most studies tend to focus on a single country, which can make it difficult to see cross-national or international patterns. As a result, it is often challenging for students who are intrigued by the power of the mass media in politics to know where to start a serious study in this area.

This book is designed to bring together a broad range of theories and analysis in order to synthesize an introduction to the field of media and politics. In particular, this text is designed to strengthen the field of comparative media studies, which looks at the relationship between the mass media and politics in ways that offer more than a description of one country's media and political system. Rather, the idea is to allow us to see how this relationship can work in a broader, more generalizable manner. Throughout this book, there is an emphasis on applying research design and method to the study of media and politics. There are two central challenges to comparative media and politics. The first is moving from being descriptive to becoming analytical. In other words, it is not enough to know that most television outlets in the U.S. are run as commercial organizations and that the main television outlet in Britain is a public body. What difference does that make? Does it mean that the journalists who produce the news at these stations work differently? How does the broadcast content differ? What do the audiences in the U.S. and the U.K. think of their own television channels? Would Americans prefer to have an influential public television station – or do British viewers really hanker for television that is more commercial? How does a system dominated by either commercial television or public television react when faced with crises such as terrorism, war, vitriolic election campaigns, or the major changes wrought by developing technology? Which system fosters more responsible citizens?

Clearly, these questions cannot be answered without relevant research. Not only are these intriguing inquiries for the citizens (and media organizations) in these countries, but they are part of larger puzzles as well. What are the strengths and weaknesses of various media systems? Are there particular media systems that better support democracy? By the same token, are there types of media systems that tend to subvert or undermine democracy? This text will give students the information to analyze these questions. The book focuses on broadcast, print, and internet media in comparative perspective, basing much of the analysis on the two influential media systems of the U.S. and the U.K. The text has a particular focus on news outlets. In addition, this book uses a range of case studies and information from other countries, particularly from the intriguing media sphere in the Russian Federation and other non-free states, to show how media operate in non-democratic systems. The text strives to give enough factual information on the workings and significant stories in these systems in order for students to assess the situation analytically. It is particularly important to realize that what is accepted as the status quo in one country might be considered a violation of norms of good journalism in another country. Media systems, media content, and audiences differ a great deal from country to country. This book looks for both similarities and differences in the interaction between media and politics to reach general conclusions. For example, it is difficult to assess whether paid political advertising has a negative impact on democracy without looking at one country that allows it and another that does not.

This chapter will begin the discussion of comparative media and politics with an introduction to various models of how the media relate to the political world. Further chapters of the book will present key points about the relationship between media and politics, including the production of news, the journalistic profession, the nature of the audience, elections, war coverage, terrorism, and the internet. The text will introduce each of the main concepts and then present important examples from the U.S., the U.K., Russia, and other countries. Readers will then be encouraged to develop their understanding of how and why there are differences – and similarities – among the media systems in these countries. Each chapter will provide a summary of central points, study questions, references, as well as websites with material suitable for further research. The goal of each chapter is to "jump-start" analytical thinking, giving students and researchers the ability to assess ideas and carry out their own research in the field.

Studying media and politics: what do we look at first?

1.2 One of the most important aspects of studying media and politics is to be very clear about which element of the relationship is under analysis. In particular, are you examining the effect that the media have on politics or the impact that the political system has on the mass media? In the first case, for example, one might be interested in the effect of television coverage on the election results in the 2004 U.S. presidential contest. In other words, how much difference did television – whether it was news coverage, paid political advertising, or the debates – make in terms of how people chose to vote? Clearly, there will be a range of other variables affecting voter choice, such as people's political party affiliations, how they are doing economically, where they live, and other factors. The media coverage would be just one of these elements in influencing choice at the polls. On the other hand, you could turn the question around to ask how television itself is influenced by a range of political factors. In that case, you might choose to undertake a study of the changes in election news coverage over the course of the 2004 campaign between George Bush and John Kerry. Once you had measured how the campaign coverage had changed, you could then consider which factors – events such as the televised debates, reports from the war in Iraq, possible new security threats, hints of scandal – might have changed the direction of this coverage. Thus, you can study the interaction between the media and politics from different perspectives.

Once you are clear about whether you are studying the impact of the media on an element in politics or the effect of politics on the media, you need to think about what part of the media sphere itself is under examination. This book generally divides the media sphere into three main categories. The first category is *news production*, which relates to all the factors that are involved in the creation of media output in the form of broadcasts, newspapers, internet content, etc., within a particular country. This includes a country's political environment, the media norms, media regulation, ownership of media outlets, as well as how the journalistic and public relations professions carry out their jobs. The second broad category to scrutinize in the study of media and politics is that of *content*. This includes studies of what is actually transmitted or printed in outlets such as the broadcast news, newspaper stories, radio broadcasts, and websites. The third category is that of the *audience*, analyzing how people react to what they see, hear, and read in the mass media. If you divide the study of the media and politics into these categories, it becomes much easier to examine the relationship between media and politics in a comparative perspective.

To return to the example above of election coverage, the first research category of news production would be concerned with all the elements that affect how news is produced. For example, you could look at whether owners of media organizations had any influence on the daily editorial meeting at newspapers. Additionally, you could study how journalists picked which events to cover and which sources they used most often. You could compare the difference in how American and British journalists followed candidates on the campaign trail. Content studies are relatively straightforward, if somewhat time-consuming. They typically involve the measurement of coverage devoted to particular issues, people, or themes. Content analysis of television, however, can be quite difficult because of the range of images and nuance in the broadcasts (not to mention the time and trouble of recording or retrieving the content). Finally, how does the audience react to news content? Do people accept it unthinkingly? What parts do they absorb and what parts do they ignore? Do they feel that they are impervious to slant or bias in the news? What media sources do they trust? Where do they turn in a national crisis, such as after an act of terrorism or during a war? Do Americans and Russians, for example, expect the same sort of coverage of terrorist acts? Does that coverage leave them feeling more secure or more vulnerable to a security threat? Finally, how does the audience reaction dictate how the news producers plan their coverage?

This three-step model of media production/environment, content, and audience is not static. The constraints of the media environment and its production will dictate, to a large degree, the type of content that is produced by a media outlet. Even when two media outlets in the same country are presented with the same event, they will cover it at least slightly differently. When various media in different systems – whether in the U.S., the U.K., or Russia – are presented with terrorism, war, elections, or other major events, they often will cover them very differently indeed. Which way is the most democratic? What effect does this approach to coverage have on content? For example, election coverage in the U.K. is far more focused on issues than in the U.S., while election coverage in Russia has become increasingly biased and propagandistic. The content, in turn, dictates the range of responses from the audience. While U.S. audiences would probably find the BBC news staid, British audiences would certainly find U.S. local television news trivial and excessively chatty. One audience might expect and welcome a level of censorship in war coverage while another audience would feel that a certain level of dissemblance on the part of war correspondents was a violation of their civil rights. Looking at media audiences in a comparative perspective will quickly reveal that norms and expectations about media content differ markedly among people in different nations. This, in turn, influences the first element in this three-step model of analysis, namely the production of news. Those who produce the news are aware of the expectations of the audience and should seek to meet the needs of that audience as consumers or as citizens – or as some combination of both.

Classic models of media and politics

1.3 It is useful to look at how people have conceptualized the relationship between media and politics, although it is also important to remain flexible to account for different types of media environments, content, and audience. One of the classic ways to attempt to model the mass media comes from work by Siebert et al. (1963). They divided the world's media into four models: libertarian, socially responsible, authoritarian, and Soviet. Siebert and his colleagues argued that the Soviet press model required that the press support the Marxist-Leninist view of reality; the authoritarian model called for a press completely subservient to the state; the libertarian model supported the notion that opinions should be aired freely; and the social responsibility model held that media should work proactively to include all segments of society in its coverage (see Table 1.1).

Although these models have been criticized as being simplistic and an artefact of the Cold War, they provide a useful starting point for a discussion of the media and the public in a generalized way. All of these models represent "ideal" situations, as opposed to actual media systems. However, the authors of *Four Theories of the Press* certainly had particular countries in mind in developing each model – and the models are useful for understanding the broad parameters of media systems. The libertarian model parallels the U.S. media market, while the social responsibility model comes closer to that of the U.K.

Table 1.1   Classic models of media systems

Model	Definition
Libertarian (Commercial)	The media are free to publish what they like. Attacks on the government are allowed and even encouraged in the interest of bettering society. Journalists and media organizations are given full autonomy.
Social responsibility	The media are not completely free to publish what they like as they have certain obligations to society to provide information and balance. The media should provide access to all groups. The media and the government are partners in constructing civil society.
Authoritarian	The media serve the needs of the state through direct governmental control. The media are not allowed to print or broadcast anything that could undermine the established authority or give offence to the existing political values. Control is by censorship and punishment of those caught breaking the rules.
Soviet	In theory, media serve the interests of the working class and the sense of limit/censorship is imposed by the consciousness of the journalists in solidarity with the workers. In practice, the Soviet media were controlled by the state as in the authoritarian model.

Source: Derived from Siebert, Peterson and Schramm (1963)

broadcasting sector. However, even with those matches, there are interesting exceptions within each country, notably the British tabloid newspapers that exploit scandal and even scaremonger in the quest for more sales. This would place the British tabloids closer to the libertarian model than the social responsibility model. The Soviet system has collapsed, but the Soviet model is still useful in understanding the poor performance of the media as a pillar of civil society in many post-Soviet states (not to mention present-day China). Finally, the authoritarian model is still recognizable in countries around the world, including Iran and Burma.[1]

Much of the discussion among people who analyze media systems focuses on either the libertarian model or the social responsibility model. Is one system better than the other? Unsurprisingly, countries tend to approve of their own system, but it is clear there are advantages and disadvantages to both systems in terms of the role the media play in democracy (see Table 1.2). For example, the libertarian system is considered to be driven by the needs of consumers, hence the chief obligation of the news media in free societies is to provide the general public with information about significant current events – as well as with entertainment. The libertarian model is also often referred to as the "commercial" model of the news. Anything that happens that seems interesting or important for media audiences may become news. It should be reported quickly, accurately, and without any attempt to convey a particular point of view. It is left to the audience to decide what to believe and what to

Table 1.2 Comparing the libertarian and social responsibility models

	Libertarian model	Social responsibility model
Definition	Driven by the needs of the consumer and often called the "commercial" model. Chief obligation of the news media in free societies is to provide the general public with information about significant current events and entertainment. Anything interesting or important for media audiences may become news. Reported quickly, accurately, and free from opinion. Left to the audience to decide what to believe and what to question.	News producers design news output to support a civil society and discourage anti-social behavior. Media output should reflect social concerns. Media should foster political action and publicize social evils. Media should not broadcast undesirable viewpoints and questionable accusations, even if sensational. Media should hold government accountable when necessary.
Role of audience	Can absorb all messages and decide what is important.	Given information to promote acting responsibly.
Role of media	Provide all information deemed of interest.	Provide information in a responsible manner.
Primary perception of audience as ...	Consumers	Citizens
Primary perception of journalists as ...	Information providers	Gatekeepers
Mostly adhere to this model	U.S. – although tends more toward social responsibility model in times of war or terrorist acts on U.S. targets.	U.K. – although its tabloid newspapers adhere to the libertarian model as do some commercial television broadcasts.

question. The libertarian media system reduces the the power of the media to serve as political "gatekeepers," making issues of media ownership and journalistic bias less important.

If the system is consumer-driven, then it is much less vulnerable to manipulation, either by a powerful group of elites or by inchoate masses. It places a high level of trust in the audience to decide what is important and to synthesize the critical messages about society. Yet, this high level of trust in the audience can be problematic, as studies suggest that people often pick entertainment over serious issues. In addition, unfiltered news can lead to panic, insecurity, or even danger such as in the deadly 1992 Los Angeles riots that were sparked by broadcasts that white policemen had been acquitted of a crime in savagely beating black motorist Rodney King. There are legitimate concerns that unfiltered information, released without regard for its societal impact, can lead to serious problems. In the short term, this can mean violence. In the long term, it can mean the erosion of the rational fabric of society.

The social responsibility model of the media should address some of these problems by having a more considered policy about the use of information in society. The social responsibility model of the news suggests that producers design their news output to support a civil society and discourage anti-social behavior (Negrine, 1994). Or, as Graber (2005: 22) phrases it, "adherents to the tenets of social responsibility believe that news and entertainment presented by the mass media should reflect social concerns". This turns the mass media into the guardians of public welfare, who "should foster political action when necessary by publicizing social evils" (such as preventing nuclear contamination or stopping child abuse). The media should not broadcast undesirable viewpoints and questionable accusations, even if they are sensational. However, if the media believe that the government is hiding information vital to the public interest, journalists should seek that information out and make it public.

The benefits of the social responsibility model of the media, when compared with the more free-wheeling libertarian model, are clear. The social responsibility model provides a level of protection to society, from everything ranging from bad taste to information that could lead to panic or violence. It protects the public from damaging, distorted, or dangerous information. Overall, it works toward building a societal consensus while the libertarian coverage of the same news might destroy that harmony. The social responsibility model of the media helps to maintain a sense of common good and, most probably, build a sense of nationhood. On the other hand, it deprives citizens of the right to act on full information – even if that could lead to injustice or violence – and gives media organizations much more power over the distribution of information in society. If the media take on a greater "gatekeeping" role, then they are more at risk of either information manipulation or control by forces such as the government.

Many modern political communication scholars reject the models developed by Siebert et al. (1963). For example, Bennett (2000: 204) finds it more useful to think about the media's relationship to political power when assessing the impact of media on societies. Bennett derives three aspects of perceptions of political power from Lukes' (1974) typology of power in society: People either accept political actions that affect them as legitimate; or they resist them; or they resign themselves to being powerless about these actions. The media can feed into these conceptions in three ways. First, media can frame coercive power within societies in ways that can "encourage, discourage, hide, or expose it" (Bennett, 2000: 205). In addition, the media can be selective in their formal political coverage, reporting on some politicians and their activities while ignoring others. Finally, media are important for "transmitting values, problem definitions and images of people in society that provide resources for people in thinking about their lives and their relations to government, politics and society" (ibid.). This final definition is particularly important in a transitional society, a country in which there has been an authoritarian regime and where democratic institutions are still weak. Yet, it is also dangerous, in the sense that an emphasis on values that divide the population or fail to foster civil society – such as a focus on nationalism of the dominant group or strong leadership over mass preference – can have a detrimental effect on the development of civil society.

However, if the mass media choose to "lead" their audience by attempting to challenge majority beliefs too vehemently, they run the risk of losing both the audience's attention and its trust. This is complicated by the fact that it is often hard to gauge the opinion or mood of an audience, particularly when journalists become somewhat isolated from average citizens. In addition, public and commercial media outlets cannot act in isolation from the competition. Even if their funding structure allows them to ignore short-term popular trends (as is technically true of the BBC), if they lose audience share to a point at which they fail to communicate messages to a significant number of people, then they become marginalized. There is compelling evidence that media pursue their own interests and traditions. Media in the U.S., in spite of growing concerns over "infotainment," still devote a relatively large amount of coverage to elections. In turn, the BBC continues to cover ceremonial state occasions such as the opening of Parliament at Westminster and the laying of wreaths for the war dead on Remembrance Day, notwithstanding their lack of dynamic viewing value. This idea is supported by work by Schudson (1995), who makes a compelling argument that media and culture are intertwined – and it is impossible to understand a media system without understanding its historical and cultural parameters.

Concerns arise when what could be termed tradition becomes too open to control by a particular group or part of the government, such as a charismatic leader and his or her following. This issue is also linked to the larger debate about media ownership. In Europe, where the consensus is that state or public-funded television is vital to society, there are quite serious conflicts about state control over news broadcasts. In addition, there is widespread criticism of the U.S. media in elections, with claims that the coverage has become little more than a "horse race" with candidates gaining less and less time to speak for themselves (Patterson, 1994). Arguably, the U.S. media are continuing the tradition of covering elections, yet offering less useful and unbiased information to the voters. If established democracies and media systems such as the U.K. and the U.S. face serious issues in terms of openness and control, the problems for less democratic systems are even starker. Sparks (2000) suggests that the whole argument about public media versus commercial media misses the point. He posits that the discussion of media and society should be re-ordered from an examination of public versus commercial media to consider who controls the media under *any* type of ownership. For example, Sparks argues that two of the classic models of the media from Siebert et al. (1963) (Soviet and libertarian) do not work because economic and political power are so intertwined in both systems. Thus, the systems can never really be contrasted since the basic component of media control is in the hands of elites, whether you are in a libertarian or authoritarian media system. For Sparks, power is more important than whether media controllers are in the state-funded sphere or the commercial sphere.

The four models listed above generally focus on how the media system relates to the ruling government and the audience. Graber (2005) finds it useful to theorize about media in a slightly different manner by categorizing them according to the manner in which they approach news coverage. This overlaps somewhat with the models from Siebert et al. (1963), yet provides an additional method of comparing media in different systems. Graber divides the news media into four models: mirror, operational, political, and professional (see Table 1.3). In the mirror model, news should simply be a reflection of reality. In the organizational model (akin to organizational theory found in management studies), news is thought to emerge from pressures inherent in the organizational processes and goals of media organizations. The political model suggests that the news reflects the ideological biases of individual journalists and their media organizations. Finally, the professional model posits that news making should be viewed as an endeavor of highly skilled professionals, seeking to create news that attracts consumers and citizens.

Graber's models are useful in terms of theorizing about how the news is made, particularly how the media environment shapes the media content (the first two steps of the three-part model outlined earlier). However, these models are slightly narrower than those suggested by Siebert et al. (1963) in that all but the political model do not really take into account the broader political context in which media must operate. This includes leaving out the third component of the model, the audience, in theorizing about the relationship between media and society. These four models delineated by Graber, however, do represent four diverse yet measurable ways in which media operate in the real world.

There are two additional media models that suggest a slightly different relationship, where the media play a less passive role in politics. A few U.S. newspapers have experimented with the democratic-participant model of having a more equal and interactive relationship between the media and the audience. This is particularly relevant when thinking about the possible role of the internet in politics. This idea of "civic" journalism involves initiating actions such as town meetings in order to stimulate political interest. However, studies suggest that it is relatively difficult to motivate disengaged citizens, even with the extra incentives of town meetings or website forums. On the other hand, the *developmental democracy model* is about making the relationship between the media and the audience less equal by giving media the power to withhold certain facts and distort other information in the attempt to support a young democracy. For example, this would involve journalists turning a blind eye to mild levels of corruption in an administration if they felt that the leader was genuinely trying to build democratic institutions. The main issue with the developmental democracy model is that it could be easily subverted to justify

Table 1.3   Models of news production

Model	Definition	Benefits to model	Flaws in model
Mirror	News should be reflection of reality.	News is not distorted or biased by production.	Unrealistic, impossible to cover all events. News producers must make choices about focus, highlighting, filtering the news, or there will be information overload. Discounts political bias and pressures.
Organizational	News emerges from pressures inherent in the organizational processes and goals of a news organization.	Differing outputs from various media organizations provide evidence for this (particularly as compared cross-nationally). Observations of journalists suggest that they are constrained by organizational factors.	Does not consider the fact that actual events also will affect the news. Discounts political bias and pressures. Ignores the notion that journalists may have professional norms that can counter organizational behavior.
Political	News reflects the ideological biases of individual journalists, as well as that of media outlets. Only high-status, approved people covered by news; those who do not support the system are ignored or vilified.	Provides strong support for a regime. Fits evidence from some media systems particularly well.	News becomes a powerful tool for oppression. Does not consider the fact that actual events will also affect the news (except in authoritarian regimes in which there is such widespread control that events can go uncovered).
Professional	News making viewed as an endeavor of highly skilled professionals. Events selected for importance, attractiveness to media audiences, and balance.	Consumer-driven and apolitical.	Skilled professionals may act as filter of unpleasant or unpopular, albeit important news. Leaves out element of civic responsibility, such as hearing about dull, yet critical economic policy or election campaigns. Could lead to dumbing-down and pandering to the audience.

Source: Derived from Graber (2005)

the undemocratic consolidation of power by elites, rather than be used as the eventual conduit for expression by the masses. While at times mass opinion can be destabilizing, a deliberate decision to distort the issues is always worrisome. This speaks to the vital question of whether the means can justify the ends – and whether democracy can be created without freedom of speech.

All of this begs the question of the role that the mass media should play in civil society. Unsurprisingly, this is a question that has intrigued philosophers for centuries and is the subject of a wide range of books (some of the classics in the twentieth century are Dahl, 1989, Habermas, 1989, and Huntington, 1991). While it is clear that the view on what constitutes democracy is culturally specific, most critics agree that the media play a crucial role in fostering civil society. Commentators vary somewhat on the exact nature of this role. While Dahl perceives democracy as an ideal rather than an actual type of governance, he sees freedom of expression, media freedom, and the right to expression as key components of civil society. Habermas argues that the media provide a critical "sphere" in which the public can debate and discuss policy as they continually forge a better society. Huntington perceives the media as important in an educative role – and the more educated the citizens, the better chance there is for democracy. There are different definitions, however, in terms of what constitutes "education" and what is really just "propaganda," definitions that vary not only from regime type to regime type, but even among countries with relatively similar political ideologies.

It is this idea that Hallin and Mancini (2003) explored by comparing media systems and trying to model the role of the media in the political sphere in ways that are more subtle and perhaps more useful than those suggested more than 40 years ago by Siebert et al. According to Hallin and Mancini, one of the central problems with Siebert et al.'s *Four Theories of the Press* is that the elements of all of the models except the Soviet model are evident in many democracies. In fact, Hallin and Mancini claim that these four theories, which had little link to actual comparative research, have "stalked the landscape of media studies like a horror-movie zombie for decades beyond its natural lifetime" and there is need for "the development of more sophisticated models based on real comparative analysis" (2003: 10). By using the study of political systems in North America and Europe, Hallin and Mancini devised the liberal model, the democratic corporatist model, and the polarized pluralist model (see Table 1.4).

As Hallin and Mancini defined and tested their models, it became clear that it is very difficult to usefully compare entire media systems. In addition, they found that the forces of commercialization and globalization were leading to "considerable convergence" among media systems in different countries, making it that much more difficult to construct models that analyzed the media and political sphere within a single country (ibid.: 12). While their three models offer a more nuanced understanding of how media systems operate today and are based on modern-day research, they also show the limitations in trying to define "models" that usefully explain the relationship between media and politics in a comparative context. This book will refer to models and use them as ways of informing broad ideas about this relationship. However, it is often more relevant to look at particular components at each of three basic levels of the media and politics relationship – the media environment, content, and audience – in a comparative context. For example, it can be more illuminating (at times) to compare war coverage on the BBC and CBS than to talk about the overall role of the media in war coverage in general.

Table 1.4 Hallin and Mancini's media models

Model name	Definition	Countries on which it is based
Liberal	Relative dominance of market mechanisms and commercial media. Relatively small role of state.	Great Britain, Ireland, U.S.
Democratic corporatist	Historical co-existence of commercial media and media tied to organized social and political groups. Relatively active, but legally limited, role of the state.	Northern continental Europe
Polarized pluralist	Integration of media into party politics, weaker historical development of commercial media. Strong role of the state.	Mediterranean countries of southern Europe

Source: Hallin and Mancini (2003)

Audience studies

1.4 How does the audience react to the various ways in which political news is presented to them? Various studies, including Berelson et al. (1954), have dismissed the notion that media consumers are easily swayed by propaganda. Rather, the relationship between the audience and media messages is perceived as a complex, interactive association. In particular, it is difficult to isolate the effect of media messages, because they are only one factor in a range of political influences. This is made even more complex by the fact that people tend to select media that support their pre-existing political viewpoints. Most people seek confirmation, rather than challenge, from their media outlets. That being said, there is a range of ways (which will be discussed in more detail in later chapters) in which audience effects can be measured. Focus groups encourage people to speak more descriptively and in depth about how they are affected politically by the mass media. In addition, there exists a range of mass public opinion surveys that ask people to report their media use and reactions. These are particularly useful in looking at variations in audience factors – such as usage, trust, interest, preferences, likes, or dislikes – that relate to political news. It is clear that understanding the audience means considering not only short-term reactions, such as being repelled by a candidate who uses negative advertising, but also conceptualizing the long-term socializing effects of how the media report on politics in general.

Assessing media freedom

1.5 One of the most compelling questions is whether the media are either contributing to democracy or helping to suppress the population's political freedoms. At times, abuses of media freedom are quite obvious, such as in the clear censorship of the mass media in China or in the high number of murdered journalists in Russia. At other times, however, it is more difficult to compare some of the more subtle elements of media freedom. Several non-governmental organizations (NGOs) track different levels of media freedom and report regularly on how various political systems are performing. For example, Freedom House publishes an annual report on media freedom, in which various elements of media systems in countries around the globe are rated on a scale of "completely free" to "completely unfree" (www.freedomhouse.org). This organization based in Washington, DC examines categories of legal, political, and economic freedoms as they relate to the media and assigns each country a score. Their findings suggest that media freedom is by no means universal. In its 2005 survey, which ranked media systems in 194 countries and territories, Freedom House judged 39 percent as free, 26 percent as partly free, and 35 percent as not free. The U.S. and the U.K. were both ranked as free, 29th and 34th in the world respectively. Russia was ranked at 151st and judged as not free. A trio of Nordic countries (Finland, Iceland, and Sweden) were ranked as having the freest media systems in the world, while North Korea was ranked as having the least free.

As the rankings suggest, there is a bias toward Western values in the system, which is not surprising given that Freedom House was very much a product of the Cold War. The international NGO Reporters Without Borders (www.rsf.org) also compiles an annual index, based on 52 criteria that affect journalists personally (including murders, imprisonment, physical attacks, and threats) and news media (censorship, confiscation of issues, searches, and harassment). In its investigation into such incidents from September 1, 2003 to September 1, 2004, the organization ranked the U.S. as 23rd out of 167 countries and the U.K. as 29th. Once again, Nordic countries were found to have the most free media systems and North Korea the least free.

While the rankings generated by Freedom House and Reporters Without Borders allow for comparisons among countries as well as over time, it is often difficult to quantify media freedom meaningfully because of the huge variation in media norms from country to country. Other international organizations routinely report on the media situation around the world. For example, Amnesty International issues regular warnings and reports about the violation of media freedom, as does Internews. In addition, Reporters Without Borders produces a "blacklist" of individuals who have isolated the human rights of journalists that have been grossly abused. In July 2005, this list included individuals in Argentina, Bangladesh, Colombia, Gambia, Guinea, Malawi, Mexico, Pakistan, the Philippines, and Peru. Ironically, places in which there is virtually complete control of media by the state tend to have relatively little violence against journalists (such as China or Uzbekistan), although journalists are vulnerable to arrest and imprisonment. The Committee to Protect Journalists publishes a list of the ten worst enemies of the press (which in May 2001 included Russian President Vladimir Putin) for the first time. In May 2005, the same organization issued a list of the top five "most murderous" countries for journalists: Bangladesh, Colombia, Iraq, the Philippines, and Russia.

Content of the book

1.6 This book will cover several important themes as an introduction to media and politics in a comparative perspective. As with any text, this book cannot reference all of the relevant work in this field, particularly as political communication is an immense area that stretches across political science, sociology, management studies, film studies, English, and beyond. As such, the chapters are designed to give students a grounding in some of the main arguments and analyzes of the field. Most of the chapters are structured around an informed discussion involving the three central case studies of the U.S., the U.K., and Russia. However, the chapters on the internet and research methods take a slightly different approach, organizing the work along more international concepts and a focus on slightly different examples. Each chapter has an introduction, subject headings with the main ideas, a synopsis of the central points in each section, a summary of the chapter, and discussion questions related to the chapter material. Each chapter also includes a section on further reading and internet resources. It should be noted that there are many excellent and exciting places on the internet to look for more information, analysis, and even raw data on comparative media and politics. The websites listed in this book were generally chosen as places that offer some valuable resources for further research and analysis. Where it is helpful, the book will include tables to summarize key concepts and information.

The central themes covered in the book are the forces that shape news production, including a separate chapter on the journalistic profession and public relations. In addition, the book covers audiences in a comparative perspective; media and elections; media and war; media and terrorism; the role of the internet in the political sphere; and an introduction to research methods in the study of media and politics. The internet, as a major communications tool, also appears in the discussions throughout the book. Much of this text is designed from experience in teaching media and politics courses to undergraduates and graduate students. In addition, the work derives from several research projects, including a comparative study of the framing of the terrorist threat in recent election campaigns in the U.S., U.K., and Russia; a ten-year study of the demise of freedom of the media in Russia; a comparative study of media freedom across the former Soviet Union; and a project that brought together 13 scholars to look at the most recent developments of the internet in politics.

Book structure

1.7 After this introductory first chapter, Chapters 2 and 3 concentrate on the first element of the three-step media and politics model, namely media production and environment. In particular, the chapters discuss the elements of the News Production Model, which theorizes that news is produced by passing through a series of filters, from political environment, media norms, regulation, and ownership of media outlets. In the final step or "filter," news content is influenced by the nature of the journalistic profession, as well as by public relations efforts. Organizing the study of the media environment around the concept of a series of steps through which news is formed allows students and researchers to consider each of these elements in a cross-national perspective.

Chapter 2 will discuss political and media environment, media norms, regulation, and ownership via the three central case studies of the U.S., the U.K., and Russia. What emerges are distinct differences that are useful in comparing and contrasting the appropriate role of the forces of media production in the formulation of a civic society. The News Production Model allows us to conceptualize the relative impact of the different elements of the news-making process on what people see, read, and hear on a daily basis in the news. A model of the news production process in a comparative perspective also allows us to filter out what is mere description, and to focus on the relative importance of different elements in analyzing the political role in the production of news.

Chapter 3 turns to the intriguing subject of the people themselves who carry out the business of news reporting: journalists and, to an increasing extent, public relations professionals. Journalists have certain established professional practices within countries, but the notions of news making vary enormously among countries. In the U.S., the idea of "objectivity" is held up as a standard and remains an important way of understanding the nature of the U.S. journalist, even though it is under threat in some ways. In the U.K., the standard held up is "balance" rather than "objectivity" in a schizophrenic system in which television is held to high standards but some segments of the print media revel in scandal and muck-raking. In Russia, journalists are perhaps best defined as political and economic pawns, although some achieve power in their own right as the voice of political forces. What are the different professional journalistic norms, particularly those of self-censorship, which have developed among journalists in different countries and media systems? What are some of the crises faced by journalists, such as at the BBC after the suicide of a key source in a story on reported flaws in the government's case to go to war in Iraq? Chapter 3 also will provide information on the craft of the journalist – such as the process of news construction and presentation – and how this varies among countries. As the relationship between public relations consultants and reporters continues to develop, does it shut out less organized (and less well-financed) voices?

Chapter 4 looks at the media audience, using studies of media consumers in the U.S., the U.K., and Russia to explore ideas about the nature of the relationship between news consumption and politics. Interestingly, the study of the media audience is often overlooked. While differences in media environment and content tend to be rather obvious, the nature of their relationship with the audience often remains somewhat hidden. We know there is some effect of media usage, but how do we define it? What does it mean in different media and political systems? Levels of usage and trust vary among different media outlets both between countries and within countries themselves. Does this matter? What does it mean if trust in a public television system erodes? Why do people trust the media so much more than many other political institutions? Varying segments of the audience have quite different relationships with the mass media. Some are empowered by the information, some are indifferent, while still others are alienated from the political sphere altogether by what they see, hear, or read. Understanding these nuances and comparing them across country boundaries will allow us to gain a better understanding of the relationship between media and politics in general.

Chapter 5 discusses elections and the media. The way in which candidates and parties are covered on the nightly news can have a relatively large amount of power in influencing undecided voters. In addition, countries have a range of approaches to allowing paid and unpaid appearances by political parties and candidates on television during election campaigns. This chapter compares and contrasts the libertarian U.S. model, in which massive amounts are spent on televising political advertising, with the U.K. system, which bans paid political advertising on TV. In addition, the chapter discusses how the Russian mass media retarded the development of political parties and subverted the construction of an electoral democracy. It is important to consider not only how media in elections can subvert, rather than support, democracy both in the specific case of Russia as well as in the broader comparative sense. Are citizens being empowered or merely duped by election campaigns?

Chapter 6 discusses and analyzes the media coverage of war, particularly how it has become controlled in a quite distinct way in democratic systems. The coverage of war has developed from the "Vietnam Model" of confrontational war correspondents to the "Gulf War" model of a docile, self-censoring media in the service of the military. This chapter traces the developments that have led to a marked decrease in openness and freedom of information in the coverage of conflict. In particular, the chapter focuses on how the British pioneered principles of media control in the Falklands War in 1982, taming journalists with a pool system, self-censorship, and the appeals to nationalism that now predominate. The chapter will include a discussion of the news coverage of U.S. and British military campaigns in Iraq. The chapter will contrast the notion of a "controlled" free media during war with that of the complete news blackout and widespread human rights violations in Chechnya.

The coverage of terrorism creates some of the same issues for media involving war and state security, yet also presents particular challenges for the media. As discussed in Chapter 7, terrorism creates an enormous tension between state security and the public's right to information. The situation is gravely complicated as terrorists target the audience as well as the actual victims of the violence, thus turning the media into unwilling players in the terrorist scheme itself. While the British media have dealt with terrorism in Northern Ireland for decades, the American media have faced a different conception of threat since the 9/11 attacks in 2001. The chapter includes material from focus groups on how the American public has reacted to ongoing coverage of terrorism since 9/11, as well as findings from British focus groups in the wake of the London bombings in July 2005. The American audience expresses frustration and patriotism in almost equal measure. On the other hand, the British audience appears more ready to discuss terrorism within a political context, long used to terrorism discussions within the political framework of Northern Ireland. Americans continue to support a balance between state security and openness that favors freedom of speech, albeit with little introspection about the causes of terrorism. Given a more socially responsible media system, British media users appear to favor more control of the media in the interest of social cohesion. Research in Russia shows that the public and the media are locked into a cycle of hatred and vilification of Chechen terrorists (and even ordinary Chechen citizens) that leaves only the most extreme political options for either the Russian military or Chechen militants.

Although the internet is discussed in specific contexts throughout the volume, Chapters 8 and 9 take an in-depth look at the internet's role in the political sphere. Chapter 8 will discuss the "civic" side of the internet, analyzing ways in which the internet functions as part of the democratic process in the U.S., U.K., and other countries. This will include an analysis of the central theories in internet studies in democracies, usage of the internet, and attitudes toward the internet. It includes case studies that illustrate the ways in which governments, parties, social groups, and others have attempted to use the internet to build what they perceive to be better societies and citizens. Chapter 9 considers the role of the internet in politics in a different way, by analyzing the internet's potential for protest and political resistance. This will include a look at the Chinese internet "Great Firewall" as a model of multi-level internet control by the state. In addition, the chapter will examine the role of the internet in the Chiapas movement, alternative views on the Chechen war, as well as the formation of the Orange Revolution in Ukraine. The chapter will weigh the evidence about the efficacy of terrorists' use of the online world.

Chapter 10 is designed to give students and new researchers in the field a quick introduction to the central ways in which to study media and politics. This chapter first provides a quick guide to hypothesis formation for studies of media and politics, allowing researchers to turn ideas into good research design. The chapter discusses key qualitative methods in the field, including in-depth interviewing, focus groups, as well as the analysis of broadcast, print, and internet content. In addition, the chapter provides a brief introduction to quantitative data, suggesting in particular how to use public opinion data in theorizing about the relationship of the media to the political sphere.

Finally, Chapter 11 will offer a brief synopsis and review of the main findings of each of the preceding chapters. In particular, the conclusions will underline the value of comparing media systems across national boundaries in order to understand the critical interaction between media and politics.

Study questions

- Why is it useful to study the media in different countries in order to understand the general relationship between media and politics?
- Describe and discuss the three-step model of media production, content, and the audience.
- What are the advantages and disadvantages of having a libertarian media system? What are the advantages and disadvantages of having media that operate under the social responsibility model?
- In what ways do the models of the media suggested by Graber and others help us to better understand the relationship between news and politics?
- What do studies suggest about how the audience is influenced by the mass media?
- How is media freedom worldwide tracked and analyzed by non-governmental organizations?

Reading guide

For a good overview of the U.S. system, which includes factual information as well as theoretical ideas in a very readable format, see Graber (2005). For the British system, see McNair (2003) or Negrine (1994). For the Russian system, see Oates (2006). To further explore some of the theories about the relationship between media and politics, consult Siebert et al. (1963) as well as Graber (2005). Hallin and Mancini (2003) provide an interesting, updated discussion about media models in a comparative context. Negrine (1994) discusses media models in the British context. For more ideas about the relationship of media to society, see Sparks (2000). In the same edited volume, Bennett (2000) discusses interesting ideas about media and politics. The edited volume itself (Curran and Parks, 2000) offers a good overview of a range of media systems. Gunther and Mughan (2000) also provide a range of key insights in their edited volume on democracy and media, particularly in the first chapter (by Mughan and Gunther).

Internet resources

www.cpj.org   The Committee to Protect Journalists is an international NGO that issues an annual list of the ten worst enemies of the press. It also publishes other reports on media abuses, including the list of the five "most murderous" countries for journalists in 2005.

www.rsf.org   Reporters Without Borders [Reporters Sans Frontières] is an international NGO that defends journalists, other media contributors, and professionals who have been imprisoned or persecuted for doing their work. It issues warnings and reports about journalists who are under threat and compiles an annual index of media freedom.

www.freedomhouse.org   Freedom House is a non-profit, non-partisan organization that promotes a "clear voice for democracy and freedom around the world," according to its website. It issues an annual report on media freedom worldwide.

www.people-press.org   The Pew Research Center for the People and the Press is a non-profit research organization that provides a wealth of survey data and reports on the media, the public, and politics in the U.S. The website provides many reports and much data (free to download) that is useful for writing scholarly work.

www.annenbergpublicpolicycenter.org   The Annenberg Public Policy Center of the University of Pennsylvania is a policy center with a particular emphasis on the role of media in the political sphere.

www.fair.org   FAIR (Fairness and Accuracy in Reporting) reports annually on perceptions of how power shapes media content.

www.amnesty.org   Amnesty International is an international, NGO that campaigns for human rights, including compiling a list of abuses of media rights.

www.internews.org   Internews is an international, non-profit organization that works to foster independent media and promote open communications policies in the public interest.

Note

1   According to media freedom rankings by Reporters Without Borders (see www.rsf.org).

References

Bennett, L.W. (2000) "Media Power in the U.S.." In Curran, J. and Park, M.-J. (eds.) *De-Westernizing Media Systems* (pp. 202–20). London: Routledge.

Berelson, B., Lazarsfeld, P., and McPhee, W. (1954) *Voting: A Study of Opinion Formation in a Presidential Campaign*. Chicago: University of Chicago Press.

Curran, J. and Park, M.-J. (2000) "Beyond globalization theory." In Curran, J. and Park, M.-J. (eds.), *De-Westernizing Media Systems* (pp. 3–18). London: Routledge.

Dahl, R. (1989) *Democracy and Its Critics*. New Haven, CT: Yale University Press.

Graber, D. (2005) *Mass Media and American Politics*, 7th edn. Washington, D.C.: Congressional Quarterly Books.

Gunther, R. and Mughan, A. (2000) *Democracy and the Media: A Comparative Perspective*. Cambridge: Cambridge University Press.

Habermas, J. (1989) *The Structural Transformation of the Public Sphere: An Inquiry into a Category of Bourgeois Society*. Oxford: Polity.

Hallin, D. and Mancini, P. (2003) *Comparing Media Systems: Three Models of Media and Politics*. Cambridge: Cambridge University Press.

Huntington, S. (1991) *The Third Wave: Democratization in the Late 20th Century*. Norman, OK: University of Oklahoma Press.

Lukes, S. (1974) *Power: A Radical View*. London: Macmillan.

McNair, B. (2003) *News and Journalism in the UK*, 4th edn. London: Routledge.

Mughan, A. and Gunther, R. (2000) "The Media in Democratic and Nondemocratic Regimes: A Multilevel Perspective." In Gunther, R. and Mughan, A. (eds.) *Democracy and the Media: A Comparative Perspective* (pp. 1–27). Cambridge: Cambridge University Press.

Negrine, R. (1994) *Politics and Mass Media in Britain,* 3rd edn. London: Routledge.

Oates, S. (2006) *Television, Democracy and Elections in Russia*. London: Routledge.

Patterson, T.E. (1994) *Out of Order.* New York: Knopf.

Schudson, M. (1995) *The Power of News.* Cambridge, MA: Harvard University Press.

Siebert, F.S., Peterson, T., and Schramm, W. (1963) *Four Theories of the Press.* Urbana, IL: University of Illinois Press.

Sparks, C. (2000) "Media Theory after the Fall of European Communism: Why the Old Models from East and West Won't Do Anymore." In Curran, J. and Park, M.-J. (eds.) *De-Westernizing Media Systems* (pp. 35–49). London: Routledge.

The News Production Model

2

Central points

- The News Production Model allows us to analyze the relative influence of the political environment, media norms, regulation, ownership, and the journalistic profession on the production of news.
- The U.S. media operate under a libertarian system with virtually no publicly funded outlets.
- The British media system is split, with social responsibility the norm for broadcasters and libertarianism in its print sector.
- The Russian media operate in a "neo-Soviet" system, in which the media remain political players in service to the state and self-censorship is endemic.

Introduction

2.1 When citizens of one realm encounter media from another country, they often are surprised or even shocked by what they find. Not only are they sometimes confronted by news they might find gruesome or just in bad taste, but they may perceive a lack of what they would consider objectivity or balance. Within our own culture, we have a tendency not to judge whether the way in which something is covered is the *best* way to go about telling a news story. However, a survey of different media systems around the world will quickly reveal that what is normal or acceptable in one country's media would be considered wrong or even offensive in another culture. For example, in local television news in the U.S., the anchors often have a cozy chat or joke, drawing the viewers in with what they consider to be a friendly appeal. Many British viewers of the more staid BBC news programs would be somewhat appalled by this bit of banter alongside serious news stories. By the same token, an American reader would be shocked to discover a topless woman on page 3 of a serious national newspaper. Yet in the U.K., the "Page Three Girl" in the *Sun* is a national institution that virtually everyone accepts as a matter of course. Opinion clearly spills over from editorial pages onto the news pages of British newspapers, in which two different newspapers may cover a single story in a very different manner. In Russia, no one is particularly surprised that prime state-run television channels devote an inordinate amount of time to the president – and ignore or belittle legitimate political opponents. Russian journalists reject the notion of objectivity or balance, perceiving themselves as political pawns or perhaps political actors – but almost never as political watchdogs.

At first glance, it would appear difficult to define and analyze how news is produced in different countries. As it is confusing to identify all of the factors that contribute to that diversity, it is useful to try to isolate what causes these variations. Central factors that create news divergence in different countries include variations in the political environment, media regulation, ownership, and the professional norms of journalists, as well as the level of development of the public relations industry. All of these elements will differ at least somewhat from country to country – and some of these factors even vary at different media outlets within the same country. What makes the study of the mass media across country boundaries so interesting is that these differences force us to think more analytically about the role of the media in the political sphere in general. There is no one standard media system, even between countries such as the U.S. and the U.K., which have relatively similar political cultures. Rather, certain traditions and characteristics of the mass media have emerged over time. These features, however, are not static. In particular, technological changes – ranging from the invention of the printing press to the introduction of television to the explosion of the internet – alter media systems. In the case of each country under study in this book, there is a media model that can usefully explain much of the relationship between news and politics, but often one single model cannot embrace an entire system, even for just one country. Rather, it is important to look at relevant factors at all three levels of media analysis outlined in Chapter 1 – news production, content, and the audience – to see which elements can be usefully compared and analyzed across country boundaries.

A central point that Michael Schudson makes in *The Power of News* is that it is impossible to separate "news" from "culture"; what journalists "produce and reproduce is not information – if there is such a thing; it is what is recognized or accepted as public knowledge given certain political structures and traditions" (1995: 31). In other words,

> Journalism is not the sum of the individual subjective experiences of reporters and editors but the source or structure that gives rise to them. It is the matrix of institutions and outlooks that produce people who understand their situations in these terms. (Ibid.: 12)

Schudson sees journalistic output as shaped by a series of factors, this "matrix" that gives rise to the particular news content that people see, hear, or read around the world. This chapter works at categorizing and defining these forces acting on the individual journalist, while the next chapter of this book specifically addresses the journalistic and public relations professions themselves. In this chapter, the text focuses on the forces that shape news production by introducing a News Production Model. This is a model of news production that allows one to measure, assess, and evaluate a range of key factors that contribute to news production. The chapter will first introduce and discuss the components of the model. It will then employ the three central case studies of the U.S., the U.K., and Russia to discuss how these factors may vary across country boundaries. The News Production Model allows us to conceptualize the relative impact of the different elements of the news-making process on what people see, read, or hear on a daily basis in the news. A model of the news-making process in a comparative perspective also allows us to filter out what is mere description, and focus on the relative importance of different elements in analyzing the production of news.

One element that pervades the study of media and politics – from news production, through content, and into audience studies – is the notion of "framing." Framing was classically defined by Ervin Goffman (1974) as the process through which societies reproduce meaning. This is interpreted by social scientists as the series of information and communication short-cuts that people take on a daily basis in order to navigate their way through a complex reality. This is paralleled in the mass media, which constantly makes these "framing" short-cuts in order to communicate the relatively entropic nature of reality in a comprehensible way. What interests those who study the media is how these frames develop, how they are expressed in media content, and how they are received by the audience. An example of media framing would be the "war on terror," a particular media frame that has been very successfully used by the Bush administration as a justification for increased security measures for the U.S. as well as the invasion of Iraq and Afghanistan (Entman, 2003). According to other work by Entman,

> to frame is to select some aspects of a perceived reality and make them more salient in a communicating text, in such a way as to promote a particular problem, definition, causal interpretation, moral evaluation, and/or treatment recommendation for the item described. (Entman, 1993: 52)

Tankard (2001: 96) defines a frame as "a central organizing idea for news content that supplies a context and suggests what the issue is through the use of selection, emphasis, exclusion and elaboration."

As these two definitions suggest, the concept of media framing varies substantially, even within the study of media and politics. While some scholars see it as a useful defining tool, others see the notion of media framing as something that stretches across many levels of the study of media and politics. Reese (2007: 150) defined frames as "structures that draw boundaries, set up categories, define some ideas as out and others in, and generally operate to snag related ideas in their net in an active process." Thus, framing is not just about how a story is presented in the final version; it also attests to how the story was conceived by those who produce the news – as well as how it is received by the audience. Framing reaches across all three levels of the study of media and politics specifically addressed in this volume. As such, framing is mentioned throughout the book.

Defining the News Production Model

2.2 This model is loosely based on the "funnel of casualty" developed by Campbell et al. (1960) to help conceptualize, measure, and understand American voting behavior. As in the voting behavior model (discussed in more depth in Chapter 5), the idea is that the way in which news is produced is contingent upon a series of filters. These filters start at the broadest category and continue to refine the news as it passed through a series of progressively narrower category filters. The Model of News Production is set out in Figure 2.1.

The model encourages us to conceptualize how news output – the media content – is shaped by these various factors. Admittedly, this is flawed in the sense that it suggests that the production of news is necessarily a linear process. In reality, the production of news may be influenced by these elements in a non-linear or rather chaotic way. However, conceptualizing news production as a series of refining filters allows us to isolate important elements that lead to divergent coverage. For example, the collapse of a national oil enterprise would no doubt be covered quite differently on NBC in the U.S., on the BBC in the U.K., or on the state-run First Channel in Russia. We know this from experience with actual coverage, but how we can conceptualize the factors that lead to these differences? The News Production Model, as outlined below and then discussed via the case studies, attempts to do just that.

Filter 1: political environment

The primary filter in modeling news production is the general political condition of the country. While this is a sweeping category, it is important to consider the overall political environment in which media organizations must function. Siebert et al. (1963) highlight this in their four models of the press as authoritarian, Soviet, libertarian, and socially responsible (discussed in

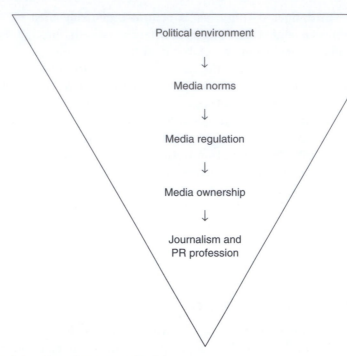

Figure 2.1   News Production Model

Chapter 1). However, these models are too broad for a useful, detailed analysis of news production in a single country. Work by Hallin and Mancini (2003) developed more contemporary models for North American and European countries that are more detailed and up to date. They struggled, however, to find models that could describe the link between media and political forces in a generally comparative way. Nonetheless, these models make an important contribution to our understanding in stressing that the media must operate within certain political parameters. For example, both the U.S. and the U.K. are essentially democratic, law-based societies with rather predictable election cycles and justice systems. Russia has regular elections, but they do not translate popular demands into an accountable government. Rather, Russia remains a society in which law is neither transparent nor predictable. Power is generated exclusively from the top down instead of from the bottom up, with a narrow group of leaders controlling the executive, legislative, legal, and economic levers of the country. All of this affects the media.

Filter 2: media norms

As discussed in Chapter 1, there are quite different convictions about the appropriate role that the media should play in politics. The definition of this role varies greatly from country to country, but generally falls into recognizable models or types. The U.S. has a libertarian media system, in which the media are almost all run as businesses and the news coverage is considered to be consumer-driven. In the U.K., there is a mixture of two models. Broadcast media are generally run under the principles of the social responsibility model, in which there is an expectation that the news should lead public opinion rather than follow it. However, much of the British print media, especially the raucous tabloid newspapers, fall more into the libertarian model of the media. Finally, the Russian media now follow a type of "neo-Soviet" model, in which all media of any significance are pressured or coerced into supporting government policies. It is closer to a reinvented type of the Soviet model, in that external pressures are generally not necessary as journalists and media outlets are typically "on message" with the current regime.

Filter 3: media regulation

Within the general political system of a country, there is specific regulation of the media. In the U.S. and the U.K., this regulation stems from the general principle of freedom of speech as the right of citizens. The right to free speech, however, is challenged in democracies in particular by issues of national security, including the climate of insecurity generated by terrorist attacks on native soil. Although freedom of speech is a right listed in the 1993 Russian Constitution, it is a principle that is not upheld by the everyday political reality of Russia. There are a plethora of laws that regulate the mass media, but very little legal protection for the rights of media outlets to publish information as they see fit in Russia. On a practical basis, media, fiscal, and other "regulation" is used as a weapon to control the media, not as a means of guaranteeing the right of free speech in Russia.

On the other hand, the U.S. is notable for a dearth of media regulation. Although the Federal Communications Commission (FCC) is tasked with the regulation and control of traditional broadcasters, in practice it has relatively little power to control the media. The British media are more tightly regulated by government institutions. In addition, the British Broadcasting Corporation (BBC) has a strong influence on broadcast norms with its detailed guidelines on public ethos, elaborate journalistic guidelines, and public oversight. In Russia there is no dearth of government bureaucracy, but there also is no tradition or concept of the media as a sphere independent from the ruling elite. As a result, the elaborate bureaucratic structure governing the media is far less powerful than the ability of the Kremlin to fire top managers at state-run media, threaten media outlets with the most restrictive application of the law, and the president's ability to issue direct legal edicts to regulate the media.

Filter 4: media ownership

In the U.S., most of the media are owned by corporations and are strictly commercial entities. This includes all types of media, from local newspapers to national television networks. The advent of new technology has brought even greater variety to the American media sphere, in terms of both explosive growth in cable television and the rapid expansion of the internet. While most of the media outlets in the U.K. are commercial enterprises, the single largest and most influential outlet is a public organization. The British Broadcasting Corporation (BBC) is funded directly by an annual fee paid by television owners and is designed to provide "public" broadcasting via television, radio, and the internet. Although other major British television outlets are commercial, they are more closely regulated by the government than are their American counterparts. Many British commercial broadcasters tend to follow, at least to a degree, the public broadcasting model. On the other hand, British newspapers generally are run as commercial entities and are both more politicized as well as more sensationalized than their U.S. counterparts.

Russia has a wide range of ownership arrangements for its media. For example, the prime television channel in Russia (The First Channel or Channel 1) is 51 percent owned by the state and 49 percent by other enterprises. However, as these enterprises are generally closely tied to the state, there is a lack of balance of interests by the owners. Russian State Television and Radio (with a television program *Rossiya* on Channel 2) is completely owned by the state. The most prominent nationwide commercial station, NTV, is a commercial enterprise and underwent a forced change in ownership under Kremlin pressure in 2001. Its editorial policy is now noticeably more Kremlin-friendly (Oates, 2006b). Throughout Russia, media outlets struggle with twin pressures of reliance on state subsidies and advertising revenue, making them vulnerable to pressures from both politicians and businesses.

Filter 5: journalists and the public relations industry

The final filter in the News Production Model receives a great deal of attention from media scholars, who perceive journalists as important "gatekeepers" in the decision of what makes the news. There is no question that individual journalists, who must produce the end product of the News Production Model, are a key element in shaping news content. However, it is critical to understand their role within the broader context of news production in general. Weaver and Cleveland Wilhoit (1996) argue that American journalists feel that the pressures emanating from their news organization are much more important in shaping news content than their individual efforts or political beliefs. Both British and Russian journalists also either report or demonstrate limited autonomy within the system. At the same time, it is clear that corporations, governments, action groups, and even individuals now employ sophisticated public relations strategies that have an effect on the news-making profession (Davis, 2002; Franklin, 2004). As the news-making profession is a particularly complex subject that also fascinates students – in particular because so many are contemplating a career in the profession – the next chapter of this text

(Chapter 3) will discuss it in greater depth. This will provide a further discussion on the News Production Model and should be considered along with the evidence provided in this chapter. In addition, Chapter 4 will include figures on media usage, which will complement the more general discussion of media outlets in each country below.

News production in the United States

Political environment in the United States

2.3 The U.S. relies on elections to translate the political desires of the public into government. In addition, the U.S. notion of democracy is based on a balance of power among the president, Congress, and the Supreme Court. In particular, the U.S. has a written Constitution with a regular review of case law by the Supreme Court. The U.S. has a wide definition of free speech. The Supreme Court has ruled that speech must incite "imminent lawless action" in order to violate the principle of freedom of speech.[1] While Americans have relatively broad latitude to express oppositional and extremist viewpoints, this is limited by issues of national security. Unsurprisingly, there is disagreement about the balance between free speech and national security. In the wake of 9/11, some analysts feel that the limits of acceptable debate and challenge in the media have been constrained by patriotic pressures (Entman, 2003; Hutcheson et al., 2004; McDonald and Lawrence, 2004). In 2001, the U.S. passed the Patriot Act,[2] which gives the federal government broader powers than the standard of "imminent lawless action" regarding possible agitation leading to terrorist acts. Although the law has been condemned by individual states and the American Civil Liberties Union, it was renewed by Congress and President Bush in 2006.

Media norms in the United States

The bulk of the U.S. media are owned by commercial entities. Although there is a range of different corporations with media holdings, the norms and principles that underlie U.S. journalism are fairly similar across different types of mass media. Major news outlets are supposed to adhere to the notions of objectivity and impartiality in reporting the news, confining opinion to clearly demarcated segments of shows or publications. The actual practice of the ideal has come under criticism and is particularly challenged by the clear bias on the newer Fox Television News (Morris, 2005). Studies of the content on Fox have shown a distinctly conservative bias and particularly patriotic approach to the current Iraq War that clearly resonates with a large number of American viewers (ibid.). In addition, critics such as Iyengar (1991) and Patterson (1993) argue that the U.S. news selects stories and edits coverage based on a news agenda that neglects critical issues in society. In addition, analysts have noted that journalists are playing a more analytical role, as sound-bites from policymakers have decreased and commentary by the reporters themselves has increased over time. Herman and Chomsky (2002) go much further, claiming that the U.S. media unfairly "manufacture" consent in the interest of a narrow group of elites. Nonetheless, the notion of objectivity is the accepted ideal for the U.S. media.

Media regulation in the United States

The Federal Communications Commission (FCC) is the central regulatory body for telecommunications, including broadcasting, in the U.S. It is over-seen by five commissioners, who are appointed for five-year terms by the U.S. president and are responsible directly to Congress. Technically, the Commission should be at least somewhat removed from political pressures, although analysts have seen a tendency to support corporate interests over public interests in many instances (McChesney, 2004). It should be noted that there is no equivalent regulatory body for the print media, which is essentially governed instead by a body of law relating to libel, sedition, and other public communication issues. The FCC has a vast remit, including telephone ser-vices, the internet, television, radio, and other communication channels.

In terms of media regulation, the FCC has three "broad goals" for both media policy and media ownership: competition, diversity, and localism (Kwerel et al., 2004: 411). As such, the FCC is charged with ensuring that U.S. citizens have a broad range of media choices without the dominance of a sin-gle media owner in one geographical location. It hears many complaints from viewers and listeners (such as about the exposure of singer Janet Jackson's breast during the 2006 Super Bowl half-time performance), but its key power lies in the regulation of commercial media enterprises. The FCC has the power to levy fines and even take away licenses from broadcasters for viola-tions of decency standards. The 1996 Telecommunications Act placed greater responsibility on the FCC in limiting concentrated media ownership (McChesney, 2004).

The U.S. broadcasting sphere remains a difficult area for the government to shape due to market forces. While large metropolitan areas have competing media sources, many less populated locales could be lucky to have one local, professionally-run media outlet. The advent of the internet, cable television, and satellite television has made it particularly difficult to try to prevent the dominance of one owner in any one market. There have been many court cases in attempting to fine-tune the FCC regulations. Overall, Graber (2005: 44) assesses the FCC as relatively weak in its ability to control the broadcast-ing output in the U.S. with a "record of setting goals and enforcing the rules [that] has earned it the reputation at best of being an ineffective watchdog over the public interest and at worst an industry-kept, pressure-group domi-nated lapdog." Other analysts such as McChesney (2004) go further, seeing some members of the FCC as consistently supporting the demands of large commercial broadcasters rather than public concerns over information provision and media ownership concentration.

When discussing the regulation of the mass media, it is important to consider the legal treatment and protection of journalists. U.S. journalists have traditionally enjoyed a particularly high level of legal protection. They are protected to a degree by the notion that they have the right to shield their key "off-the-record" sources from public exposure, even when they have information needed by the legal system to pursue a court case. About half of the U.S. states bolster this with formal "shield laws" to protect journalists (Graber, 2005), although it is problematic because the definition of exactly who is a journalist is not always clear. In addition, the Supreme Court decision in the case of *New York Times vs. Sullivan* (1964) made it relatively hard to sue publications for libel. This case involved a full-page ad protesting the actions of a city official in the arrest of civil rights activist Martin Luther King Jr. The case established that the publication must have known the facts to be wrong and that the publication of the facts must have damaged the individual in order to win a libel case. This interpretation of the law protects journalists who are lied to by sources or who may get the facts wrong in the rush to deadline. In addition, once people are deemed to be "public individuals" in the U.S. system, it becomes very difficult for them to complain about press treatment. However, celebrities and politicians have successfully sued journalists and media organizations for biased, inaccurate, and damaging reports.

It should be noted that the traditional protection offered to U.S. journalists from naming their sources was violated in a recent high-profile case involving reporters from *The New York Times* and *Time* magazine. *The New York Times* reporter Judith Miller was sent to prison for almost three months in 2005 before she agreed to testify in the case of White House official accused of deliberately leaking the name of a CIA agent. An article in *The New York Times* claimed this has "changed the landscape of relations between journalists and official sources, as many of Washington's prominent political reporters were forced to testify in a criminal trial."[3] Thus, even in a relatively open and stable system, journalists often find themselves in difficult legal situations.

Media outlets and ownership in the United States

Most media outlets in the U.S. are owned by corporations. These corporations must satisfy two diverse yet important constituents. In terms of news production, they must satisfy their audience in order to attract and maintain their popularity. In terms of their shareholders, they are expected to make a profit. These often conflicting goals create the ongoing challenge for a news organization to pursue simultaneously both excellence in news and good fiscal performance. Media outlets need to craft a product that creates a wide audience, but doesn't alienate any advertisers. This is all the more challenging because as the number and type of media outlets grow with the technological advancements, the competition for advertising becomes increasingly fierce. The only public broadcaster of note is the Public Broadcasting System (PBS), which produces in-depth, analytical radio broadcasts and television programming that is arguably influential among the political elites. However, PBS does not have a daily mass audience or the power consistently to set the national news agenda in the same way as the main commercial broadcasters.

While U.S. analysts posit that the plurality of the commercial media market in the U.S. contributes to democracy, there are many who argue that commercial ownership of the media inhibits democracy. Particularly prominent among the critics of the commercial media system are Herman and Chomsky (2002), who assert that the corporately owned media "manufacture consent" for the capitalistic, unfair status quo in countries such as the U.S. It is quite common to see warnings of the danger that media outlets might reproduce the political, social, and economic agenda of their owners – particularly in systems such as the U.S., in which major media corporations own numerous media outlets.[4] There are several challenges, however, to counter the argument that media owners control media content. First, media owners need to attract a steady audience in a highly competitive media marketplace. This should mean that media owners would avoid an overt political bias that would damage credibility or – more worrying for their financial fortunes – popularity. The "corporate-influence" argument also assumes that media owners have a strong, stable political agenda that can readily be translated into news production. With the possible exception of certain individual media owners (such as Rupert Murdoch), it is relatively unusual to be able to determine a particular political "line" on the part of a media owner, particularly if it is a multi-faceted corporation. Finally, this model of media owners being able to disperse propaganda also would depend on an absence of other factors – such as political environment, media norms, the legal structure, the journalistic culture – that dictate the shape of news coverage. As Graber writes, while there have been troubling examples of specific news stories that were influenced by media owners, there is no "solid evidence that the media giants routinely suppress diversity among the news outlets under their control, squelch anti-business news, and stress anti-labor, pro-Republican, and jingoist stories" (1997: 45).

Graber wrote those words, however, before the advent of Fox News. For decades, the American media sphere was dominated by the "Big Three" television networks: ABC, CBS, and NBC. In the 1970s, *NBC Nightly News, CBS Evening News,* and *ABC World News Tonight* together attracted 90 percent of the national audience (Morris, 2005: 58). While these half-hour evening news programs are still a dominant part of the news sphere, they are now challenged by cable and satellite news (as well as offerings via the internet). Figures from the Pew Research Center for the People and the Press (2004) show that viewership of network news and cable news was starting to converge by 2004, with about 33 percent of Americans watching network television news regularly, compared with about 20 percent for CNN and

23 percent for Fox News. Cable news started with the advent of CNN (Cable News Network) in 1980, with other corporations following suit. The fortunes of Fox News have been bolstered by its jingoistic coverage of the second Gulf War, although Fox News was starting to "consistently beat" CNN in the ratings by 2001 (Morris, 2005: 60, citing Collins, 2004).

Fox News is owned by the Fox Entertainment Group and is a subsidiary of Rupert Murdoch's News Corporation. It was launched in October 1996 to 17 million cable subscribers and now reaches 85 million households in the U.S. Unlike the other major news networks, Fox News has a measurable conservative, pro-Republican bias: what some observers have termed a more "patriotic" or "nationalistic" approach to news coverage (Oates and Williams, 2006). This has upset many media observers, who perceive this as a violation of U.S. media norms of objectivity, while others claim that Fox merely balances a more covert liberal bias in much of the U.S. media. In any case, the content of Fox News is clearly more dramatic, particularly with its emphasis on bright graphics, emotive music, and outspoken hosts. But is the choice of Fox News producers to be more pro-Republican than their network counterparts an economic or a political decision? While departing from the U.S. norm of objectivity in the nightly news, Fox is breaking with American news tradition. On the other hand, this approach is also finding resonance with a large number of viewers in an increasingly competitive media marketplace (Morris, 2005). Hence, is Fox News responding to a Republican, pro-war, and "patriotic" constituency in the U.S. or is it abusing the trust of its viewers that television news should be as objective as possible?[5] Another point that challenges the notion that owners influence media content is that the Fox Network produces a range of programs, including the satirical and rather politically left-wing cartoon *The Simpsons*.

While a review of the national networks is important to understanding the American media sphere, comprehending the role of the local media is also key. As Tip O'Neill, former speaker of the U.S. House of Representatives is famous for saying, in America "all politics are local." Local issues and personalities are particularly important, especially in a vast country of 300 million people with distinctly different political, economic, social, and ethnic patterns. Typically local network affiliates present the local news from 6 pm to 6.30 pm and the national news broadcasts compete from 6.30–7 pm.[6] This means even relatively small communities are covered by local television news, unlike in the U.K. where major British cities with populations in excess of half a million (such as Glasgow and Liverpool) do not have their own local news programs.

Radio remains popular in the U.S., although many smaller stations were merged into large media companies due to a relaxation in broadcasting monopoly rules by the 1996 Telecommunications Act. There have been some nationally syndicated radio stars with political agendas, such as conservative commentator Rush Limbaugh. Radio, however, mostly remains important as a local information source. The relatively low cost of broadcast on radio has meant it is still an affordable medium for local news broadcasting and a vibrant, grass-roots radio station system still exists in the U.S. National Public Radio (NPR) is the most successful "public" broadcaster in the country. Funded by a not-for-profit membership organization, NPR news and entertainment broadcasts reached up to 26 million people a week in 2007 via more than 800 independently operated, non-commercial public radio stations.[7]

There are several U.S. newspapers that are held up as models of good journalistic practice. Interestingly, the Pew Research Center for the People and the Press (2005) reports that U.S. readers are less enamored of these outlets than in the past (discussed in more detail in Chapter 4), but they remain an example of journalistic aspirations and good practice. In U.S. journalism, media outlets fiercely compete for the annual Pulitzer prizes, which judge the best output for editorial, opinion, photos, investigative journalism, and a range of other categories (see www.pulitzer.org). *The New York Times, Washington Post, Boston Globe,* and *The Wall Street Journal* remain amongst the most authoritative newspapers in the country, particularly among elites. In general, though, newspapers serve a more mundane, albeit important daily function of disseminating local information. Very few areas can support more than a single daily newspaper – and sometimes not even that, as advertising revenue continues to shrink in the face of competition from satellite, cable, and internet outlets.

The Project for Excellence in Journalism suggests that the entire premise of the libertarian (a.k.a commercial) model of the news model may be challenged by the continuing decline of the general-interest media in the U.S. In a 2007 report, the non-profit organization questioned whether "the business model that has financed the news for more than a century – product advertising – still fits the way people consume media" (Project for Excellence in Journalism, 2007). Faced with increasing competition and stagnation in media use, media outlets may now pursue "hyper-localism," in which they attract and retain relatively narrow audiences (based on location, ethnicity, special interests, or other factors). Arguably, these financial pressures and resulting strategy could provide far more of a threat to in-depth news coverage and meaningful diversity than the possible bias of media owners.

Key points about news production in the United States

- The U.S. is a democracy, with freedom of speech guaranteed by the Constitution and a robust legal system.
- There is tension between the limits of freedom of speech and national security, particularly in the wake of 9/11.
- U.S. media outlets are almost all run as commercial enterprises and adhere to the libertarian model of the media.
- Although the general norm in the U.S. media is "objectivity," this is challenged by some critics as well as by the overt bias on the popular Fox News.

News production in the United Kingdom

Political environment in the United Kingdom

2.4 The U.K. does not have a written Constitution in the same way as the U.S., but freedom of speech is one of the central tenets of the country's democratic tradition. However, the British government takes a more active role in the regulation of free speech and the media than does the U.S. administration. Part of this has been due to security concerns, notably in the past with terrorism in Northern Ireland. British media outlets are subject to D Notices, edicts issued by the Ministry of Defense that ban the release of certain information. In the 1990s, the government's Broadcasting Ban prohibited anyone affiliated with a cause linked to terrorism from speaking on television. In addition to a lack of a written Constitution and a regular system of judicial review through court cases, Britain does not have the same separation of powers in the executive and legislative branches of government as in the U.S. The political party that wins the largest number of seats in elections for Parliament has control of the House of Commons and appoints ministers to run the country – including the prime minister. The locus of power lies far more with political parties than with individual politicians, particularly as political parties select who runs for office and what jobs they get in government. There are checks on the party system, such as the House of Lords and the existence of the Queen as nominal head of state, but these are very weak compared with the division of power in the U.S.

There are some important political differences linked to a far greater role of the state in the economic and social life of the U.K.[8] Britain has higher taxes and a much broader social welfare system than the U.S. As the British government tends to be more involved in the daily life of its citizens – as most of the health care system and higher educational system is run by the state – British citizens find that government policy often has far more impact on their daily lives than does government policy for U.S. citizens. Yet, how would any of this affect the media system? There are several ways in which the links between particular political institutions and the media become clear. In the U.S., election campaigns focus on candidates rather than political parties. In Britain, where political parties are much more powerful, there is far greater emphasis on the parties themselves. As the state is more involved in the daily life of the citizen – whether through health care, housing, or higher education – there is arguably a more intense day-to-day interest in state policy.[9]

Media norms in the United Kingdom

Britain's news landscape is schizophrenic, with the television industry adhering to the social responsibility model and much of the print industry coming close to a politicized libertarian model. Thus, journalists at the BBC and its chief commercial rival Independent Television News (ITN) are careful to craft their journalistic messages within a framework that supports societal reflection and consensus. At the same time, the television producers feel an increasing pressure to maintain market share as they are challenged by both the internet and an explosion of broadcast alternatives via cable, satellite, and digital channels. The central normative question about British media is to what extent the "public" media really reflect the wishes of the masses – and to what extent they maintain the social and political status quo for the elites (Philo, 1995). For example, Schlesinger claims that the BBC is particularly powerful for having a "perceived credibility" while really functioning as a propaganda arm of the government (quoted in McNair, 2003: 60). Those who already have some degree of power get access, but only one part of society is really covered by the news: "Impartiality and objectivity ... stop at the point where political consensus ends – and the more radical the dissent, the less impartial and objective the media" (ibid.: 61). This is a charge levelled at both the U.S. and British media, but it is particularly thought-provoking if the media are supposed to be "public."

Even with the norm of public broadcasting, the news has changed to reflect the times. As a result, even the staid BBC has started to "liven up" its broadcasts (to a degree) while commercial Channel 5 news has introduced a radical format of more casual newscasters who eschew the anchor's desk altogether for a stand-up performance. Meanwhile, the tabloid newspapers produce scaremongering headlines on everything from child molesters to the unlikely side-effects of childhood vaccinations. The "broadsheet" newspapers have a more dignified approach, but still typically have a very readily identifiable political slant that permeates much of the news content. The terms "tabloid" and "broadsheet" can be confusing as some papers (such as the *Independent* and *The Times*) are broadsheet in *content* but publish in a smaller format that is tabloid in *size*. These are known as "compacts" to distinguish them from the traditional tabloids. British papers that focus more on scandal than hard news are often also called "red tops" because of the red printing on the top of tabloids such as the *Sun*. In Britain, it is somewhat easier to prove libel than in the U.S., but it is very expensive to bring a case through the courts. British print journalists take more liberty with their sources, and it is acknowledged that "direct" quotations from sources do not have to be exact.

Media regulation in the United Kingdom

Media regulation in the U.K. is far more extensive than in the U.S. The Department for Culture, Media and Sport (DCMS) is the branch of the British government that must "foster fair and effective competition, promote high quality broadcasting from a diverse range of sources, provide a high level of consumer protection and safeguard freedom of expression" (see www.culture.gov.uk). Complaints about media content are handled by the British Office of Communication (Ofcom). Ofcom is the independent regulator and competition authority for the British communications industries, with responsibilities across television, radio, telecommunications, and wireless communications services (see www.ofcom.gov.uk). The Press Complaints Commission (PCC) is an independent body which deals with complaints from members of the public about the editorial content of newspapers and magazines.[10]

The centralized hand of the government in media regulation has a significant role in shaping media output in the U.K. For example, both public and commercial broadcasters are regulated by government rules that require them to maintain standards of public service in their output. Although commercial broadcasters do not carry as heavy a responsibility in this area as the BBC, they still have a requirement of editorial balance and must include some socially useful programming in their schedules. In the U.S., viewers, listeners, and readers can complain about content to individual media outlets or corporations – but they often have little recourse without expensive lawsuits that may not succeed.[11] In Britain, the discussion about the appropriate role and behavior of the media is far more regulated and – especially as complaints and their resolutions are now published on various governmental websites – far more visible. Overall, the impact of government regulation is far more evident in the British media sphere than in the American media sphere. At the same time, British journalists do not enjoy as broad a protection under the law in terms of avoiding libel as their U.S. counterparts.

Media outlets in the United Kingdom

What is distinctive about the British media system is the structure and funding of the British Broadcasting Corporation (BBC). The BBC, formed initially for radio, was founded with the notion that no commercial entity or government should control the broadcast industry. It was deemed too important for the national interest to fall into commercial hands. As a result, the BBC is funded by a television tax, in which citizens who have a television in their household pay an annual licensing fee (£135.50 or about $270 in the fiscal year beginning April 2007). According to the BBC's annual financial report, there were 25 million licenses in effect as of March 31, 2006. This brought in an income of about £3.1 billion (roughly 6 billion dollars) as there were some discounts for the elderly or those with black-and-white sets. In addition, the BBC receives income from other ventures, but carries no advertising and hence has no advertising revenue. Overall, the BBC spent about 60 percent of its income of £4 billion in 2006 on eight television network channels, 27 percent on radio, and 2.5 percent of its revenue on its website (which also shares news gathering with television and radio services).[12] The rest of the funding is spent on administration, transmission costs, interactive services, and educational broadcasts linked to the school curriculum.

The BBC has an extensive set of guidelines and is overseen by the BBC Trust, a group of 12 individuals who are appointed by the Queen on advice from ministers.[13] Anyone can apply for the part-time job of serving as a member of the BBC Trust, although in practice it is clear that the appointments are given to experts in the field of media, finance, regulation, or other areas of expertise relevant to overseeing a huge media corporation (see www.bbc.co.uk/bbctrust). This Trust replaced the former BBC Board of Governors, a similar institution, in January 2007. In theory, the BBC is responsible directly to those who pay the licensing fee, as well as to the high standards of balance and fairness set down in the BBC Charter. This makes it a "public" broadcaster as opposed to a "state" broadcaster (such as Channels 1 and 2 in Russia that have direct government control of policy and personnel). Although the BBC is supposed to operate at arm's length from the government, in reality the BBC is both a public and a state broadcaster. Not only does the ruling government appoint the members of the BBC Trust, but the prime minister is involved in the appointment of the top BBC executive, the director-general.

There are examples from periods in which both the Conservatives and the Labour government have been in power to show that the BBC is vulnerable to government pressure. Studies by the Glasgow Media Group have shown a pervasive pro-government, anti-union bias on the BBC in the 1970s and 1980s (Philo, 1995). Bill Miller (1991) found the BBC biased towards the Conservative government in election coverage. During Margaret Thatcher's government, the BBC banned the voices of certain Northern Irish political figures who were considered terrorists by the British government. In addition, the BBC readily subscribed to censorship during the Falklands War in 1982. In the most recent famous case, Prime Minister Tony Blair's administration became furious over a report by a BBC freelance correspondent that the Labour government had "sexed up" the evidence of weapons of mass destruction in Iraq in order to build public consensus for sending British troops to war. Although it later became apparent that evidence of these weapons was inconclusive, an inquiry into the matter (which also involved the suicide of a government official responsible for unauthorized comments) led to the resignation of both the head of the BBC Board of Governors and the BBC director-general (Hutton Inquiry, 2004; Dyke, 2005).

Despite these documented problems with the lack of barriers between government influence and BBC content, the BBC still has an enviable structure, reputation, and high level of funding. In particular, the BBC is able to devote considerable resources to traditionally unprofitable areas that are still important to many segments in society, including children's programming, cultural shows, programming in Welsh and Gaelic, coverage of minority issues, and in-depth analysis of societal problems. In a study of the framing of terrorist threat in election campaigns in Britain, the U.S., and Russia, it was clear that British television had the most systematic dissemination of information and focus on important policies of the three national television news systems (Oates, 2006a).

The BBC was formed initially as a company by a group of radio manufacturers in Britain in 1922. It was transformed into a public broadcaster by the government in 1927, as it was convinced after widespread labor strikes in 1926 that public broadcasting could not be left in private hands.[14] The BBC enjoyed a monopoly on television news in Britain until the launch of commercial Independent Television (ITV) in 1955. However, the British commercial television news sector differs markedly from its U.S. counterpart as news across much of the sector is produced by the same agency, Independent Television News (ITN). As a result, there is less focus on competition and more on fulfilling the norms of the social responsibility framework (albeit within an intensively competitive framework among the BBC, ITV, and the rest of the media sphere). In addition, radio is still a powerful news force in the U.K., in particular as it is part of the well-funded public media organization of the BBC. BBC radio reaches 53 percent of the adult population in the country, broadcasting a staggering 4,000 hours of national news, current affairs, and documentary features on five channels each year (McNair, 2003: 12). Commercial radio news is negligible on a national basis, but can play an important role regionally.

As in the U.S., a relatively small group of owners control the newspaper sector in the U.K. In particular, the commercial sector has been led by Australian media entrepreneur Rupert Murdoch (ibid.). Like television, the British print media is centered around London, although there are some influential papers that are based elsewhere (such as the *Herald* in Glasgow). The main division is between the more solemn "broadsheets" (such as *The Times* and *The Financial Times*) and the more raucous "tabloids." Although the label is from the size of the newspaper page – tabloid pages are smaller, close to the size of a large magazine – it is not only size that matters. The tabloids have a tradition of outrageous headlines, attention-grabbing stories, and scandal-mongering. At the same time, virtually all broadsheets and tabloids in the U.K. have an overt political agenda that is clear throughout the paper in the way that stories are chosen, covered, and displayed. Whereas a U.S. paper with a very liberal editorial page will still cover conservative politicians, a left-wing tabloid in Britain feels no compunction at even giving Conservative politicians meaningful coverage at all. The same is true for Conservative newspapers, which give little fair coverage to politicians from the left.

It should be remembered that a key difference in the media landscape is that the media market in the U.K. is highly centralized. Although the BBC has a remit to provide local and regional news, the London-based broadcast news agenda dominates.[15] McNair notes that all of the ITV news production is based in London (although the BBC has regional news offices). With only one capital city dominating the political landscape – as opposed to several major cities with strong media outlets in the U.S. – news interest is not as well distributed throughout the regions and nations of the U.K. as it is in the U.S. On the other hand, more than 8 million people (or about 13 percent of the country's population) live in the British capital, which is a world financial center as well.[16] So it comes as no surprise that the concentration of power, wealth, and population in a corner of southern England has led to a focus of media interest as well.

Key points about news production in the United Kingdom

- Although the U.K. has no written Constitution, there is a strong tradition of freedom of speech.
- The norm in the British media is "balance," but this is adhered to far more in the socially responsible broadcast sector than in the more commercialized, libertarian elements of the press.
- There are a greater range of government controls on the media in Britain than in the U.S.
- The BBC is a major influence on journalistic norms for broadcasters, both public and commercial.
- The BBC is designed as a broadcaster in service to the public, but there is evidence that it comes under pressure from the ruling government.

News production in Russia

Political environment in Russia

2.5 The Russian political landscape is markedly different from either that of the U.S. or the U.K. While both the U.S. and the U.K. have shown their development as liberal states over the centuries, Russia has few traditional liberal values. The country was ruled by a monarchy until the 1917 revolution swept away the old ruling class and established the regime of the Communist Party of the Soviet Union. Although in theory a "dictatorship" of the working class, in fact the Soviet Union was ruled by a relatively narrow group of repressive elites. One of the key factors in the Soviet regime was strict censorship, including internment in prison camps and death sentences for those who questioned the authority of the Communist Party. It is interesting that changes in the limits on free expression were a significant factor in the collapse of the Communist Party monopoly on power in 1991.

In the mid-1980s, Soviet leaders introduced a policy of "glasnost" (transparency) aimed at allowing citizens to discuss ways to improve Soviet society. This limited discussion quickly escalated into a broad-ranging attack of the repressive Soviet system, exacerbated by sharp divisions in the leadership who used media outlets to push their own agendas (Oates, 2006b). After the introduction of limited elections in 1989, the Communist Party lost control of the legislature, public opinion, and finally the mass media and the military as well. In a nearly bloodless revolt, future Russian President Boris Yeltsin took control of the Russian Federation[17] in August 1991. Russia and the other 14 Soviet republics formed into independent countries by the end of that year.

Media norms in Russia

It is important to reflect on the role that the media sphere itself played in the huge political changes that transformed the Soviet Union into 15 independent countries. Initially, analysts tended to equate glasnost with freedom of speech. However, this freedom to speak politically generally remained with the elites. Although the stories were of enormous interest to the public during the glasnost era (1985–91), a fundamentally new notion of the media's role in society did not develop. In Soviet times, the media served the interests of the ruling elite in the Communist Party as delineated in the Soviet model of the press in Siebert et al. (1963; see Mickiewicz, 1980, for an in-depth discussion of the Soviet media). In glasnost, the media served the interests of a broader segment of the elites, but did not fundamentally change their role as a voice for political players to a voice of the citizens. Although some diversity of media remains in Russia, the notion of the media as "objective" or "balanced" has never been widely applied. Russian politicians, journalists, and the public alike view the mass media as a political player rather than as a watchdog that can provide a check on political power.

Although analysts initially labeled Russia as a "developing democracy," it has not developed democratic institutions. Rather, there is the appearance of democratic institutions in *form*, including media outlets, elections, parliament, and a popularly elected president, but these institutions lack democratic *content*. As a result, much of the mass media simply repeat the fable of democratic interaction. Any attempt to challenge the government on key issues such as corruption at the top, the progress of war in Chechnya, bribery, or the unfairness of the leadership, is not tolerated. The majority stockholder of the most prominent commercial television station was arrested in 2001 and his station was then "sold" to forces friendly to the government (Oates, 2006b). As discussed in Chapter 1, Russia has been labeled by international media freedom organizations as particularly bad in terms of its treatment of journalists, for whom there is a real fear of menace, physical threat, and even death. As a result, the media work virtually unanimously to support the policies of the central leaders in a disturbing echo of the Soviet model of the media. This could be termed the "neo-Soviet" model of the media as this captures the idea of the media in service to the state leaders (as opposed to the citizens).

Media regulation in Russia

Freedom of speech is guaranteed in the 1993 Russian Constitution, but this does not serve as a basis for media laws that protect this concept. Rather, the law tends to work against the interests of free speech in Russia. There are serious flaws in the legal system in terms of protection of free speech (Oates, 2006b). Surprisingly, Russia lacks a contemporary law on broadcasting, the key media sector. In addition, there is a "war" of laws in the country – affecting the media sector and beyond – because the president can issue edicts that conflict with laws passed by the parliament. Essentially, the president has the ability to rule by decree. In particular, the president can effectively limit the freedom of speech with edicts that address specific issues. The situation is further confused by the fact that the 89 regions of Russia also regulate the media locally and can impose further or even contradictory laws on the media. As much of the local media funding comes from the local government (and its very existence often depends on the goodwill of local leaders), the media are quite vulnerable to local legislation. The Moscow Media Law and Policy Center found that some regional media legislation conflicts with national law, making it impossible for media outlets to operate within both legal boundaries (European Institute for the Media, 2000: 19). As a result, the law does not provide a framework for the media sphere; rather, it supplies another way for local and national politicians to threaten the media with closure for adverse coverage. There have been some occasional legal victories for the media, but they are relatively rare and insignificant.[18]

Media outlets in Russia

Russia has a mix of ownership across all levels of print and broadcasting. However, the most dominant media outlet is television in Russia. The primacy of central television stations in Russia remains relatively unchallenged, unlike in the U.S. and the U.K., due to several factors. First, the internet is underdeveloped in the country as both the telecommunications infrastructure and personal income to buy extra media services lag behind the West. National newspapers are relatively expensive and many people simply cannot afford the luxury of a subscription. The same is true for satellite television, which is generally for well-off people in the urban centers. As a result, the central television stations in Russia retain a particular political influence that they now lack in the U.S. and the U.K. The dominant networks (broadcast on Channels 1 and 2 on the television dial) are the state-run First Channel and state-owned *Rossiya* (Russia) Channel. Technically, only 51 percent of the First Channel is owned directly by the Russian state, but much of the rest of the ownership is in the hands of state enterprises controlled by the Kremlin. As a result, the Kremlin retains the right to hire and fire the director of the channel. Since the founding of the Russian state in 1991, this ability has been exercised many times. In the more settled authoritarian regime of Putin, however, constant hiring and firings are no longer necessary. Employees of all media outlets are well aware of the limits of what can be said on air or in print. This parallels the Soviet experience of journalists, in which the action of a censor was rarely needed, as Soviet journalists understood the party "line" and the way all stories should be formulated by the time they received their first jobs.

Even if there are certain topics that get little meaningful coverage, there is a lot of news in general. There are more than 400 newspaper titles (more than during the Soviet era), but most of them are quite small and struggle financially (BBC, 2007).[19] In addition, all prominent newspapers toe the Kremlin line. There is some radio news, including the relatively liberal Echo of Moscow radio station, but radio nationwide provides little serious alternative news. While there are well-known, professional websites that address Russian news and politics, many of them reflect the limited news spread found in the mainstream media. In any case, internet access and its authority in the news sphere remains relatively low in Russia. In the most popular sphere of television, there has been steady growth (Kachkaeva et al., 2006). The number of non-subscription channels that half of the Russian nation could receive increased from five in 2004 to nine in 2006 (ibid.).

Key points about news production in Russia

- Russia has a constitution that guarantees free speech in theory, but in practice there is limited opportunity for free media expression.
- The media model in Russia could be described as "neo-Soviet" in that the media contribute to the illusion of a progressive society.
- The law does not protect freedom of speech.
- There are a range of media outlets, both state and commercial, but little media freedom in Russia as those major media outlets that challenge the Kremlin line are forced to change their line or go out of business.
- Central television stations are still vastly influential, as there has been relatively little penetration by satellite, cable, or internet options.

Chapter summary

The News Production Model shows there are differences in various broad factors that will affect the content of news. Specifically, this chapter has looked at the political environment, media norms, regulation, and ownership to show the variation in these elements across three countries. The final elements of the model, the journalistic profession and public relations, will be examined in the next chapter (Chapter 3). The American media operate in a democratic environment, albeit with limits imposed for reasons of national security as well as laws such as those for libel. The norm of American journalism is "objectivity," although this norm is challenged by the rising popularity of Fox News with its clear pro-Republican, patriotic slant on the news. The bulk of the media are run as commercial organizations, and the American media fit into the libertarian model. Regulation of the media is rather weak, particularly in that the Federal Communications Commission is considered by some analysts to favor the rights of media owners over those of media consumers. Television is still dominant, although cable television news has risen to challenge the supremacy of the "Big Three."

There is significant variation in the key factors of the News Production Model in the U.K. Although there is respect for freedom of speech, there are some central differences in governance. These differences in the political environment include stronger political parties, the lack of a separation of powers, and a larger role in general for the state. This is echoed in the institution of the BBC, a huge broadcasting service that is funded by a direct fee paid by the viewing public. Although the BBC is designed to be free from government control, there is evidence that it must cope with political influences. However, the model of social responsibility inherent in the BBC Charter permeates the British broadcasting industry, both public and commercial. In the broadcast industry, the notion of "balance" remains important. At the same time, Britain has a lively tabloid press that embraces the commercialism and sensationalism to echo the libertarian model.

The key elements of the News Production Model are significantly different in Russia. Russia is not a democracy, as it does not have transparent institutions nor the rule of law. The media are part of the "appearance" of democracy favored by Russia's oligarchic rulers. There is no notion of balance or objectivity – even with all of their flaws – in Russian journalism. Russia has both commercial and state-funded media, but neither function as a watchdog of the state. Rather, Russian media outlets are perceived as pawns in the political system, seen as either partners to those in power or merely in service to political elites. Power remains much more important than law in Russia. Although there are laws regarding freedom of speech and media freedom in Russia, they are not useful in terms of providing support for media organizations. Rather, it is more likely that the Russian government will deploy media, financial, tax, or other laws in punitive and unfair ways to punish or even shut down media outlets that are critical of Kremlin policy.

Examining these elements of the News Production Model reveals a range of constraints that will shape news content. These constraints start long before a journalist arrives at his or her desk in the morning to begin the task of covering events and gathering news. All of these elements will dictate the shape, direction, and final form of news coverage. That, in turn, will influence the citizens and the public sphere. The next chapter (Chapter 3) will discuss journalists and public relations as the final step of the model.

Study questions

1 Describe the News Production Model and analyze its usefulness in the study of media and politics in comparative perspective.
2 How does media regulation affect the ability of media outlets to cover politics and politicians?
3 Does it matter who owns the media?
4 What are the significant differences among commercial media, public media, and state media?
5 Describe and discuss key media outlets in the U.S., Britain, and Russia.
6 What key elements in news production produce a media system that is free and fair?

Reading guide

As noted in Chapter 1, Graber (2005), McNair (2003), and Oates (2006a) are useful for looking at the elements of the News Production Model discussed above in the U.S., the U.K., and Russia respectively. An interesting account of the rising popularity of the Fox News Network as well as a discussion of news viewing patterns has been written by Morris (2005). One of the most interesting documents on the British media is the Hutton Report, which was an inquiry into the suicide of a government source after a BBC report that the Blair administration had exaggerated the threat of weapons of mass destruction in Iraq. The full report can be downloaded from the inquiry website at www.the-hutton-inquiry.org.uk. For insight into news production in Russia, see media monitoring reports from the former European Institute for the Media or the Organization for Security and Co-operation in Europe's Office of Democratic Initiatives and Human Rights. The European Institute for the Media reports are archived at www.media-politics.com/eimreports.htm. The OSCE/ODIHR website is at http://www.osce.org/odihr/ – please see their section on election monitoring for comments on the media in Russian and other elections.

Internet resources

www.journalism.org   The Project for Excellence in Journalism is a research organization that specializes in using empirical methods to evaluate and study the performance of the press. It is non-partisan, non-ideological, and non-political. It is a project of the Pew Research Center (based in Washington, D.C.) and is funded by The Pew Charitable Trusts. The website provides many reports with in-depth analysis on the U.S. media.

www.cjr.org   The *Columbia Journalism Review* is the journal of the journalism industry in the U.S. Its articles provide key updates on the state of the industry.

www.bbc.co.uk   The British Broadcasting Corporation website provides not only news, but detailed information about this public service broadcasting organization.

www.terramedia.co.uk/law/index.htm   This site gives access to the full text of laws relating to the media in the U.K.

www.culture.gov.uk   The British Department for Culture, Media and Sport is the branch of the government that covers the regulation of broadcasting and the print media.

http://www.rferl.org/reports/FullReport.aspx?report=573   Radio Free Europe/Radio Liberty *Media Matters* reports cover the latest news and developments in the media industry, including Russia.

Notes

1 This is from the decision of the case, *Brandenburg vs. Ohio* (1969). A summary of the case can be assessed on FindLaw at http://caselaw.lp.findlaw.com/scripts/getcase.pl?court=us&vol=395&invol=444.

2 The full name of the act is the Uniting and Strengthening America by Providing Appropriate Tools Required to Intercept and Obstruct Terrorism Act of 2001.

3 "Libby Guilty of Lying in CIA Leak Case", March 7, 2007, *New York Times*. The official, I. Lewis Libby Jr., was eventually convicted of lying to a grand jury about the leak.

4 This is a very common theme from British undergraduates in their essay and exam answers.

5 Fox News labels itself as "fair and balanced", but also seems comfortable with a pro-war, pro-Bush stance – thus sending out a rather confusing message.

6 While the three major networks compete at the same time in the U.S., in other countries the news is deliberately staggered so that viewers can see more than one news program on major channels on the same night.

7 http://www.npr.org/about/.

8 The U.K. consists of four nations: England, Scotland, Northern Ireland, and Wales. There is a rising sense of national identity in all of the separate nations, fostered by the current government's decision to devolve power (to a degree) from the central government to the individual nations. There is a robust debate within the U.K. about the need for more national media for the four nations, as opposed to public and commercial media heavily based in London with a perceived pro-English bias. This book does not cover these issues in depth, but it is important for students to remember that England is not synonymous with the U.K. or Great Britain. The term "Great Britain" refers to England, Wales, and Scotland only. This text deals primarily with the overall picture in the U.K., although arguably Northern Ireland is somewhat slighted because the book does not cover the Irish media (an important influence on their neighboring nation).

9 There are virtually no private universities in Britain – even Oxford and Cambridge are now state institutions. As a result, British students follow party educational policy, campaign promises, and debates surrounding state tuition fees with great interest.

10 In addition, Britain has the Advertising Standards Authority (www.asa.org.uk) to help ensure that ads meet national standards. This gives citizens a central site to complain about advertising that they find offensive, immoral, or in other ways unacceptable.

11 Although the FCC does take complaints from viewers, it does not regulate content on paid broadcasting services (such as cable and satellite) as it does on the terrestrial channels. As a result, complaints to the FCC are relatively ineffective in influencing broadcasters, although overt obscenity or clearly offensive material on a main channel can lead to fines and other sanctions.

12 This information and a wealth of additional detail are available in the 2005–6 annual report from the BBC Board of Governors, available online at http://www.bbcgovernorsarchive.co.uk/annreport/.

13 For those not familiar with British politics, the Queen's role in this is ceremonial as she considers the advice of ministers of the ruling party of the day to be binding.

14 For the BBC's description of its history, see http://www.bbc.co.uk/heritage/story/index.shtml (last accessed March 22, 2007).

15 This is only countered to a degree by regional news broadcasts, such as Reporting Scotland on BBC Scotland. For example, observers have noted that BBC reports often mislabel the Scottish parliament as an "assembly" and seem to ignore the devolved powers gained by Scotland since devolution. In addition, BBC reports on education, law, and religious issues often ignore the fact that the systems are very different in Scotland – which can be confusing for Scottish viewers.

16 In contrast, the 19 million people who live in and around New York City only make up about 6 percent of the U.S population – and the U.S. capital is in completely separate location.

17 There are 89 regions (including Chechnya) that make up the Russian Federation, which is the full name of the country. However, in this book and in general it is referred to as Russia (just as most say "the U.S." instead of "the United States of America" except in rather formal contexts).

18 For example, the media did successfully challenge a quite restrictive election coverage law that was passed in 2003, that would have made it essentially impossible for them to carry any discussion of party policy or ideology in the election coverage. The law was overturned.

19 As part of its remit, the BBC monitors media outlets from around the world. This report is available online at http://news.bbc.co.uk/1/hi/world/europe/4315129.stm

References

Berelson, B. and Lazarsfeld, P.F. (1954) *Voting: a Study of Public Opinion Formation in a Presidential Campaign.* Chicago: Chicago University Press.

British Broadcasting Corporation (2007) *The Press in Russia.* Available online at http://news.bbc.co.uk/1/hi/world/europe/4315129.stm.

Campbell, A., Converse, P., Miller, W., and Stokes, D. (1960) *The American Voter.* Chicago: University of Chicago Press.

Collins, S. (2004) *Crazy Like a FOX: The Inside Story of How Fox News Beat CNN.* New York: Penguin.

Davis, A. (2002) *Public Relations Democracy: Public Relations, Politics and the Mass Media in Britain.* Manchester: Manchester University Press.

Dyke, G. (2005) *Inside Story.* London: HarperPerennial.

Entman, R. (1993) "Framing: Toward Clarification of a Fractured Paradigm." *Journal of Communication* 43 (4): 51–8.

Entman, R.M. (2003) "Cascading Activation: Contesting the White House's Frame after 9/11". *Political Communication* 20 (4): 415–32.

European Institute for the Media (2000) *Monitoring the Media Coverage of the December 1999 Parliamentary Elections in Russia: Final Report.* Düsseldorf: European Institute for the Media. Available online at http://www.media-politics.com/eimreports.htm.

Franklin, B. (2004) *Packaging Politics: Political Communication in Britain's Media Democracy*, 2nd edn. London: Hodder Arnold.

Goffman, E. (1974) *Frame Analysis: An Essay on the Organization of Experience.* London: Harper and Row.

Graber, D. (2005) *Mass Media and American Politics*, 7th edn. Washington, DC: Congressional Quarterly Books.

Graber, D. (1997) *Mass Media and American Politics*, 5th edn. Washington, DC: Congressional Quarterly Books.

Hallin, D.C. and Mancini, P. (2003) *Comparing Media Systems: Three Models of Media and Politics.* Cambridge: Cambridge University Press.

Herman, E. and Chomsky, N. (2002). *Manufacturing Consent.* New York: Pantheon Books.

Hutcheson, J., Domke, D., Billeaudeaux, A., and Garland, P. (2004) "U.S. National Identity, Political Elites, and a Patriotic Press Following September 11." *Political Communication* 21 (1): 27–50.

Hutton Inquiry (2004 *Report of the Inquiry into the Circumstances Surrounding the Death of Dr David Kelly CMG.* London: The Stationery Office. Available online at http://www.the-hutton-inquiry.org.uk.

Iyengar, S. (1991) *Is Anyone Responsible? How Television Frames Political Issues.* Chicago: University of Chicago Press.

Kachkaeva, A., Kiriya, I. and Libergal, G. (2006) *Television in the Russian Federation: Organisational Structure, Programme Production and Audience*, a report prepared by Internews Russia for the European Audiovisual Observatory. Moscow: Educated Media.

Kwerel, E., Levy, J., Needy, C., Perry, M., Uretsky, M., Waldon, T. and Williams, J. (2004) "Economic Analysis at the Federal Communications Commission". *Review of Industrial Organization* 25: 395–430.

McChesney, R.W. (2004) "Media Policy Goes to Main Street: The Uprising of 2003". *The Communication Review* 7: 223–58.

McDonald, I.R. and Lawrence, R. (2004) "Filling the 24×7 News Hole: Television News Coverage Following September 11th." Paper presented at the Annual Meeting of the American Political Science Association, Chicago, Illinois.

McNair, B. (2003) *News and Journalism in the UK*, 4th edn. London: Routledge.

Mickiewicz, E.P. (1980) *Media and the Russian Public*. New York: Praeger.

Miller, D. (1995) "The Media and Northern Ireland: Censorship, Information Management and the Broadcasting Ban." In Philo, G. (ed.) *Glasgow Media Group Reader, Vol. II: Industry, Economy, War and Politics*. London: Routledge.

Miller, W.L. (1991) *Media and Voters: The Audience, Content and Influence of Press and Television in the 1987 General Election*. Oxford: Clarendon Press.

Morris, J.S. (2005) "The Fox News Factor." *The Harvard International Journal of Press/Politics* 10 (3): 56–79.

Oates, S. (2004) "From the Archives of the European Institute for the Media: Analysing the Results of a Decade of Monitoring of Post-Soviet Elections." Paper presented at the British Association for Slavonic and East European Studies Conference, Fitzwilliam College, Cambridge, England.

Oates, S. (2006a) "Comparing the Politics of Fear: The Role of Terrorism News in Election Campaigns in Russia, the United States and Britain." *International Relations* 20 (4): 425–38.

Oates, S. (2006b) *Television, Democracy and Elections in Russia*. London: Routledge.

Oates, S. and Williams, A. (2006) "Comparative Aspects of Terrorism Coverage: Television and Voters in the 2004 U.S. and 2005 British Elections". Paper presented at the Annual Meeting of the American Political Science Association, Philadelphia, Pennsylvania. Available online at www.media-politics.com/publications.htm.

Patterson, T.E. (1993) *Out of Order*. New York: Vintage Books.

Pew Research Center for the People and the Press (2004) *Cable and Internet Loom Large in Fragmented Political News Universe*. Washington, DC: Pew Research Center for the People and the Press. Available online at http://people-press.org/reports/display.php3?ReportID=200.

Pew Research Center for the People and the Press (2005) *Public More Critical of Press, But Goodwill Persists*. Washington, DC: Pew Research Center for the People and the Press, available online at http://people-press.org/reports/display.php3?ReportID=248.

Philo, G. (ed.) (1995) *Glasgow Media Group Reader, Vol. II: Industry, Economy, War and Politics*. London: Routledge.

Project for Excellence in Journalism (2007) *The State of the News Media 2007: An Annual Report on American Journalism*. Washington, DC: Project for Excellence in Journalism. Available online at http://www.stateofthemedia.org/2007/.

Reese, S.D. (2007) "The Framing Project: A Bridging Model for Media Research Revisited." *Journal of Communication* 57 (1): 148–54.

Schudson, M. (1995) *The Power of News*. Cambridge, MA: Harvard University Press.

Siebert, F.S., Peterson, T. and Schramm, W. (1963) *Four Theories of the Press: The Authoritarian, Libertarian, Social Responsibility, and Soviet Communist Concepts of What the Press Should Be and Do*. Chicago: University of Illinois Press.

Tankard, J.W. Jr. (2001) "The Empirical Approach to the Study of Media Framing." In Reese, S.D., Gandy, O.H. Jr., and Grant, A.E. (eds.), *Framing Public Life: Perspectives on Media and Our Understanding of the Social World* (pp. 95–106). Mahwah, NJ: Lawrence Erlbaum Associates.

Weaver, D.H. and Cleveland Wilhoit, C. (1996) *The American Journalist in the 1990s*. Mahwah, NJ: Lawrence Erlbaum Associates.

Journalists, Public Relations, and Politics ③

Central points

- American journalists feel more constrained by their media outlets than by their personal views in reporting the news.
- British journalists have become progressively more educated as well as increasingly the target of public relations tactics.
- The British Lobby system for briefing journalists fosters a symbiotic relationship between top British journalists and politicians.
- Russian journalists, mired in a dangerous and difficult profession, are more political pawns than political observers.
- Russia has developed some particularly aggressive "public relations" tactics, including mud-smearing and the spread of comprising material about political opponents.

Introduction

3.1 Understanding what Everette Dennis whimsically labels the *homo journalisticas* (Weaver and Wilhoit, 1996: ix) is an important part of comprehending the relationship between news and politics. Like variant types of the same species, journalists exhibit quite different behaviors in various countries. Within countries, however, there are generally well-understood norms and practices that structure how journalists go about doing their jobs. In the U.S., there has long been a tradition of striving toward "objectivity." Although there are many cases of failure to meet that standard – and a trend towards ignoring it in some major outlets such as Fox News – it is still an important way of understanding how U.S. journalists approach the news. Opinion is supposed to be relegated to clearly defined sections of a newspaper or a broadcast, although critics claim that bias can pervade media output. In the U.K. the standard is better understood as "balance" rather than "objectivity". This norm is apparent in much of the broadcast industry and is regulated both by BBC guidelines and broader broadcast rules. But in the British print media, especially tabloid newspapers, the notion of "balance" is generally ignored. It is accepted that British newspapers will have a particular political bias shaping virtually every aspect of news coverage, including the choice and treatment of news stories and particular politicians. In Russia, it is generally understood that a journalist is a political player, rather than a political observer. Coverage in Russian media outlets is dictated by political necessity rather than the perceived needs of citizens or society in general.

If there is one element that is consistent across all three case studies, it is the escalating pressures on journalists from various factors. As discussed in Chapter 2, journalists carry out their jobs in radically different political, legal, and media environments. Although there is at least some respect for the craft of the journalist in democracies, there is little protection from pressure, intimidation, and even physical violence against journalists in non-democratic states. Given the difficult job of being society's critic, journalists often find themselves unloved by elites and citizens alike, negotiating a thorny path between providing healthy criticism yet stopping short at undermining societal confidence. The increasing competition among the rising number of types of media outlets – from the proliferation of television stations via cable and satellite to the explosion of the number of internet websites – means that journalists cope with job insecurity, pay cuts, and a newsroom budget that is often stripped to the bone. They often work long hours and find it difficult, if not impossible, to reconcile their jobs with a family life. At the same time that many newsroom budgets have been slashed, the amount of money spent by governments, corporations, and even individuals on public relations is on the rise. As a result, journalists may find it increasingly difficult to resist relying on the resources of well-funded PR campaigns instead of careful independent reporting.

Ironically, the state of Russian journalism throws into relief some of the very real strengths of the journalistic profession in the U.S. and the U.K. While journalism training could be said to be flawed in democracies, it is virtually non-existent in Russia. In addition, although American and British journalists may sometimes fail to fulfill the lofty ideals of journalism, at least the ideals exist. In Russia, growing evidence shows that many journalists consider themselves political pawns rather than political observers, with their loyalties firmly tied to the entity supporting the existence of their publication. With the growing intolerance toward dissent from the Kremlin's rule, it is clear that it is not simply about financing. A political "line" has been well established, with Russian journalists almost universally complying with a system of internal censorship. As result, there are elements of the current Russian media system that suggest it is "neo-Soviet" in nature. It also shows that – no matter how flawed – there is a distinct difference between a democratic media system and an authoritarian media in service to the state rather than the citizens.

The role of the journalist in shaping political news is the final step in the News Production Model outlined in Chapter 2. Along with a study of the journalistic profession itself, this chapter will include a discussion of public relations. Public relations, in particular from corporations and politicians, has been part of the U.S. political sphere for decades. However, as Davis (2002) notes, public relations tactics have also been on the rise in the U.K. In Russia, aggressive public relations tactics developed at the same time as the media organizations in the post-Soviet era, but the line between reporting and propaganda is far less distinct in Russia than it is in the U.S. or Britain. In addition, some of the more aggressive Russian tactics of mud-slinging and "black" PR make British and American PR specialists look very tame in comparison. This chapter provides the information to fill out the final filter of the News Production Model, the last step as the formation of news is shaped by political environment, media norms, media regulation, and ownership.

The journalistic profession and public relations in the United States

3.2 One of the most in-depth looks at the thoughts, habits, and backgrounds of U.S. journalists comes from a survey of more than 1,000 journalists conducted in 1992 (Weaver and Wilhoit, 1996). The survey asked a range of questions about background, education, salary, job attitudes, and how journalists felt about their ability to report on the world around them. Weaver and Wilhoit found journalists to be typically male. They were on average 39 years old in print journalism and 33 years old in broadcast journalism (which was somewhat older than in a similar survey in the 1980s). Ideologically, journalists were more likely than the general U.S. population to consider themselves left of center and to support the Democratic Party. However, as Weaver and Wilhoit point out, there is convincing evidence that the organizational characteristics of a media outlet are more important in shaping news coverage than the personal attributes of the individual journalists. The social scientists found that journalists were attracted to the career for a number of factors, including the notion of "helping people" (ibid.: 121). However, American journalists were increasingly frustrated by a range of factors that limited their ability to pursue in-depth, meaningful stories, including inadequate staffing; media outlet concern for profits over quality; limits on travel; as well as formal and informal policy restrictions on what is considered newsworthy (ibid.: 65–7). While Weaver and Wilhoit's research found that low pay was less of an issue since a similar study of the profession in the 1980s, pay rises were apparently not enough to make the job universally attractive. Other frustrations were leading to two out of ten journalists considering a change in profession. This is at odds with a societal perception in the U.S. of journalists as glamorous or powerful members of a sought-after profession.

A key point addressed by Weaver and Wilhoit is that the ownership of media outlets by a particular corporation or even an individual did not automatically spawn a particular type of coverage. As Graber (2005) also notes, media owners rarely have the luxury of pursuing personal or corporate agendas at the expense of losing credibility or market share. In this sense, she is suggesting that good business practices will guard against bad journalism, at least to a degree. A more subtle and perhaps more relevant problem in the libertarian model of journalism is underlined by Weaver and Wilhoit in highlighting the conflicting sense of duty for the American journalist. He or she is expected to serve society by being both critical and descriptive (Graber, 2005: 170). Finding the elusive balance between the two is extraordinarily difficult, particularly for journalists who are increasingly pressured for time because of cutbacks in the newsroom. As more media outlets develop via the internet, satellite outlets, and cable, the dominance of traditional media organizations begins to fade (although television networks remain quite profitable). As a result, the share of advertising revenue diminishes for a wide range of media outlets and staff numbers fall at newspapers and traditional broadcasters.

Faced with mounting work pressures and less time, reporters are forced to rely more on single sources, public relations material, and other information provided by sources. There is less opportunity to challenge an employer about how stories are covered, particularly as many media outlets are "the only game in town." The ability to carry out thought-provoking or carefully balanced reporting is severely limited. This is a particularly difficult problem in the U.S., which lacks public funding for any large media organization.

Work pressures and time constraints aside, a lack of a sense of professional standards is a problem as well (Weaver and Wilhoit, 1996; Macdonald, 2006). Journalism schools have a long tradition in the U.S., but they have been based more on teaching skills than on inculcating ethics (Macdonald, 2006). Journalists have not developed the same sense of professional identity and industrial clout as doctors and lawyers. There are no formal qualifications, such as the state exams sat by other professionals. As a result, although journalists can be powerful political players, their lack of cohesion or political awareness as a profession can make them more pawns than watchdogs of the political sphere (Macdonald, 2006; Weaver and Wilhoit, 1996). Macdonald notes that journalism schools in the U.S. and Canada "bypass an analysis of the powerful media industries, downplaying the significance of journalists" working conditions and encouraging students to think idealistically about journalism" (2006: 746). In other words, market forces will overwhelm ideals in terms of shaping how journalists carry out their news-gathering and writing tasks in North America.

There is anecdotal evidence that journalists are under enormous personal and professional pressure. Some high-profile cases of journalists who have falsified stories have been widely discussed by the media themselves; in particular the case of *Washington Post* reporter Janet Cooke who made up a story of an 8-year-old boy addicted to heroin (and won a Pulitzer Prize in 1981 for the story before editors realized that it was false). In addition, the case of Jayson Blair, a reporter at *The New York Times*, who was found by 2003 to have plagiarized and fabricated parts of numerous articles, attracted attention to the fact that it is possible to work for a powerful media outlet and fail spectacularly to adhere to good journalistic practices.[1]

At the same time that journalists are struggling, public relations remains a thriving field and profession in the U.S. Public relations – the notion that a party, cause, or individual would need to have an organized media strategy – has a long tradition in the U.S. Another tradition is that the professions of journalism and public relations are quite distinct. While it is not unusual for former reporters to become public relations consultants (journalism is viewed as good preparation for the career), it is unusual for a public relations specialist to become a journalist again. The most benevolent view of public relations in the American sphere is that "flaks" serve as useful sources of information, particularly as a deadline looms. In a more negative light, public relations specialists can be both very aggressive and rather insidious in pursuing coverage or obfuscating problems. This is particular true in corporate communications, where it is noted by Davis (2002), a negative spin on company news can wipe millions or even billions of dollars off share prices. While the PR industry is viewed as a key part of the corporate hold on the media agenda by some analysts (such as Herman and Chomsky), there is also compelling evidence that slick, expensive PR does not translate into media dominance. Rather, as Davis (2002) suggests, journalists often respond to popular causes and grass-roots public relations efforts more readily than well-financed campaigns by big business or central government. Thus, the role of public relations in shaping political news must be considered within the framework of the other factors, especially within the News Production Model.

All of these somewhat pessimistic findings, however, should be balanced by the fact that journalists remain a very important part of American democracy. Since the era of Watergate in the mid-1970s, the profession has pursued many stories that challenge powerful elites. In particular, with the power of internet reports to penetrate every aspect of the public (and sometimes private) life of a politician, it is difficult for politicians to get away with a façade of democracy. Although often blamed for being too sycophantic to political leaders – especially the president – American journalists have not been intimidated from following stories that have led to heart of the White House and other citadels of power in the U.S. Prey to enormous pressures and struggling with a lack of resources, U.S. journalists sometimes fail to reach lofty ideals, but in striving for the goals of objectivity and service to society, they are a key factor in democracy.

Key points for American journalists and public relations

- Journalists feel that the pressures of their media outlets, rather than their personal viewpoints, are more important in shaping the news.
- Fierce competition and cuts in the media have brought more pressure for journalists, with two out of ten contemplating a career change.
- The U.S. has a long tradition of public relations.
- Despite often failing to meet lofty standards, American journalists serve a key function in American democracy.

The journalistic profession and public relations in the United Kingdom

3.3 When attention is turned to the British journalist, it is clear that the profession has changed profoundly in the past few decades. Journalism was regarded as a trade rather than a profession for longer in Britain than in the U.S. Journalists generally started in their teens,[2] received all of their training on the job, were relatively poorly paid, and had little prestige. By the 1990s, this concept of the journalist had changed radically (Delano, 2000; McNair, 2003): "Even when they worked at the less scrupulous end of the occupational spectrum or in the most menial of jobs, journalists came to be seen by many as privileged and powerful beings who possessed knowledge denied to others" (Delano, 2000: 262). One of the complaints about U.S. journalists is that there is no real national body for accreditation, control, or lobbying. While this is not true in the U.K., it is still arguable that the journalists themselves have less power than the media organizations. A survey of British journalists carried out in the mid-1990s showed that although most of them viewed their job as a profession rather than a trade, more than half of them belonged to a trade union called the National Union of Journalists. The union was very visible in the struggle to maintain jobs for many of the newspaper production workers made redundant by advancing technologies in the 1980s, but does not explicitly control journalists or their content. The union continues to represent journalists in pay and other disputes, but as with most of the other unions in Britain, it has lost a considerable amount of political influence in the past decades.

On the other hand, there is compelling evidence that British journalists are better able to translate their positions into significant political influence than their U.S. counterparts. For example, one of the chief architects of the New Labour political message and the "packaging" of former Prime Minister Tony Blair is former journalist Alastair Campbell. Campbell consistently used his network of former journalistic colleagues and his knowledge of the profession to manipulate the news to the prime minister's advantage. While some might see this as simply good political marketing, Campbell and other key advisers to the Labour Party spent decades working as top-level journalists before becoming political advisers. As Campbell himself emphasizes, he perceives his role as political adviser and a journalist as two sides of a coin. As both reporter and editor (of a now defunct national newspaper), Campbell has sought to produce news favorable to the cause of the Labour Party. Although many in Britain would view Campbell as a particularly powerful example of the very close relationship between journalists and politicians, there is nothing extraordinary in the British system about his perception of the need for a journalist to support his or her political convictions. Further convincing evidence of the lack of barriers between journalists and politicians in Britain is the fact that at least 30 out of 646 members of the British Parliament elected in 1997 were journalists[3] (Delano, 2000: 262).

Who are these British journalists, some of whom play such a significant part in the political life of the country? According to the data cited by Delano, almost 80 percent of British journalists are university graduates. Not only has Britain seen the introduction of undergraduate programs in journalism, there are now a range of postgraduate degrees as well. Whereas women were once very rare in British newsrooms, they are now common – albeit not in the highest editorial posts. Delano speculated that the average British journalist is a well-educated, 36-year-old, white, Protestant person with just one child or no children. He or she is left-wing, listens to Radio 4, and reads the *Daily Telegraph* or the *Guardian*. It is likely that this person voted for the Labour Party at the last election. The data also suggest that the journalists are generally better educated than their audience. Delano claims that journalists lack a common ethos (a comment echoed by Macdonald for American and Canadian journalists), seemingly content to "allow the issues of ethics, regulation, prerogatives, levels of skill and conditions of employment and reward to be decided entirely by their employers" (Delano, 2000: 271). Delano and others find this ironic, in that it would appear that while journalists are ready to investigate other political actors, they are reluctant to achieve political consciousness as a profession.

One of the institutions of British journalism that underline the close relationship between politicians and journalists is the "Lobby" system. While elite American journalists are called to public press conferences at the White House and other key government institutions, much of the national political news in Britain is gathered through meetings in the lobby of the Houses of Parliament in London. Through the Lobby system, an elite set of 220 journalists are allowed into briefings (typically twice daily at 11 am and 4 pm) with the prime minister's press secretary. They are encouraged to report stories on a non-attributed basis (often on the basis of one source, i.e. the press secretary himself or herself). In addition, privileged media organizations and journalists who are thought particularly favorable or influential will be given special access to the prime minister or other government officials. This access comes with strict rules, however. Journalists who break the agreement by identifying sources, asking difficult questions, or failing to report on political issues in a way favorable to the government can be excluded from the Lobby – and hence from the central source of political information in the country. In times of crisis, such as the Falklands War, the government has suspended even these press briefings.

The Lobby system draws British journalists and politicians into a symbiotic relationship that is much closer than that of the Washington journalists to the politicians "inside the Beltway" in Washington, D.C. While British politicians rely on journalists to raise awareness of their public policy, provide favorable coverage, and denigrate their opponents, journalists have an unusually close relationship with the leaders of the country. This means a steady supply of key information to write their stories. Although politicians and journalists could perhaps be considered natural enemies, in the Lobby system they typically work as partners in the political sphere. This has led to criticism of the system from some analysts such as Franklin (2004), who suggests that British journalists are so reliant on government for information that they can become government mouthpieces' instead of watchdogs. The system strongly discourages investigative journalism that could challenge the policies, personalities, or success of the current government. In addition, the rules of secrecy can lead to a lack of accountability, including rumor, gossip, and the ability of politicians to undermine colleagues without being held accountable. For example, the Lobby system is used extensively by both Labour and Conservative politicians to discredit political "dissidents" who fail to toe the party line. The Lobby system can foster the "packaging of politics" as it manipulates while it disseminates information, which "impoverishes political debate because it oversimplifies and trivializes political communication" (Franklin, 2004).

Despite the influence of the Lobby system, there is evidence of conflict between a fast-growing media sector and the traditional norms of deference to central political power by much of the media. One of the largest conflicts that illuminate these tensions arose over a BBC radio report broadcast on May 29, 2003 by freelance correspondent Andrew Gilligan, who suggested that the government's dossier on the weapons of mass destruction in Iraq had been "sexed up" to make a more compelling case for the war in Iraq (Hutton Inquiry, 2004: 12). The Blair administration was furious, in particular as the report suggested that the government had tried to manipulate sensitive security reports for political causes. Eventually, the source of the report was traced to a government defense adviser named Dr David Kelly, who committed suicide after his name as the source of the report was leaked to the media by other government officials. An official parliamentary inquiry – somewhat akin to a U.S. congressional hearing – was ordered. As part of the report, the exact workings of the BBC, its news-gathering techniques, production oversight, and relationship to government sources were scrutinized. When the parliamentary report was published in January 2004, the BBC was criticized for broadcasting Gilligan's item without proper editorial oversight and fact-checking. Both the head of the BBC Board of Governors and BBC Director-General Greg Dyke resigned, although Dyke and others later argued that the report was unfairly critical of the BBC (Dyke, 2005). The report on the Inquiry provides a fascinating study of the inner workings of journalists and politicians in Britain.

The other major change in the journalism sphere has been the rapid growth and professionalization of the public relations industry in the U.K. (Davis, 2002). The PR industry grew tenfold between 1979 and 1998, according to a study by Miller and Dinan (2000: 10). As the British government extended its professional public relations, so did other segments of society, including unions, pressure groups, religious organizations, charities, local governments, and other state institutions (Davis, 2002: 3). All of this has led to a much broader range of information and pressure on journalists from groups wishing to shape the news agenda in their own interests. In addition, as Davis points out, there are concerted efforts to keep some news away from the public. Although Davis and others (for example, see Schlesinger et al., 2001) see the rise of the public relations industry as worrying for democracy, Davis sees limits on the influence of corporate or government public relations. Although public relations efforts can put pressure on journalists, news logic and a focus on the media audience can balance these efforts. For example, a somewhat ragged and disorganized campaign with genuine grass-roots appeal can have more effect than a slick, well-financed publicity effort for a major corporation or unpopular government. The large exposure to public relations has made British journalists – just as their American counterparts – possibly more immune to the effects of publicity campaigns and personal pressures.

Key points for British journalists and public relations

- Journalists have become better educated and have achieved a higher social status have in the past in the U.K.
- Although British journalists are represented by a national trade union, they feel more influence from their media outlets than their profession in terms of shaping their daily work.
- There is a close, symbiotic relationship between journalists and the government in the U.K., as exemplified by the involvement of journalists in politics and the Lobby system.
- Public relations as an industry has grown massively in the U.K.

The journalistic profession and public relations in Russia[4]

3.4 What has been the fate of journalists across the former Soviet Union (including Russia)? An analysis of the performance of the media in 18 elections in Russia, Ukraine, Belarus, Moldova, and Armenia from 1993 to 2001 highlights that the central problem lies in the lack of professionalism on the part of the journalists (Oates, 2004). While all of the countries struggled with problems of state influence on the media, unfairness, bias, lack of financial backing, and other issues, the central dilemma of the dearth of an independent journalism profession resonates throughout all of these former Soviet countries. In particular, Russia would appear to be reverting to a Soviet-style relationship, with the media as an actively co-opted player in repressive governance rather than a factor in moving forward to a situation in which the media are a part of a burgeoning civil society. It is important to point out that journalists in Russia are struggling with massive barriers to pursuing their profession, including a lack of proper financing, inordinate pressure from officials and, most worryingly, violence against them that has led to murder in many cases. Russia is one of the deadliest countries in the world for journalists, as measured by international groups such as Reporters Without Borders.

The key question about Russian journalists is whether they have fundamentally changed their role in politics from the Soviet era. Under Communist rule, the Soviet media fulfilled the political function as outlined by Siebert et al. (1963) in the "soviet" model of the press. The media were the political communication wing of the ruling Communist Party of the Soviet Union, existing not to provide information to the public so that they could make political decisions, but to educate the public in the tenets of Marxism-Leninism. In reality, this took the form of presenting an idealized view of society to the masses, showing them Soviet society as it ought to be, and ignoring aspects that did not fit the government image. Although there were censors, they were not the key part of the formation of political news. Rather, journalists were well inculcated with the norms of self-censorship, producing news that fitted the "frame" of the Soviet government. Although there was some variation across different publications, as well as a waxing and waning of the strictness of the proper "line," the central Soviet media never functioned as anything but a propaganda wing of the Communist Party. At the end of the Soviet period, the introduction of the policy of glasnost (transparency) by Soviet leaders led to an increase in the variety of opinions expressed, but not to a fundamental, permanent change in how post-Soviet journalists perceived their role (Oates, 2006). They continued to see themselves as political players, rather than political observers in service to the citizens.

It is understandable that journalists who worked as propagandists in the Soviet era might have trouble adjusting to change. However, there is fairly strong evidence that the post-Soviet generation of journalists do not interpret their role as disinterested supporters of civil society (Pasti, 2005; Voltmer, 2000). Much of the problem is simply practical. Journalists in Russia must adhere to the news agenda set by the forces that control their media outlet, as discussed in Chapter 2. While the post-Soviet period initially allowed some variation in opinion, this has become increasingly limited as the Kremlin tolerates less and less opposition to its policies. State-funded media outlets face losing their subsidies. When commercial media outlets criticize the presidential administration on key issues (such as opposition to Putin, corruption, or the war in Chechnya), they often lose financial control through government sanctions (such as strict application of tax or finance laws). Even when individual journalists choose to pursue controversial issues, they will quickly find that cautious editors and publishers will be quick to set limits. When interviewed in March 2004, the host of the political talk show *Freedom of Speech*, Savik Shuster, complained that his NTV bosses constantly called him to complain about his plans to book outspoken guests.[5] A few months later, his show on commercial television was cancelled. The toleration for a free and fair media became even more remote in April 2007, as security forces seized the computer servers of a Russian media freedom organization, Educated Media (formerly the Russian office of Internews).[6]

Practical issues aside, there is substantial evidence that Russian journalists do not view themselves as political watchdogs or challengers of the political status quo. It is unsurprising that Russian journalists would view their role differently from their American and British counterparts; after all, American and British journalists differ a great deal from one another. However, while American and British journalists differ significantly, they both view their role as independent political actors in society. Most Russian journalists view themselves as political players and do not seek to change that role (see reports from the European Institute for the Media listed below, also Oates, 2006); they work for their particular political "patron." Viewers, readers, and listeners will be presented with "news" that is essentially propaganda from the point of view of the political patron. As the presidential apparatus has consolidated power in Russia to a large extent (discussed in more detail about elections and the media in Chapter 5), there is now little deviation from the Kremlin line. In particular, this means that there is virtually no meaningful news from Chechnya. Generally, it means that Russian citizens have little ability to debate meaningfully political issues or to participate in civic life.

There remains some variation in the media sphere in Russia, as a wide range of opinion and news is expressed in smaller outlets. In particular, a Moscow newspaper called *Novaya Gazeta* [The New Newspaper] and a Moscow-based radio station called Echo of Moscow continue to report on issues such as the war in Chechnya, opposition to Putin, protest marches, and the lack of basic social services in post-Soviet Russia. They do this is an atmosphere of menace and personal threat. The most prominent opposition journalist, *Novaya Gazeta* reporter Anna Politkovskaya, was assassinated in October 2006 in the elevator of her apartment building. Although her death caused world-wide comment and outrage, President Putin was fairly dismissive of her work, saying she had no influence on political life in Russia. There was relatively little interest in her death in Russia. This is unsurprising, as the Committee to Protect Journalists has estimated that 29 journalists were killed in a decade in post-Soviet Russia. Many have died covering the wars in Chechnya, but the organization estimated that at least 11 (not including Politkovskaya) were murdered in contract-style killings in the four years after Putin came to power.[7]

With this sort of example of the fate of investigative journalists, it is not surprising that most Russian journalists have a finely developed sense of self-censorship. Unfortunately, many also freely accept bribes (particularly during elections) to write favorable articles on some candidates and publish scurrilous rumors about others (see European Institute for the Media reports; Oates, 2006). This reflects the development of the Russian PR system, with a host of non-democratic tactics. While arguably the unfair influence of money and power makes PR undemocratic in the U.S. and Britain, the Russian PR sphere is far more Machiavellian. Although tactics include "white propaganda" – the dissemination of positive information about an organization, party, political candidate, company, etc. – far more popular in election campaigns is "black propaganda." This includes planting negative information, rumors, or even lies about individuals and organizations, usually via journalists who are either bribed or under political influence. This is called "hidden advertising" and is particularly prevalent at election times, as "news" articles or items appear that are actually planted by PR "technologists," as they are known in Russia. By the 1999 elections, the Russian media – and state-run Channel 1 television in particular – had developed a compelling system of *kompromat* (an abbreviation of "compromising material" in Russian). With *kompromat*, the media provide dodgy "evidence" that a political or business figure has been involved in shady dealings (such as by insinuating a link between the murder of American businessman Paul Tatum and the Moscow mayor standing in opposition to Putin). There is no attempt to present a balanced report or seek a reply from the individual involved. Often the "evidence" is just quick flashes of financial documents on the television screen or insinuations from the television host on a political chat show (see reports by the European Institute for the Media; Oates, 2006).

Research suggests that it is unlikely that the next generation of Russian journalists will bring great change, as few journalists have either the ability or the desire to perceive themselves as "watchdogs" for the public (Pasti, 2005; Voltmer, 2000). Although freed from the censorship of the Soviet state, Russian journalists now must operate within a constrained and dangerous profession. In a study of the newspaper *Izvestiya*, Voltmer did find some change in the way the newspaper covered political news. Using qualitative content analysis of front-page stories, she found "clear signs of growing professionalism with the news becoming more factual, more timely and broader in the selection of topics" (2000: 469). At the same time, however, her research found a "high degree of subjective evaluations indicating the persistence of the historical legacy of Russian journalism" (ibid.). In a number of interviews, discussions, and studies over the years by the author, it is clear that Russian journalists remain much more fragmented and disempowered as a profession than their U.S. or British colleagues.

Key points for Russian journalists and public relations

- Russian journalists perceive themselves as political players (or pawns) but not as observers or watchdogs.
- Journalism in Russia is a dangerous profession, with many killed in recent years.

- Very few journalists choose to oppose the dominant Kremlin political line.
- Public relations in Russia utilizes a range of aggressive tactics, including vicious smear campaigns of political opponents during elections.

Chapter summary

Just as there is variation from country to country in the first four categories of the News Production Model (political environment, media norms, media regulation, media ownership), there are significant differences in the professional lives of journalists in the U.S., the U.K., and Russia. U.S. journalists have come under significant pressure due to shrinking newsrooms and report feeling relatively powerless in their news organizations. At the same time, there is evidence that American journalists continue to strive for "objectivity" and pursue politically sensitive stories in the watchdog tradition.

Evidence suggests that there is a quite close, symbiotic relationship between British journalists and politicians, particularly due to the Lobby system. In addition, the public relations profession has grown enormously in Britain in recent decades, providing new challenges to journalists who would fend off "flaks" in their daily professional lives. At the same time, British journalists themselves have become increasingly more educated, although not particularly well-organized as a profession (echoing a problem with their American counterparts). The Hutton Inquiry, stemming from a report accusing the Blair administration of "sexing up" a report on weapons of mass destruction in Iraq, revealed significant tensions between the government and the journalistic sphere in the U.K.

In Russia, the situation is much starker, as Russian journalists have failed to develop into a facet of civil society. Rather, they are overwhelmingly obliged to serve their political and financial masters, with investigative journalists facing intimidation, threats, and even assassination. The dire situation in Russia throws into relief the fact that the American and British journalistic profession, albeit flawed, serves as a critical element of civil society. It is possible to design a system in which you have journalists without democracy; however, democracy cannot exist without a vibrant core of journalists in service – at least much of the time – to informing the public.

Study questions

1 How do the working principles of journalists differ in the U.S., the U.K., and Russia?
2 What is the largest threat to journalists functioning as political observers rather than political pawns in these three countries?
3 What is the role of self-censorship in the journalistic profession?
4 Is the role of public relations fundamentally different in the U.S., the U.K., and Russia?
5 In thinking back to the first four factors of the News Production Model presented in Chapter 2 (political environment, media norms, media regulation, and ownership), how do the different attributes of journalists and public relations in the three case studies round out the model?

Reading guide

A thoughtful and well-written book that questions the nature of journalism in general and studies the American journalist in particular is *The Power of News* (1995) by Michael Schudson. *The American Journalist in the 1990s* details the findings of Weaver and Wilhoit (1996) from a survey of U.S. journalists and makes interesting reading. McNair (2003) discusses journalists in Great Britain in his book. For a discussion of a survey of British journalists, see Delano's (2000) article about a century of British journalism, which includes his profile of the profession. In terms of academic journals, *Journalism Studies,* the *European Journal of Communication,* and *Political Communication,* as well as the *Harvard International Journal of Press/Politics,* all include articles addressing the trials and tribulations of the profession in the U.S., the U.K., and other countries. The Harvard journal also regularly includes commentary from journalists themselves. The *Columbia Journalism Review*, as the journal of the profession in the U.S., covers the state of American profession thoroughly as well. *Public Relations Democracy* by Aeron Davis (2002) is a useful blend of an intellectual overview of the political science literature on public relations – as well as a specific case study of Britain. First-hand evidence of the experiences of Russian journalists can be found in several reports by the European Institute for the Media (now defunct, but their archive of reports is available online via www.media-politics.com). In addition, the nature of Russian journalism is discussed in various reports on the role of the media in election campaigns by the Organization for Security and Co-operation in Europe (OSCE), with the full citation for one of the most relevant reports listed in the references below. Others are available via the OSCE's Office of Democracy Initiatives and Human Rights at www.osce.org/odihr.

Internet resources

www.rsf.org   Reporters Without Borders is an international NGO that defends journalists and other media contributors and professionals who have been imprisoned or persecuted for doing their work. It issues warnings and reports about journalists who are under threat and publishes an annual index of media freedom.

www.internews.org   Internews is an international, non-profit organization that works to foster independent media and promote open communications policies in the public interest.

www.cjr.org   The *Columbia Journalism Review* is the central journal of the journalism profession in the U.S.

www.nuj.org.uk   The National Union of Journalists is the British union for journalists.

http://www.osce.org/odihr/   The Office for Democratic Institutions and Human Rights, part of the Organization for Security and Co-operation in Europe (OSCE), monitors election fairness, including media performance and provides reports online.

Notes

1 See "Correcting the Record: Times Reporter Who Resigned Leaves Long Trail of Deception", May 11, 2003, *New York Times.*
2 British students can choose to leave school earlier than U.S. students, gaining credit for national exams passed rather than for a set number of years of study.
3 Identified by the fact that they were members of the National Union of Journalists.
4 Much of the information in this section is based on the author's research, including dissertation fieldwork in 1995 and 1996 that was funded by a Fulbright award. Research and fieldwork also was funded by grants from the British Economic and Social Research Council (R223250028 and R000223133). Some of the most interesting insights came from work as a member of a team that analyzed media performance in the 1999 Russian Duma elections for the European Institute for the Media. For more details on the research, see Oates, 2006.
5 Interview with author, NTV offices, Moscow, March 2004.
6 The Russian procurator claimed that the organization, which receives funding from overseas, was involved in financial fraud. This author has worked with the individuals involved in this organiza-tion for more than ten years and observed much of its work. The government's action was clearly a case of harassment to stop the work of the organization in training journalists to better serve Russian society.
7 See *Journalists Killed in the Line of Duty in the Last 10 Years*, a report from the Committee to Project Journalists. Available at http://www.cpj.org/killed/Ten_Year_Killed/Intro.html. The figures only include those for which there is evidence to suggest that a journalist was likely killed in direct reprisal for his or her work or in crossfire while carrying out a dangerous assignment. The figure does not include journalists who are killed in accidents – such as car or plane crashes – unless the crash was caused by hostile action (for example, if a plane were shot down or a car crashed trying to avoid gunfire).

References

Davis, A. (2002) *Public Relations Democracy: Public Relations, Politics and the Mass Media in Britain.* Manchester: Manchester University Press.

Delano, A. (2000) "No Sign of a Better Job: 100 Years of British Journalism." *Journalism Studies* 1 (2): 261–72.

Dyke, G. (2005) *Inside Story.* London: Harper Perennial.

European Institute for the Media (1994) *The Russian Parliamentary Elections: Monitoring of the Election Coverage of the Russian Mass Media.* Düsseldorf: European Institute for the Media. Available online at http://www.media-politics.com/eimreports.htm.

European Institute for the Media (February 1996) *Monitoring the Media Coverage of the 1995 Russian Parliamentary Elections.* Düsseldorf, Germany: The European Institute for the Media. Available online at http://www.media-politics.com/eimreports.htm.

European Institute for the Media (September 1997) *Monitoring the Media Coverage of the 1996 Russian Presidential Elections.* Düsseldorf, Germany: The European Institute for the Media. Available online at http://www.media-politics.com/eimreports.htm.

European Institute for the Media (March 2000) *Monitoring the Media Coverage of the December 1999 Parliamentary Elections in Russia: Final Report.* Düsseldorf: European Institute for the Media. Available online at http://www.media-politics.com/eimreports.htm.

European Institute for the Media (August 2000) *Monitoring the Media Coverage of the March 2000 Presidential Elections in Russia (Final Report).* Düsseldorf: European Institute for the Media. Available online at http://www.media-politics.com/eimreports.htm.

Franklin, B. (2004) *Packaging Politics: Political Communications in Britain's Media Democracy.* London: Hodder Arnold.

Herman, E. and Chomsky, N. (2002) *Manufacturing Consent.* New York: Pantheon Books.

Hutton Inquiry (2004) *Report of the Inquiry into the Circumstances Surrounding the Death of Dr David Kelly CMG.* London: The Stationery Office. Available online at http://www.the-hutton-inquiry.org.uk.

Macdonald, I. (2006) "Teaching Journalists to Save the Profession: A Critical Assessment of Recent Debates on the Future of U.S. and Canadian Journalism Education." *Journalism Studies* 7 (5): 745–64.

McChesney, R.W. (2004) "Media Policy Goes to Main Street: The Uprising of 2003." *The Communication Review* 7: 223–58.

McNair, B. (2003) *News and Journalism in the UK*, 4th edn. London: Routledge.

Miller, D. (1995) "The Media and Northern Ireland: Censorship, Information Management and the Broadcasting Ban." In Philo, G. (ed.) *Glasgow Media Group Reader, Vol. II: Industry, Economy, War and Politics.* London: Routledge.

Miller, D. and W. Dinan. (2000) "The Rise of the PR Industry in Britain, 1979–1998." *European Journal of Communication* 15 (1): 5–35.

Oates, S. (2004) "From the Archives of the European Institute for the Media: Analysing the Results of a Decade of Monitoring of Post-Soviet Elections." Paper presented at the British Association for Slavonic and East European Studies Conference, Fitzwilliam College, Cambridge, England.

Oates, S. (2006) *Television, Democracy and Elections in Russia.* London: Routledge.

Organization for Security and Co-operation in Europe/Office for Democratic Institutions and Human Rights (OSCE/ODIHR) (2004). *Russian Federation Elections to the State Duma 7 December 2003 OSCE/ODIHR Election Observation Mission Report.* Warsaw: Office for Democratic Institutions and Human Rights. Available online at http://www.osce.org/item/8051.html.

Pasti, S. (2005) "Two Generations of Contemporary Russian Journalists". *European Journal of Communication* 20 (1): 89–115.

Project for Excellence in Journalism (2007) *The State of the News Media 2007: An Annual Report on American Journalism.* Washington, DC: Project for Excellence in Journalism. Available online at http://www.stateofthemedia.org/2007/.

Schlesinger, P., Miller, D., and Dinan, W. (2001) *Open Scotland? Journalists, Spin Doctors and Lobbyists.* Edinburgh: Polygon.

Schudson, M. (1995) *The Power of News,* Cambridge, MA: Harvard University Press.

Siebert, F.S., Peterson, T., and Schramm, W. (1963) *Four Theories of the Press.* Urbana, IL: University of Illinois Press.

Voltmer, K. (2000) "Constructing Political Reality in Russia: *Izvestiya* – Between Old and New Journalistic Practices". *European Journal of Communication* 15 (4): 469–500.

Weaver, D.H. and Wilhoit, G. (1996) *The American Journalist in the 1990s.* Mahwah, NJ: Lawrence Erlbaum Associates.

The Media Audience in Comparative Perspective

4

Central points

- The propaganda model – the idea that the audience can be easily swayed or manipulated by the news media – is not very useful.
- Just as media systems vary across country boundaries, so do media audiences.
- It is important to consider not only the usage of various types of media, but the amount of trust and attention paid to different media outlets.
- Viewers still love television, even though media audiences are becoming increasingly fragmented in advanced industrial democracies by the explosion in media choice fostered by technological advancements.
- The media provide a key rallying point for national identity and patriotism for citizens.
- The relationship among news production, content, and the audience is perhaps seen most clearly in times of political crisis and change.

Introduction

4.1 Just after the Second World War, there was great interest in testing the power of propaganda on citizens. Having watched the rise of Adolf Hitler in Germany, social scientists wanted to analyze how the influence of the mass media could drive a nation into the extremism that had fostered the Holocaust and a global war. What they found, however, was both puzzling and alarming to those who would dismiss the rise of Nazism as a public brainwashed by cunning words and images. Studies by Berelson and Lazarsfeld (1954) in the U.S. quickly established that the media actually have a relatively weak ability to bring leaders to power. Instead, voters rely on cues from their sociological backgrounds, party identification, stands on issues, and even conversations with family and friends before listing media as a key influence. This understanding of the role of the media in voting behavior (discussed in more detail in Chapter 5) influenced much of the scholarship on measuring possible political manipulation by the media in the second half of the twentieth century. Similar studies in the U.K. by Butler and Stokes (1969, 1974) came to roughly the same conclusions: The role of the media was just one factor nested in a range of other influences. At the same time, the Soviets remained very confident in the efficacy of propaganda – so convinced that they rapidly lost power when they mistakenly believed in their on-going ability to manipulate the audience in the face of elite change.

It is clear that there is some effect from media usage. It is, however, not at all like the Soviet conception of the "hypodermic syringe," in which the information is injected into the individuals and the audience is automatically convinced. Levels of usage and trust vary among different media outlets both between countries and within countries themselves. Varying segments of the audience have quite distinct relationships with the mass media. Some are empowered by the information, some are indifferent, while still others are even alienated from the political sphere altogether by what they see, hear, or read.

Understanding these nuances and comparing them across country boundaries will allow us to gain a better understanding of the general relationship between the media and the audience. With the rejection of the propaganda theory in the West, social scientists have struggled for decades to try to define just how media messages can affect an audience. It is apparent that people do not think in a certain way just because a newspaper, a broadcast, or an online news site has told them to think in that manner. On the other hand, it is apparent that political beliefs of individuals often parallel the political messages found in their favorite media outlets. However, as social scientists like to emphasize, correlation is not causality. In other words, just because one thing follows another, it does not mean that one *caused* the other. Just because a Republican supporter watches Fox News, this does not mean that the more patriotic, pro-Bush coverage on Fox "turned" the individual Republican. There is a synergetic relationship here, in that it is likely that a more conservative, pro-Bush American would tune in to Fox News in the first place as it tends to agree with – as well as reinforce – his or her world view. Thus, there is a relationship between the political messages of a media outlet and the recipient – but it is more dynamic than a simple propaganda model would suggest.

It is within these particular boundaries of understanding news reception that some of the most interesting work on understanding the audience can be found. For example, if people tend to select a media outlet that supports their world view, then they are less likely to hear opposing or challenging viewpoints. This can make it difficult for a society to find solutions to problems that must involve an entire community, such as reaching peace agreements in places including Northern Ireland or post-war Iraq. Media outlets face challenges not only in attracting an audience, but also in maintaining the interest and trust of that audience. Overall, an examination of the media audience illuminates the interactive and complex nature of the relationship between news producer and news receiver.

There is a long tradition of research into media audiences. Much of this stemmed from concerns about propaganda, but became much more sophisticated over time (McQuail, 1997). McQuail (p. 21) usefully divides research concerning media audiences into three areas. First, there is structural research, in which social scientists define the size of the audience and describe who makes up the audience – as well as how the audience relates to society. This helps researchers to understand who is using the media at any given point, as well as trends over time. This type of audience research is typically carried out through opinion surveys and statistical analysis (as in the Pew Center reports cited in this volume). A second strand of research is behavioral in nature. In these studies, using surveys and other methods, social scientists seek to explain and predict audience choices, reactions, and media effects on society in general. Finally, McQuail discusses cultural research, in which analysts try to understand how audiences understand the content that they receive and how that understanding is translated into social change or action. Researchers often use qualitative methods such as focus groups in this type of cultural research of audiences. This chapter discusses findings in the case studies that stretch across all three of those strands in audience research.

Overall, a central theme to the work by McQuail and others on audience research is that the concept of "audience" is complicated and growing even more difficult to study with the proliferation of new communication technologies. Not only do people have different media habits, the same people will have varying habits at different times. In addition, for some the media is essentially "wallpaper," just background to everyday activities, while to others viewing a particular news report or program can change opinions or even (more rarely) galvanize people into action. Thus, earlier assumptions that a message sent would be a message received have long since been debunked by media research. For example, at different times, members of a media audience can respond to media messages as voters and citizens – and sometimes as viewers, listeners, and consumers (Avery, 1993). Audience reception is "not a matter of checking out whether or not audience members had managed to get the meaning of items, but instead a matter of looking at the different meanings which they constructed from items" (Corner, 1996: 282). McQuail summarizes work by Clausse (1968) to underline six specific hurdles that a media message must cross in order to have a meaningful impact on a member of the audience (McQuail: 49): 1) the message must be created and offered; 2) it must be able to be received by the audience; 3) it must actually be received; 4) it must be registered by the audience member; and 5) it must be internalized by the audience member. In order for it to have political impact (step 6), the message must then lead to some sort of political behavior – ranging from compliance to an existing regime, to voting in an election, to protest, to possibly even taking to the streets in protest (as in the 1991 Russian counter-coup).

When attempting to compare audience reception, understanding, reaction, and behavior across various countries, the nature of the study becomes even more complex. As such, the information presented below is a comparison of media consumption, with some references to particular characteristics of attention, trust, and relative political influence of the media in the U.S., the U.K., and Russia. This provides useful information on the potential of the media to reach and influence its audience. More direct linkages between media use and political action will be explored in subsequent chapters on the media and elections, terrorism, war, and the internet.

The U.S. audience is particularly fond of broadcast journalism, while print journalism is losing ground. At the same time, the advent of the internet has significantly widened the information available to one part of the population, but has little influence on others. Some Americans even reject the internet, feeling that it further erodes the social fabric. In the U.K., there is a particularly strong trust in the BBC, even while the viewers are attracted to the ever-increasing array of entertainment and information programs on other channels. The British remain much more interested in their national newspapers than their American counterparts. While the internet has surged in use, studies suggest that the British are somewhat less likely to view it as the central source of news and information it has become for many Americans.

The Russian case provides us with some of the most intriguing audience behavior of all. Despite clear evidence that state-run channels are badly biased, Russian viewers still both like and trust their central television. The revolution in the media driven by cable, satellite, and the internet has touched far less of the population in Russia, where most of the population cannot afford to pay for the extra services. The use of the internet – and its role in the information sphere – remains limited in Russia when compared with the U.S. and the U.K. While there is still an array of political viewpoints found in some small publications and on some radio outlets, they do not reach a mass audience. Russians show a duality that is at first puzzling to Western observers, in that they can love and trust media they know to be untruthful. However, this set of attitudes is particularly enlightening, as it underlines the idea that the audience relationship with media in all countries is both complicated and sometimes contradictory.

The U.S. media audience

4.2 The Pew Research Center for the People and the Press carries out extensive research into the nature of the U.S. media audience and regularly monitors where Americans get their news. In a survey for one week in March 2007, 65 percent of the respondents said their news came from network television news (ABC, CBS, or NBC) and 59 percent from cable channels such as Cable News Network (CNN) or the Fox News Channel.[1] In addition, 40 percent of the American audience reported getting news from the radio and 36 percent from the internet. Fifty-three percent said they regularly obtained national and international information from newspapers. When asked about their *main* source of news for national and international issues, 29 percent of the American respondents listed network television news, 29 percent cable television news, 14 percent the internet, 11 percent newspapers, and 10 percent radio.

These figures provide an important snapshot of the U.S. news audience in a changing environment. They show that television remains central to the news audience – but the dominance of the "Big Three" networks is now gone. According to this survey, the central television networks of ABC, CBS, and NBC now share equal audience attention and interest with the far newer offerings on CNN and Fox News. In particular, the rise of the Fox Network is intriguing as Fox News clearly departs from the norms of objectivity and offers a far more patriotic, pro-Republican view of the news (see Chapter 2 for more discussion of this). As well as competing with their cable rivals, the Big Three news programs also now must compete with the internet. However, while the internet offers competition, it also offers the opportunity for the traditional mass media to adapt its products to the new technology and potentially increase its audience reach. In other words, if a news network is losing viewers on television, it can try to get them back online.

In a detailed survey of the U.S. media audience, the Pew Research Center explored the relationship between Americans and their media (Pew, Center, 2005). While the respondents had plenty to complain about some media outlets and journalistic behavior, overall they were very supportive of their media and approved of the attempts to make the news balanced. They did, however, make significant distinctions between different types of media. In their daily local newspapers, they liked the local news, sports, entertainment, the useful classified advertising, and the editorials that gave opinions on particular issues. On their local television news, the viewers reported approval of the focus on area events, the connection to their community, the personalities on the television screen, the weather, and the "hometown factor." As the survey indicated, Americans were looking for something different in the national network news: a broad scope, a concise format, and in-depth coverage. They were more likely to turn to cable television news for up-to-the-minute breaking information on a wide range of topics. Overall, they felt well-served by the vast variety offered up by the U.S. media sphere.[2]

The Pew survey lists the internet as "central" to U.S. media use, in that one in four Americans picked the internet as a main source of news. Almost a quarter of Americans (23 percent) go online for news daily, up from 15 percent in 2000. Although younger people are more likely to use the internet for news, use is not limited to the younger generation. While internet use is often cited as a reason for the declining interest in newspapers, it would seem that internet users are in some ways champions of the traditional American newspaper. This is because many of the online news gatherers are in fact using the internet version of printed newspapers. In addition, it would appear that internet use can contribute to positive feelings about newspapers – and more negative feelings about some other news outlets. The Pew survey found that people who read newspapers online have a far less favorable opinion of network and local television news programming than do people who read the print version of the paper. At the same time, readers of online newspapers feel far more favorable toward large national newspapers, such as *The New York Times* and *The Washington Post*. This could suggest a particular synergy: those who read the more in-depth news coverage in newspapers and seek out extra information online find more to challenge in the generally shorter coverage on television. On the other hand, those who are naturally more cynical might choose to seek out additional information, hence it could be less an "internet and newspaper effect" than another case of self-selection toward particular media use. Overall, newspaper circulation is rather low (considering that there are 300 million people in the U.S.) and has stagnated or fallen in the many markets (see Table 4.1). This may be compensated by those who are picking up the news from websites of traditional newspapers, but this information is not released by the Audit Bureau of Circulations in the same way as the print distribution.

The U.S. news paradox is that while the American public faults the media coverage in many ways, people generally remain favorable toward media organizations. The Pew survey found that public attitudes toward the media, which have been increasingly negative in recent years, were the worst since the mid-1980s. Perceptions of political bias in the media had increased in the past two years. However, the American public still viewed most media outlets quite favorably (see Table 4.2). Daily newspapers, local television news, and network television news had all slipped slightly in favorability – but none of them as much as the Supreme Court, President Bush, Congress, or the Democratic Party. The only media to slip fairly far in favorability were the major national newspapers, which is worrying for those who consider large, prestige newspapers such as *The New York Times* as the "backbone" of American journalism.

Table 4.1   Top daily newspapers in the U.S.

Rank	Title	Place of publication	Publisher	Average Paid Circulation
1	USA Today	McLean, Virginia	Gannett Co. Inc.	2,272,815
2	The Wall Street Journal	New York City	News Corporation	2,049,786
3	The New York Times	New York City	New York Times Company	1,142,464
4	Los Angeles Times	Los Angeles	Tribune Company	851,832
5	The Washington Post	Washington, D.C.	Washington Post Company	724,242
6	New York Daily News	New York City	New York Daily News	708,477
7	New York Post	New York City	News Corporation	673,379
8	Chicago Tribune	Chicago, Illinois	Tribune Company	579,079
9	Houston Chronicle	Houston, Texas	Hearst Newspapers	513,387
10	Arizona Republic	Phoenix, Arizona	Gannett Co. Inc.	438,722

Source: Audit Bureau of Circulations data reported in USA Today, on May 9, 2006.

Table 4.2   U.S. audience view of media institutions (percentage with favorable view)

Favorable opinion of …	2001	2005	Change
Daily newspaper	82	80	−2
Local TV news	83	79	−4
Cable TV news*	88	79	−9
Network TV news	76	75	−1
Major national papers	74	61	−13
Supreme Court	78	66	−12
Democratic Party	63	57	−6
Congress	65	54	−11
George W. Bush**	64	55	−9
Republican Party	54	52	−2

Notes
* In 2001, this question listed only CNN and MSNBC; Fox News was added in 2005
** Figures on Bush's popularity date to March 2005

Source: Pew, June 26, 2005 report. The percentages are based on those who chose to rate each category.

However, overall it is clear that media institutions are generally more popular than political institutions.

Americans reported liking many factors in their news, including the ability to get information in a timely fashion as well as staying informed about a wide range of news developments both locally and globally. However, although they were provided with the same media environment as American Democrats, Republicans reported less affection for the news media. This raises an intriguing question – given the broad choices available and the alleged objectivity in news, why would Republicans like it less? This is a difficult question to answer, but information from focus groups held in 2004 provides some clues. Eleven focus groups, part of a project to look at the framing of the terrorist threat in the media, discussed media use, feelings about terrorism, coverage of terrorist acts, the role of security concerns in the recent election, and other issues (Oates and Williams, 2006).[3] As the participants were screened to ascertain that they had at least moderate media use, they did represent a rather more media-savvy sample than the general population. What emerged, however, was concern and frustration that any sense of security was so often challenged by the media. They were generally annoyed at the reporting of various "threat" levels, with little moderating information. In particular, those who were more likely to vote for Bush were more concerned with a notion of a strong, safe nation. This would suggest that Republicans may have less tolerance for media discussion and debate, particularly when it can descend into sensationalizing threat.

The notion of American media objectivity is certainly criticized (and sometimes defended) by scholars and analysts, but is it still relevant for the American audience? The conviction that their news is objective is clearly far less widespread in the U.S. than in the past, as the percentage of those who believe most of what they read in daily newspapers dropped from 84 percent in 1985 to just 54 percent in 2004 (Pew, Research Center, 2005). Overall, Americans do feel fairly confident that they are receiving facts rather than merely opinion from their media outlets, although this varies a great deal from outlet to outlet (see Table 4.3). The respondents to the 2005 Pew survey perceived more fact than opinion from local television, local newspapers, the network evening news, and cable news networks. However, they were less convinced of fact over opinion for the more casual format of the television network morning news. In addition, they felt they were receiving more opinion than facts on internet news blogs and talk radio shows. These figures challenge the notion that the standard of objectivity has truly widespread resonance for the U.S. audience. This is underlined by the evidence in the Pew survey showing that Americans have distinct opinions about the patriotism of the U.S. media. Forty-two percent felt that news organizations "stand up for America," while 40 percent believed that news organizations were "too critical of America." Other Pew surveys have found that the U.S. media audience becomes more negative about the media during political crises, such as during the February 1999 impeachment trial for former U.S. President Bill Clinton. Thus, attitudes about political events seem to get conflated with the news organizations that report them. This would suggest that some of the U.S. audience perceive the media as "creating" these events – and that their attitudes about the media tend to reflect their general attitude about politics.

Certainly, general political ideology tends to shape perception of the media. The gap between the way Democrats and Republicans perceive the news media has increased dramatically, according to a Pew survey. More than twice as many Republicans as Democrats (67 percent versus 24 percent) believe that

Table 4.3   Where do Americans feel they get the most facts?

Media type	Mostly facts	Mostly opinion	Both/neither	Don't know
Local TV news	61	25	7	7
Local daily newspapers	54	31	7	8
Network evening news	53	31	7	9
Cable news networks	45	29	9	17
Major national newspapers	45	30	6	19
Network morning news	39	33	6	22
Internet news blogs	20	32	3	45
Talk radio shows	10	68	5	17

Source: Pew Research Center, June 26, 2005. The question asked was: "Does each media outlet named mostly report the facts about recent news developments, or mostly give their opinions about the news?"

the media are too critical of America. Slightly more Republicans are convinced that the media hurt democracy (43 percent) rather than protect democracy (40 percent). On the other hand, Democrats are more convinced that the media are a force for democracy: 56 percent of Democrats believe the media protect democracy while only 27 percent believe they harm democracy. Pew surveys have noted that Republicans – unlike Democrats – are becoming increasingly disillusioned with the democratic value of the media. This is particularly inter- esting as Republican policy has dominated in recent years, particularly with the election of Republican President George W. Bush in 2000.

What causes this difference in perceptions of the media in a single society? Democrats certainly seem more comfortable with the more critical role of the media, but does this mean that the media are somehow pro-Democratic? This would violate the notion of an objective American media, but certainly chimes with many conservative commentators, who see a persistent "liberal bias" in the media. The point is, however, the differences are more on the level of the audience than the level of the news production or content. Confronted with identical media content (although they will tend to use outlets they find polit- ically sympathetic), different individuals have varying reactions to the "objec- tivity" of the information. This difference is generated by the individual reactions, rather than differences in the content.

However, Americans seem particularly comfortable with one facet of their media environment, according to the Pew survey. Most Americans (75 percent) agree that attracting the biggest audience is more important than keeping the public informed (19 percent). This resonates with the libertarian model of the media, which embraces the ethos of news distributed as the audi- ence demands (rather than what journalists perceive that the audience needs to know, as in the social responsibility model). More Republicans (90 percent) believe this – but so do people who label themselves liberal Democrats (67 percent). They see the coverage on the war on terror as generally neutral (68 percent), although about a quarter see it as pro-American. Overall, the U.S.

audience supports the idea of the media as a watchdog of society, as 60 percent approve of criticizing political leaders. It would appear, however, that the line between "watchdog" and "negative commentator" is somewhat blurred – making it difficult to tell if the public will find the media doing their job or actually undermining faith in the U.S. political system. Party affiliation is only one filter that audience members use when viewing the news. Evidence over time suggests that those who are less educated also use the media less frequently. This means that those people with less political information are using fewer information sources – but ironically may be more likely to be persuaded by a narrower range of messages (Zaller, 1992). Other filters include age, gender, race, degree of religious faith, and a host of socio-economic indicators. Thus, a single news program can have quite a different effect on a range of individuals, making it clear that there is no such thing as a single "audience." Rather, there is a range of "audiences" within a particular country.

Key points about the U.S. media audience

- Network television news and cable television news are tied as the main source of information on national and international issues in the U.S.
- Fox News, which has departed from the accepted norm of "objectivity" with a Republican bias, has quickly gained a strong following.
- The internet is now central to the U.S. audience, with almost a quarter of Americans going online for news daily but in some ways the internet supports the traditional mass media as well.
- Americans tend to view the news through the lens of their own political beliefs.
- Americans are comfortable with the notion of a libertarian media system, but they differ on attitudes about media objectivity.

The British media audience

4.3 The central channels in the U.K. (BBC1, BBC2, ITV1, Channel 4, and Channel 5) still dominate, although their audience share fell from 80.5 percent in 2001 to 70.4 percent in 2005.[4] The newest central commercial offering, Channel 5, managed a modest increase and Channel 4 lost less than a percentage point of its viewing share. However, both the BBC and ITV1 saw their market shares decline by about 20 percent. Although they still dominate the television market, together they now share just over half of the audience. This is no surprise to anyone who has lived in Britain in the past decade, as the pace of new offerings via satellite, cable, and digital television is fast and furious. The British Office of Communications (Ofcom), which regulates telecommunications in the U.K., reported issuing more new licenses for television stations in 2006 than in any other year. The advent of digital television has provided more channels to more viewers. In addition,

Table 4.4   Television channel rankings in the United kingdom (2005 and 2001)

Channel	Description	2005 rank	2001 rank
BBC One	Public television. Flagship BBC news and entertainment	1	2
ITV1	Commercial news and entertainment	2	1
Channel 4	Commercial news and entertainment	3	3
BBC Two	Public television. BBC news and entertainment	4	4
Five	Commercial entertainment and news	5	5
ITV2	Commercial entertainment and news	6	60
Sky One	Entertainment	7	6
Sky Sports 1	Sports	8	9
E4	Entertainment	9	22
CBeebies	Public television. BBC children's entertainment	10	140

Source: 2006 Ofcom Report

subscription to paid television services (cable or satellite) has grown after Britain's relatively late entry into the cable business. In its 2006 report, Ofcom found that about 43 percent of the television sets in the country were receiving programming via paid services on satellite or cable. Ofcom estimates that the daily television audience peaks at about 9 p.m., with an average of 23.5 million people (in a country of 60 million) tuned in.

The media audience in Britain is coping with a range of rapid changes in the services available via the broadcast sector. As a 2006 Ofcom report underlined, the availability of different options is growing at a bewildering rate. In particular, the media market is being changed by the national switch from analog to digital provision, which includes a new range of channels that are available on the digital system. As Table 4.4 shows, the provision of a new range of channels has changed viewership patterns, albeit not as sharply for the most popular channels. It is interesting to note, however, that channels such as ITV2 and CBeebies (the BBC channel for very young children), which barely registered in 2001, now figure in the top ten. It does not appear, though, that choice is necessarily making people happy. Ofcom found that there was a significant change in the public's perception of programming standards, with an 18 percent rise in those claiming that standards had deteriorated. Overall, 47 percent of the respondents to the Ofcom survey believed standards on television had remained the same, while 40 percent believed those standards had fallen. A small minority – 10 percent – believed that broadcasting standards on television had improved.[5] On the other hand, the percentage of viewers who claim they were offended by television content has held steady at about 32 percent.

What was it that the British viewers didn't like in their broadcast world? According to the 2006 Ofcom report, more than half the respondents felt there was too much violence (56 percent), swearing (55 percent), and intrusion into other people's lives (56 percent). More than a third (36 percent) of the viewers felt that there was too much sex on television. Women and older people were more likely than men to claim that there were excessive levels of sex, violence, swearing, and intrusion. Interestingly, the combination of sex, swearing, and intrusiveness are features of some of the most popular types of programming – particularly reality programs such as *Big Brother* – which suggests that people don't necessarily stop watching something just because they find it offensive. In fact, the distasteful elements may also lead to the popularity. While these comments generally referred to entertainment television, research suggests that more people in the U.K. continue to rely on television as their primary news source.

Reliance on television as the central news source has increased as fewer British people turn to newspapers. When asked for the Ofcom report about their main source for news in their local area, 46 percent of the respondents listed television, 29 percent newspapers, 10 percent radio, and 4 percent talking to people (the survey did not include the internet). In terms of more global information, television had a far greater dominance. Seventy-two percent of the respondents listed television as their primary source of information for what was going on in the world, compared with 10 percent for newspapers, and 9 percent for radio. In spite of the reliance on television for both local and global information, the centrality of the early evening national news bulletins is in decline in Britain. BBC and ITV1 have competed head-to-head for years for dominance in this area, but viewer share is declining for both. Share of the audience fell from roughly 33 percent for BBC1 and about 28 percent for ITV1 in January 2000 to about 25 and 22 percent respectively by January 2006. Ofcom speculated that this is due to the proliferation of other television choices, including 24-hour rolling news services on Sky and BBC24. In addition, serious news junkies can now turn to the internet (including the expansive BBC website) for immediate and in-depth coverage of events. Although there may be diffusion in the television market, there is relatively strong support for regulation of television in the U.K. one of the most common concern about television cited by the British audience is that regulation is needed to protect children. In the 2005 Ofcom survey, 71 percent of the respondents agreed that television should be regulated in order to protect children and young people. Other reasons included the need to protect the public in general (25 percent), shield vulnerable people (16 percent), and control content (6 percent).

In 2007, Ofcom reported three key findings about the possible "fragmentation" of the British media audience (see www.ofcom.org.uk/media/news/2007/07/nr_20070704). The research found that: i) the British audience still expects high-quality, well-funded television news on both the BBC and central commercial broadcasters; ii) the amount and type of broadcast news is changing rapidly; and iii) some people are increasingly disengaged from mainstream television news. It is clear that the British audience wants *both* the high-quality, socially responsible news they have come to expect from the BBC and ITN, as well as an array of newer offerings from satellite, cable, digital and internet outlets. According to the report, central broadcasters fret that they won't be able to afford to continue to provide expensive, high-quality news production for a

Table 4.5   Top ten newspapers in Britain, 2007

Rank	Title	Type	Publisher	Circulation
1	News of the World	Tabloid	News International Newspapers Ltd	3,371,369
2	Sun	Tabloid	News International Newspapers Ltd	3,072,392
3	Daily Mail	Tabloid	Associated Newspapers Ltd	2,339,733
4	Mail on Sunday	Tabloid	Associated Newspapers Ltd	2,263,980
5	Daily Mirror/Daily Record	Tabloid	Trinity Mirror plc	1,976,926
6	Daily Mirror	Tabloid	Trinity Mirror plc	1,564,082
7	Sunday Mirror	Tabloid	Trinity Mirror plc	1,374,786
8	Sunday Times	Broadsheet	News International Newspapers Ltd	1,245,483
9	Daily Telegraph	Broadsheet	Telegraph Group Ltd	896,476
10	Sunday Express	Tabloid	Express Newspapers	816,351

Source: Audited circulation from January 29, to February 25, 2007 by the Audit Bureau of Circulation (www.abc.org.uk)

shrinking audience, particularly for regional and local news. The research also underlined different perceptions of the news from various elements of the British audience. For example, the research showed that those aged 16 to 24 watched less than half as much television news as the average British viewer, tuning in every year for an average of less than 40 hours of news (compared with around 90 hours a year for the rest of the viewing public). In addition, qualitative research found that some members of minority groups felt news coverage reinforced unfair stereotypes (such as linking blacks with crime or Muslims with extremism). The report also found a drop from 2002 to 2006 in the British audience's perception of television news as impartial – but an increase in the trust in news on the internet over the same time period.

While dependence on television remains strong, the circulation of most newspapers is in decline in the U.K. (McNair, 2003). That being said, the figures show that the British can still be considered a nation of enthusiastic newspaper readers, particularly in terms of the tabloids. Together, the top three British tabloids have a daily circulation of almost 8.8 million copies. In a country of about 60 million, this means that the British are reading far more daily newspapers than their U.S. counterparts (where the top three daily newspapers have a circulation of 5.6 million in a country that has five times the population). It is clear from figures from the British Audit Bureau of Circulation that a single company – News International Newspapers Ltd – dominates the print sphere by owning the first, second, and eighth largest newspapers in the country (see Table 4.5). While there is a broad range of more introspective and less sensationalist newspapers, it is clear that the tabloids dominate. The picture for regional newspapers, however, is not as bright. While U.S. media consumers value newspapers for local information, it would appear that British readers are not as interested. For example, the two most prestigious broadsheets in Scotland – the *Herald* in Glasgow and the *Scotsman* in Edinburgh – have experienced a steady decline in readership. The *Herald*, arguably the key national newspaper of Scotland, has a circulation of just 70,000[6] – ranking it with relatively small regional newspapers in the U.S. Yet, while serious newspapers may be losing a grip on news influence, radio remains strong and influential in the U.K. This is a function of the BBC system, which supports detailed news and analytical programs across different national radio programs.

Key points about the British media audience

- Central television channels in the U.K. still dominate, although their market share is slipping as the number of channels proliferate.
- About a third of the viewers claim they are offended by some aspect of television, but viewership remains high.
- Newspaper readership is in decline, but overall still quite popular when compared with the U.S.
- British citizens are comfortable with the notion of a socially responsible broadcast system linked with a libertarian print industry.

The Russian media audience

4.4 The single largest incorrect assumption about the Russian media audience has been that Russian citizens crave an American-style media system. To this end, enormous propaganda efforts were made to broadcast Russian-language programs produced by the U.S. into the Soviet Union during the Communist regime. However, once the Soviet system collapsed and free exchange of information became possible, it became clear that the post-Soviet audience's expectations and needs were far different from those of U.S. audiences – or even of those closer to home in European countries. Inculcated in the Soviet norms of direction rather than debate in the mass media, the Russian audience has shown a great deal of support for censorship, government control of journalists, and the general suppression of "negative" news about topics ranging from the war in Chechnya to political opposition to Putin. There is a majority consensus among Russian citizens that the media should support a strong, stable state and help the country move on from the political and economic chaos of the 1990s. This means that Russian citizens, trained to perceive the most subtle signs of change in the relatively monolithic Soviet media, can reconcile the fact that they know the media fail to give them meaningful information with the idea that the media are supporting their society.

While Russian viewers have experienced a very different political history, they do share the same pace of change in their media offerings as audiences in the U.S. and the U.K., according to a report by the Educated Media organization (Kachkaeva et al., 2006). As the report highlights, Russian viewers have a relatively wide selection of broadcast offerings. The prime state-run channel

Table 4.6   TV ratings of top Russian channels (2005)

Channel	Ownership and content	2005 rating (%)
First Channel	State-run, news and entertainment	22.9
Rossiya [Russia]	State-owned, news and entertainment	22.6
The respondent's local TV company	Commercial and state	12.3
NTV	Commercial, news and entertainment	11.2
CTC	Commercial, entertainment	10.3
TNT	Commercial, entertainment	6.7
REN TV	Commercial, entertainment, and news	5.0
TV-Center	Moscow administration, news, and entertainment	2.6
Kultura [Culture]	State-owned, culture programming	2.5
Sport	Commercial, sports only	1.8
DTV Viasat	Commercial, entertainment, sports	1.5
MTV	Commercial, music television	1.1
Muz TV	Commercial, music television	1.0
Domashny [Home]	Commercial, home shows	1.0

Source: Kachkaeva et al. (2006)

called the First Channel maintains the highest market share, but only by a tiny margin ahead of the state-owned *Rossiya* on Channel 2 (see Table 4.6). The commercial NTV was in third place, with 11 percent of the television share in 2005, although studies have shown that its political coverage is now relatively unchallenging of the Kremlin elites. The other major television channel is TV-Center, which is owned and run by the Moscow city administration. The Educated Media study reports on several trends in television coverage, notably the growth of Russian productions over Western imports as well as a heavy interest in crime drama.

At the same time, financial constraints and infrastructure problems in Russia mean that cable television penetration remains relatively low at 11 percent (Kachkaeva et al., 2006: 76). The same percentage of Russian respondents reported having a computer at home although internet access is available for some in offices, universities, or via internet cafés. Meanwhile, newspapers are relatively expensive, particularly for those earning lower wages outside of the urban centers. Despite the relatively higher barriers to getting access to a full spectrum of the media, there is evidence that many Russians are news junkies. In a 2001 survey of 2,000 Russian citizens, about 80 percent reported tuning in to television seven days a week –and almost 70 percent of them watched for at least two hours a day on weekdays and even more on their days off (Oates, 2006). While this survey tracked general viewing, the respondents ranked watching the news as particularly important. In addition, 57 percent of the respondents said that they picked up a local paper several times a week and 36 percent of them reported reading a national newspaper at the same rate. Newspapers remain relatively expensive for many Russian consumers and there has been a large decline in circulation since the heady days of glasnost and the first years of the Russian state. A report by the BBC, which monitors media worldwide, estimated that just over 100 papers are sold in Russia for every 1,000 inhabitants, which is about one-third the figure for the U.K.[7] At the same time, there is a wider variation of opinion and news in newspapers than on television, particularly in papers such as *Novaya Gazeta* (which openly criticizes the Kremlin and covers events in Chechnya).[8] The handful of "opposition" media, which included the Echo of Moscow radio news in 2007, remain relatively small and are not considered major mass media outlets.

In the 2001 survey in Russia, 65 percent of the respondents picked national state television as one of the "most unbiased and reliable sources of information" – far more than those who selected local newspapers (20 percent), national newspapers (18 percent), Russian radio stations (16 percent), commercial television (13 percent), or even relatives and friends (14 percent). It was particularly surprising that Russians expressed such a high level of trust in state television, even though propaganda and the obvious manipulation of the news had increased steadily in recent years. In particular, the Kremlin forced a management change at commercial NTV in the midst of this particular survey. Despite this – and many Russians clearly showed they were aware of government interference – the respondents believed in state television more than in any other media outlet in the country. In another survey question about trust and political institutions, this bias toward the state media was again clear. More of the respondents (57 percent) said they had full or considerable confidence in state television than in any other institution on the list. Other rankings for full or considerable confidence were 52 percent for radio, 50 percent for the armed forces, 48 percent for the church, 47 percent for the print media, 38 percent for commercial television, 30 percent for the government, 16 percent for the parliament, and a mere 11 percent for political parties.

Many Russians, like many Europeans, believe that television is such an important national asset that it should be owned (if not controlled) by the state. This could go a long way toward explaining the gap in trust between state-run and commercial television. For example, few Russians believe that commercial television news content is not influenced by its owners. Half of the respondents felt that commercial television *did* reflect the owners' views either to a full extent (14 percent) or to a significant extent (33 percent). A mere 7 percent of the survey respondents believed that commercial television companies did *not* reflect the point of view of their owners. It is true that commercial television channels, most notably NTV, have used their formidable national presence to pursue their own political agendas rather than strive to give viewers objective information. In addition, it took considerable political influence and favoritism to secure a national broadcasting license in the early 1990s in Russia. Thus, while NTV could in many ways be said to have been more even-handed and objective than the main state television channels by mid-2001, nonetheless its news could not be trusted to present disinterested information in all situations. In fact, NTV producers deliberately distorted facts and hid Russian President Boris Yeltsin's illness in his battle against a Communist contender in 1996. As such, Russian viewers appeared to be much more comfortable with the state-run media, which they see as clearly biased, but perceive not to be pursuing the agenda of commercial owners.

People in Russia often see the media more as a *pillar* of the state than as a *watchdog* of the state. For example, while 68 percent of the respondents in the 2001 survey said that the most important role of the mass media in Russia was "to give citizens unbiased and objective information," 28 percent responded that its most important role was "to strengthen the feeling of national unity of the Russians". These two goals may seem contradictory, yet the respondents did not necessarily perceive them as incompatible: 23 percent of the respondents who felt that the unbiased and objective information was most important also felt that the media should strengthen national unity.[9] This is a paradox. Unless the media choose only to report good news (objectively) and ignore the bad, fulfilling these two roles simultaneously would be impossible. In addition, 20 percent of the Russian respondents felt that the most important role of the mass media was "to elucidate the position and views of our leaders." Only a third of the respondents picked entertainment as a critical role of the media.

But when they switch on television, are Russians truly interested in news or do they seek to escape some of the pressing economic, military, and political problems of their society? In fact, Russians rely quite heavily on the television for news, in particular spending a lot of time comparing and contrasting news coverage from various sources. In this way, they re-create the Soviet habit of "gleaning" the news from a variety of channels. Not only do Russian viewers claim this activity in focus groups, but they also reported it in the 2001 survey. Over one-fifth of the survey respondents (22 percent) reported watching more than one news program a day on different channels, and almost half (45 percent) reported doing this from time to time. Only about a quarter of the respondents reported that they never bothered to tune in to different channels to check out the reporting from competing news teams. It would seem that many Russians are news junkies, as similar numbers reported watching more than one news program a day on the *same* channels. In addition, when asked about their level of trust in the television news, those who watched the main commercial competitor (on NTV) were more likely to question the veracity of the main nightly news on the prime state channels.

Thus, although many of the Russians seen to be dismissive of the bias in commercial news, it does allow them to question state broadcasts. As content analysis in different studies (including those from the Organization for Security and Cooperation in Europe and the European Institute for the Media) has shown increasing bias and distortion in the Russian news on state-run channels, this is evidence that the commercial news was serving to provide some balance. Unfortunately, commercial news has become increasingly wary of the Kremlin political influence. This has led to the cancellation of political shows such as NTV's *Freedom of Speech* and *Lately* [*Namedni*], which discussed more controversial issues such as Chechnya. Although other outlets some-times attract relative popularity and strength in providing less Kremlin-friendly coverage, they are curtailed if they start to have political influence.[10]

Russian participants in 32 focus groups in 2000 and 2004 showed a wide array of knowledge and insight into news coverage (Oates, 2006). In fact, when compared with participants in similar focus groups in the U.S. and Britain (Oates and Williams, 2006), the Russian audience was particularly aware of various nuances and issues surrounding the problems in the mass media. In particular, they were aware of the specific "slant" of various news outlets, in relation to who had financial control of a television station, a newspaper, or a radio station. They were less interested or concerned about the internet, as many of them did not view the internet as an authoritative, alternative source for news. They also faced a paradox in terms of the relative freedom with which they could receive news from overseas. Although technically overseas sources could balance their views in a way that was not possible under Soviet censorship, the foreign news media have little coverage of Russian domestic affairs (including Chechnya, where it is now too dangerous for Western journalists to work on a regular basis). In addition, the Russian focus group participants, unsurprisingly, showed a marked preference for following their own domestic media.

Overall, the Russian media system has many of the apparent features of the Western media, but the audience as well as other elements are quite distinct. As the discussion in Chapter 2 showed, Russian media organizations do not operate as relatively independent political institutions. Rather, both state-owned and commercial media outlets are very much aware of the boundaries on "free" speech in Russia (Kachkaeva et al., 2006; Oates, 2006). This raises the question of whether the Russian audience is still so inculcated in the norms of the Soviet media of censorship and untruth that they form a type of "neo-Soviet" audience. The key factors in this media model would be (i) a rejection of the notion of balance or objectivity in news reporting; (ii) flaws in mass media law; (iii) self-censorship; (iv) government interference and harassment of media outlets; (v) the influence of commercial interests; (vi) a worrying lack of journalistic professionalism; and (vii) an atmosphere of condoned violence against journalists.

Comments in focus groups conducted in 2000 and 2004 in Russia highlight some important characteristics of the media audience in Russia (Oates, 2006).[11] The focus groups, which asked Russians about their attitudes toward the media, elections, and security issues, found that the state-run First Channel remained trusted, valued, and very popular. At the same time, the Russian focus-group participants were also relatively convinced that most media outlets, including the First Channel, were neither objective nor balanced. The main concerns of the Russian audience are not focused on liberal concepts such as freedom of speech; rather the audience is concerned that television should uphold a sense of national pride. While the focus group participants differed in their opinions, a surprisingly large number of them were unconvinced that the media could serve as a watchdog for society. Rather, they perceived media as important players with each media outlet – state and commercial – pursuing its own agenda. The participants felt it was critical to employ a personal filter on the news rather than rely on what they considered the quite shaky concept of media objectivity. In this way, their attitude toward television was perhaps not markedly different from the attitude of Soviet times – and lends credence to the notion of a "neo-Soviet" audience.

It is particularly interesting that in these focus groups and in numerous surveys on the media, Russian respondents have shown a marked distrust or even dislike of commercial television. In many democracies (aside from the U.S.), there is a great deal of concern over whether public broadcasting can continue to serve as a pillar of civil society in the wake of commercial globalization (Aldridge and Hewitt, 1994; Avery, 1993; Curran and Park, 2000; Tracey, 1998). In Russia, the case would appear to be inverted. With public broadcasting firmly in the grip of a narrow group of elites in Moscow, the best chance of breaking the information monopoly would appear to be a national commercial station with a reputable news team. Local and even regional television channels in Russia lack the ability to formulate national opinion, although they can challenge the information hegemony at a local level when they can escape control by local bureaucrats. This creates problems at the theoretical level – except for scholars such as Doris Graber (2005), who eloquently defend the value of a commercialized media system – as public broadcasting is assumed to be in the service of the public, albeit often flawed and now somewhat commercialized. This is an assumption that cannot be made in Russia.

These discussions in Russian focus groups that suggest emotions ranging from wariness to downright distrust of commercial media find resonance in the work of Colin Sparks (2000). Sparks argues that the discussion of media and society should be reframed from an examination of public versus commercial media to consider who controls the media *under any type of ownership*. Sparks posits that two of the classic models of the media, in this case Soviet and Libertarian, are not useful because economic and political power are so intertwined in both systems. Thus, the systems never could be juxtaposed and compared as they share a basic component of media control in the hands of elites.[12] Rather, Sparks sees any media system in which elites control the means of communication as fundamentally flawed, perceiving no useful distinction between political and economic elites. In this sense, the Russian respondents agree with Sparks, as they repeatedly point to the interdependence of top economic and political elites in Russia. Yet, even if the Russians respondents are wary of commercial television, wouldn't they appreciate the diversity brought to the media sphere by a range of commercial media outlets? Kachkaeva et al., show that the pace of new broadcast licenses is growing, but political diversity is not. Thus, while Russians can enjoy a range of new entertainment programs that highlight the talent of Russian filmmakers and producers, there is little challenging political content.

What makes Sparks's conceptualization of a convergence between state and commercial media so compelling is how well it fits the Russian experience and the focus-group findings discussed in this chapter. Despite initial optimism on the part of Western and some Russian analysts, the Russian mass media have failed to develop into any sort of political tool for the masses. Rather, after a brief period of plurality, they remain firmly entrenched as a tool for the elites, as in Soviet times. The people who remain unsurprised – and surprisingly accepting – of this fate of the Russian media appear to be the Russian audience. Through focus group discussions and survey responses, it is clear that they expect a certain collusion between the power elite and the media. Like Sparks, they see little to recommend the possible disinterested community service of a commercial media owner. In fact, they prefer state-run television to all other major types of media and a wide range of political institutions. They imbue state-run television with a relatively high level of trust. While some evidence makes it clear that the Russian viewers are aware of the distortion and lies in the state media, other discussion shows that they accept this as a part of the state-building exercise. Weary of the political and economic chaos of the late 1980s and 1990s, many are ready to accept state television as a political Leviathan. Sparks recognizes that his theory fits the Russian situation particularly well, citing the long-term dean of the Moscow School of Journalism Yassen Zassoursky, who identified television as critical "political capital" (Sparks, 2000: 43).

Key points about the Russian media audience

- The Russian audience values the role of the central media as consolidating, rather than challenging, state power.
- There has been a growth in television offerings, although cable television has relatively small penetration.
- Newspaper circulation is relatively low.
- Use of the internet is far less common in Russia than in the U.S. or the U.K..
- State-run television enjoys a high level of trust and influence, even though Russian viewers are aware of the increasing bias on the news.
- Components of the Russian audience suggest that a "neo-Soviet" model of audience reception may be appropriate.

Chapter summary

Just as media outlets are diverse, so is the relationship between media audiences and the political sphere. In studying the patterns of media audiences across three countries, several interesting points emerge. What one audience would accept as strange, others find a normal and even commendable part of their media mix. Thus, Americans favor objectivity, British people feel comfortable with balance, and Russians accept a certain amount of image over truth in their mass media. In all three societies, there is a vast range of media offerings. In particular, television programming continues to expand at a fast pace, changing and reshaping long-held dominance by a handful of broadcasters in the U.S. and the U.K. Although Russia is also experiencing rapid growth in the broadcasting industry, the relatively low penetration of cable and satellite programming as well as the high favorability of state-run television means that central, state-run television dominates in terms of media influence in the political sphere.

Newspapers and radio round out the media mix, but enjoy different levels of success and political influence in the three countries. In the U.S., national prestige newspapers are apparently losing political influence while local publications remain valued, particularly for fostering a sense of community. National newspapers have more influence in the U.K., which has a less-developed strength in local or regional newspapers. National radio news via the BBC is immensely popular and relatively influential in the U.K., while national radio news generally does not set the political agenda in the U.S. or Russia.

Overall, however, it is clear that the notion of a single, dominating voice of propaganda is much too simplistic to fully understand the media audience in comparative perspective. It is not surprising that Sparks finds the audience a large part of the solution to understanding the role of media in the political sphere:

> the attention of students of the media interested in finding ways in which they may be democratized would be better directed at the relationships between the media and their audiences, and the fault lines within media organizations between those who give orders and those who are forced to take them. (Sparks, 2000: 47)

Thus, Sparks suggests, those who are interested in the relationship between democracy and the media need to shift their attention away "from these debates about the relatively empowering virtues of the state and the market and turn to the relations between the media and the mass of the population" (ibid.: 47). This chapter has presented several findings that are relevant to that understanding. Notably, the American, British, and Russian audiences have quite distinct patterns of usage, trust, and influence relating to their media systems.

Study questions

1 How do the usage patterns of the mass media vary for the citizens of the three countries under study (the U.S., the U.K., and Russia)?

2 What political and social factors appear to influence audience patterns in the three countries?

3 Why would Americans approve of a libertarian television sphere and British citizens prefer a socially responsible broadcasting system if both countries are democracies?

4 Why would Russians trust their media if they know it doesn't tell the truth?

Reading guide

McQuail (1997) offers a good overview of audience analysis. The case studies of the U.S. and the U.K. are based respectively on figures from the Pew Research Center for the People and The Press (see link below) and the British Office of Communication (web link also below). The most recent Russian audience research is based on Kachkaeva et al. (2006), which unfortunately is not available online. However, many articles in the Russian media can be found via the Radio Free Europe/Radio Liberty Newsline, at http://www.rferl. org/newsline/. For an in-depth study of the Russian audience, see Chapters 3, 7, and 8 of my own book, *Television, Democracy and Elections in Russia*.

Internet resources

http://people-press.org/   The Pew Research Center for the People and the Press provides information on U.S. elections, attitudes, and the media in detailed, but comprehensible reports (free access).

http://www.annenbergpublicpolicycenter.org/naes/   The Annenburg Public Policy Center of the University of Virginia provides this National Annenburg Election Study. It includes information on a large survey during the 2000 and 2004 U.S. elections, with a particular focus on media impact and use.

www.ofcom.org.uk   The British Office of Communication regulates broadcasting in the U.K. The website includes statistics and many reports on the British telecommunications industry.

www.rferl.org   This non-profit organization (funded largely by the Soros Foundation) follows daily news about Russia, including in-depth reports on the media.

Notes

1   This survey and a wealth of other information about media, politics, and the public are available for free download at the website for The Pew Research Center for the People and the Press; see http://people-press.org/.
2   The survey consisted of 1,464 Americans in June 2005.
3   The groups were held in Florida, Missouri, and near Washington, D.C. just after the 2004 U.S. elections. The project was founded by the British Economic and Social Research Council.
4   Ofcom, August 10, 2006.
5   The Ofcom report posited that part of the problem was linked to a single Channel 4 program, Brass Eye (July 26, 2001), a spoof documentary that outraged many viewers by lampooning scaremongering reporting about child molesters.
6   Audit Bureau of Circulation.
7   British Broadcasting Corporation (February 2007) *The Press in Russia*. Available online at http://news.bbc.co.uk/1/hi/world/europe/4315129.stm.
8   Anna Politovskaya, one of the few reporters providing in-depth coverage of Chechnya, worked for Novaya Gazeta. She was assassinated in 2006, although her killers have not been identified.

9   Respondents were allowed to pick both answers, which was arguably a design flaw in the survey, but one that yielded interesting results.
10 For example, news on the commercial channel REN-TV became fairly popular in 2006, but the channel soon changed hands. Since the switch in ownership, Russian observers have perceived the news content as less challenging to the Kremlin "line."
11 This information is from 255 people who participated in 32 focus groups in Moscow, Ulyanovsk, and a small town near Voronezh in 2000 and 2004. The research was funded by grants from the British Economic and Social Research Council and carried out by Russian Research Ltd under the supervision of the author.
12 This is a more extreme argument than those such as Tracey (1998) who see decay in public broadcasting due to commercialization and globalization.

References

Aldridge, M. and Hewitt, N. (eds.) (1994) *Controlling Broadcasting: Access Policy and Practice in North America and Europe.* Manchester: Manchester University Press.

Avery, R.K. (ed.) (1993) *Public Service Broadcasting in a Multichannel Environment.* White Plains, NJ: Longman.

Avery, R. (1993) *Public Service Broadcasting.* New York: Longman.

Berelson, B. and Lazarsfeld, P.F. (1954) *Voting: a Study of Public Opinion Formation in a Presidential Campaign.* Chicago, IL: Chicago University Press.

Butler, D. and Stokes, D.E. (1969) *Political Change in Britain: Forces Shaping Electoral Choice.* London: Macmillan.

Butler, D. and Stokes, D.E. (1974) *Political Change in Britain: The Evolution of Electoral Choice.* London: Macmillan.

Corner, John. Reappraising Reception: Aims, Concepts and Methods. In Curran J. and Gurevitch M. (eds) *Mass Media and Society,* 2nd edn. London: Arnold, pp. 280–304.

Curran, J. and Park, M.J. (2000) "Beyond Globalization Theory." In Curran, J. and Park, M.J. (eds.) *De-Westernizing Media Systems* (pp. 3–18). London: Routledge.

European Institute for the Media (2000). *Monitoring the Media Coverage of the December 1999 Parliamentary Elections in Russia: Final Report.* Düsseldorf: European Institute for the Media. Available online at http://www.media-politics.com/eimreports.htm

Graber, D. (2005) *Mass Media and American Politics,* 3rd edn. Washington, DC: Congressional Quarterly Books.

Livingstone, Sonia. (1996) On the Continuing Problem of Media Effects. In Curran J. and Gurevitch M. (eds.) *Mass Media and Society,* 2nd edn. London: Arnold, pp. 305–24.

Kachkaeva, A., Kiriya, I., and Libergal, G. (2006) *Television in the Russian Federation: Organisational Structure, Programme Production and Audience.* Report prepared by Internews Russia for the European Audiovisual Observatory. Moscow: Educated Media.

McQuail, D. (1997) *Audience Analysis.* London: SAGE.

McNair, B. (2003) *News and Journalism in the UK,* 4th edn. London: Routledge.

Oates, S. (2006) *Television, Democracy and Elections in Russia.* London: Routledge.

Oates, S. and Williams, A. (2006) "Comparative Aspects of Terrorism Coverage: Television and Voters in the 2004 U.S. and 2005 British Elections." Paper presented at the Annual Meeting of the American Political Science Association, Philadelphia, Pennsylvania.

Office of Communication (Ofcom) (2006) *The Communications Market 2006.* London: Ofcom. Available online at http://www.ofcom.org.uk/research/cm/cm06/.

Pew Research Center for the People and the Press (2005) *Public More Critical of Press, but Goodwill Persists*. Washington, DC: Pew Research Center for the People and the Press. Available online at http://people-press.org/reports/display.php3?ReportID=248.

Siebert, F., Peterson, T., and Schramm, W. (1963) *Four Theories of the Press*. Urbana, IL: University of Illinois Press.

Sparks, C. (2000) "Media Theory after the Fall of European Communism: Why the Old Models from East and West Won't Do Anymore." In Curran, J. and Park, M.J. (eds.) *De-Westernizing Media Systems* (pp. 35-49). London and New York: Routledge.

Tracey, M. (1998) *The Decline and Fall of Public Service Broadcasting*. Oxford: Oxford University Press.

Zaller, J.R. (1992) *The Nature and Origins of Mass Opinion*. New York: Cambridge University Press.

Media and Elections

Central points

- How much do media matter to election outcomes?
- What opportunities do candidates and political parties have to present their ideas and images via the mass media?
- How do media in various countries broadcast electoral images and ideas, whether through paid political advertising, free time, or the nightly television news?
- Which elements of media coverage seem to make a difference and which seem to be largely irrelevant to the voters?
- Do the media support or subvert democratic elections?

Introduction

5.1 During election campaigns, three of the most important political components in a country – the media, candidates, and the public – all intersect as public representation are chosen at the polls. Elections are times when politics become defined more as a "horse race," reduced to a collection of winners and losers, than as a way of organizing political institutions for the long-term good of society. As a result, election coverage is often more focused on the short-term elements of the campaign rather than the deeper issues confronting a nation. Across various societies, observers now complain that elections are little more than an exchange of insults among political contenders, a series of vague sound-bites and the saturation of television with images. All this is said to replace the provision of useful information to the electorate. At the same time, studies of voting behavior since the Second World War in the U.S. and the U.K. suggest that many citizens are not particularly influenced by the scenes and drama of the election campaign coverage itself. Rather, they rely on long-term political affinity and identification, which are formed from political socialization in their early years. Yet, as recent U.S. presidential elections have shown, close elections often can hinge on the persuasion of a relatively small number of voters. This has brought the importance of the campaign – and the study of the role of the mass media in influencing voters – into sharp focus in modern politics. At the same time, it is clear that the media's role is especially influential in times of political flux, as when political parties scrambled for power in Russia after the collapse of communism, or when American voters chose between two competing visions of the U.S. role in the world in the 2004 elections.

This chapter will first discuss classic models of voting behavior, to assess what social science research has discovered about the relative importance of the media in making voting choices. The chapter will then analyze political parties, electoral systems, campaign rules, and media performance in elections in the U.S., the U.K., and Russia. Finally, the chapter will balance this information by pointing out that the media can play an extraordinary role in electoral outcomes at pivotal moments in history.

Classic models of voting behavior and the media

5.2 In order to understand the influence of the media on electoral outcomes, you need first to look at the role of political parties and electoral rules on voter choice. When scholars consider campaign effects, they will place them within this broader context of how people make their choices at the ballot box. In the U.S., this study grew from concerns over the effects of propaganda (the "propaganda model") to a focus on the relative role of fixed and enduring attachment to political parties. Most of the research focuses on national elections in the U.S., particularly the presidential race held every four years. While Americans elect a vast number of officials at every level of governance – from the local school board in some communities to the state governor to congressional representatives – the U.S. presidential elections are the most visible and most important elections in the nation.

U.S. presidential elections were first used after the Second World War to test the effects of the "propaganda model," i.e. that citizens would be inclined to change their voter choice because of media influence. At the time, the skillful propaganda of Hitler and the Nazis was seen as one of the key factors in explaining the rise of the repressive German regime that had slaughtered millions. In fact, researchers (Berelson et al., 1954) found exactly the *opposite* effect among American voters, as public opinion surveys showed that people were more likely to be influenced by discussions with friends and family than by what they heard or read in the mass media. Berelson and his colleagues described this phenomenon as the "minimal effects model" of the media in elections. This left unanswered, to a degree, the extent to which media coverage mattered to Germans in their choice to support Hitler, but suggested that the post-war American electorate were relatively protected from the forces of extremist propaganda. Three years later in 1957, Anthony Downs published his classic work on voting behavior, *An Economic Theory of Democracy*, which theorized that political parties could best find voters by determining the range of public opinion and searching for voters in the middle. This suggests that parties (and election campaigns) should avoid extremism, chasing public opinion rather than formulating it.

These theories were suggesting that media messages during the campaign were not particularly relevant for persuasion, although no doubt important for informing voters where parties or candidates stood on particular positions. The classic study of U.S. voting behavior is *The American Voter*, published in 1960 by Angus Campbell and colleagues, which looked further at the relationship among parties, media, and the electorate. Their work examined how voters responded to the issues in the campaign and found that the issues themselves were less important than long-term sociological attachment to political parties, dubbed "party identification." Campbell and his colleagues developed a model of voting behavior called the "funnel of causality," which is still both influential and useful today in the calculus of vote choice in the U.S. and beyond. The scholars imagined the structure of voter choice as a large funnel. Starting at the wide end, the vote is filtered through a series of sections of the funnel, beginning with socio-economic status (such as age, education, ethnicity, gender, and income), which in turn influences party identification (i.e., wealthier people have tended to be Republicans in the U.S. while poorer people have tended to be Democrats). The funnel then moves on to issues and then to the events of the campaign itself. While the media permeate political life on many levels, in this model it is clear that their only significant impact could be in the final stage of the vote process. As voter choice is linked to long-held sociological conditions and beliefs, the media have relatively little chance to change voting decisions in the short term. Work in Britain (Butler and Stokes, 1969) found a similar syndrome in that country, as identification with a political party has been the most reliable predictor of voter choice in parliamentary elections.

More recent studies of voting behavior in the U.S. (for example, Miller and Shanks, 1996) have suggested that issues have risen in salience as the strength of party identification has eroded over time – although the debate about the nature and the endurance of party identification still continues (Farrell and Schmitt-Beck, 2002; Holbrook, 1996; Niemi and Weisberg, 1993). Other research suggests that while some issues – particularly the economy – are quite important, voters remain confused and relatively uninfluenced by more complex and subtle issues (Carmines and Stimson, 1980). In addition, there is evidence that voters are able to look beyond immediate, personal needs and vote for longer-term policies in important policy spheres such as economics (Kinder and Kiewit, 1979). So, even within a broad understanding that voters aren't easily swayed into large ideological shifts by the media in election campaigns, the media matter because (i) they provide information to allow voters to match their preferences with particular candidates or parties; (ii) they give long-term political information that helps to socialize voters into particular party preferences; and (iii) in close elections or on critical issues when voters are confused or even angry, media coverage can sway an election.

Although the notion of partisan identification, as defined in *The American Voter*, remains an important part of how political scientists think about the relative role of the media in elections, a lot has changed since the 1950s and 1960s. While much of the scholarly debate has been over how much people have really remained attached to political parties (whether the Democrats or the Republicans in the U.S. or Labour or the Conservatives in the U.K.), more than just partisan identification has shifted over 40 years. These foundational studies were done at a time of relative consensus in U.S. politics, before the mass protests over Vietnam and race relations in the late 1960s or the general disenchantment with the president and politics after the Watergate scandal in the mid-1970s. British society experienced a massive shift after the Second World War away from the tradition of class-based politics. At the same time, the media have changed dramatically since the 1950s. The post-Second World War era has encompassed not only the rise and saturation of television in the 1960s and 1970s, but the introduction of cable and satellite channels in the 1980s, and the growth of the internet in the 1990s.

In addition, there has been a great deal of change in the conduct of parties and candidates in recent decades. For example, the campaign team for Bill Clinton for the 1992 presidential elections pioneered a new, more proactive media approach, aggressively challenging media outlets on negative news about the candidate (Kurtz, 1998). The Labour Party in Britain is particularly centralized, deciding who gets to stand in a particular constituency and demanding that party members vote according to the party line on key issues. There are those who contend that modern political parties are so concerned with controlling the "message" and "spin" that real concerns for citizens and policies are neglected. As a result, there are fears that people in countries such as the U.S. and the U.K. are choosing parties or candidates based on clever marketing ploys rather than sound policies.

This has been a particular criticism of Britain's "New" Labour as the party has remarketed itself to be more centrist and less socialist since Tony Blair became party leader in 1994. There is convincing evidence that British politicians, like their American counterparts, pursue a much more active strategy than their predecessors to control and influence the messages that are transmitted in the election and beyond. In particular, studies suggest that British politicians and journalists enjoy a particularly symbiotic relationship. However, well-balanced and reasoned studies (for example, Norris et al., 1999) suggest that British voters are not so easily duped by media "spin." Rather, researchers found evidence that there was relatively little influence of "spin" in the 1997 British campaign, in which Labour finally won back power after 18 years of Conservative rule. In addition, evidence presented below suggests that the relationship among parties, candidates, and voters is too complex to allow for the overwhelming dominance of PR in a campaign.

While newspaper circulation and readership have declined in many places, the use of the internet has exploded, particularly among the younger generations in the U.S.. Internet users clearly have greater capacity for electoral campaign involvement. The internet offers them the ability to communicate directly with candidates and parties – from contributing to party war chests to making comments in blogs to posting articles about politics on websites. Since the 1996 presidential elections, the Pew internet & American Life Project has found a rising influence of the internet on political choice. Can internet use really fit into the "funnel of causality," if online use can influence political choice and awareness in far more powerful and meaningful ways than merely listening to news broadcasts or reading newspapers? Social scientists are still not convinced that the internet plays a critical role in electoral choice, although evidence suggests that even online entertainment use – especially among young people – often leads to greater political knowledge and engagement (Owen, 2006). Much of what purports to be political news on the Web is more about scandal and entertainment (Davis and Owen, 1998), although this may be changing more quickly than researchers' ability to keep pace. Yet the internet, while not fundamentally changing politics, does have the ability to reinforce messages, mobilize activists, and strengthen the views of political partisans (Bimber and Davis, 2003).

Despite the increase in media outlets in the Western world, researchers are relatively unconvinced that the electorate is becoming better informed. Although there may be more sources of information, these sources are focusing more on the "horse race" qualities of the elections and less on substantive issues (Patterson, 1994). Studies show other worrying trends – such as the rise in negativity in political ads as well as journalists talking more and politicians themselves being allowed less time to put across their views (Ansolabehere and Iyengar, 1995; Kaid and Johnston, 2001; Patterson, 1994). Even in the U.K., where paid political advertising on television is not permitted, there are well-documented problems of political bias in televised election reporting (Miller, 1991). Not all commentators, however, feel that the media are an obstacle to democratic choice. For example, Pippa Norris (2000) found in a multinational study that media use is linked to improved political knowledge and participation.

In addition, there is compelling evidence that the internet is particularly effective at engaging younger people in politics, in ways that were not possible with the traditional media (Owen, 2006). Although there is a great deal of grumbling about media performance, there remain no better alternatives to broadcasting messages about candidates and parties during elections. Political parties do pursue direct contact with their potential voters, especially via the internet, but news coverage remains a particularly influential part of an election effort. This is true both in countries that allow paid political advertising on television (such as the U.S. and Russia) and in countries that ban this practice (such as the U.K.).

As national elections vary so much from country to country, cross-national comparisons make it possible to analyze the relationships among candidates, media, and voters in a more generalized way. In particular, this suggests that different media systems generate distinct roles for the media that can strongly influence not only the outcome of particular elections, but also the general level of democracy within each country. In the U.S., the central concern is that the media detract from a sensible political debate, encouraging candidates to attack one another through expensive ad campaigns on television. As a result, voters become alienated not only from particular candidates, but also from politics in general. However, the marked increase in turnout and higher level of citizen interest in the 2004 presidential election suggests that it may be events and the saliency of political choices, rather than media coverage, that drive political engagement. In the U.K., much debate has focused on whether the American disinterest in "serious" politics is contagious and whether British electoral politics are becoming "dumbed down" or "Americanized" (Kavanagh, 1995) in the same way. Elections in Russia are a study in how the media can fail to aid in democratization when journalists and media organizations put their own interests before unbiased, or even balanced, reporting of political events (Oates, 2006).

Elections and media in the United States

5.3 The lack of a central platform for political parties means that candidates need to reiterate their positions on key policies and issues at each election. This is less complicated – albeit still expensive – for candidates at the sub-national level. As all U.S. congressional representatives are elected through single-member districts, most constituencies are relatively compact. However, races in the larger states such as California and New York can be massively expensive, as candidates strive to cover multiple media markets with their advertisements. The U.S. media system is generally well designed for local politics, with local media markets interested in focusing on "hometown" candidates and issues. At the same time, the fact that the races are localized means that national policies are often ignored or marginalized. This fragments not only national policy, but also the way in which electoral politics are discussed in the mass media. Ironically, despite the expense and noise of the campaigns, the single greatest predictor of electoral success for a candidate remains incumbency. If you are a popular candidate already in office and there is no scandal or serious problem of policy, it is quite difficult for a challenger to win the race no matter what the media coverage.

None of the congressional campaigns, however, compares with the logistics and expense of running a national presidential campaign. The final Republican and Democratic candidate must each be selected through primary ballots in the states to win the place on the national party ticket. Typically, the incumbent president will run for a second term or the vice-president will become the national candidate if the president already has served the limit of two four-year terms in office. That leaves the competing party – the Republicans in 2000 and the Democrats in 2004 – with long, expensive primary campaigns before the general election on the first Tuesday of November every four years. It also means that the public are saturated with media messages, many of them negative, before the general campaign even starts. The long primary campaign can expose weaknesses in candidates – ranging from past indiscretions to television gaffes – which can make them unpalatable to some voters. As that candidate may go on to win the primary, many party loyalists are then confronted with a candidate for whom they have little enthusiasm as a leader.

There are four key issues to consider when analyzing the role of the media in U.S. elections: party identification, paid political advertising, news coverage, and the growing influence of the internet in elections. Overall, looking at these issues can help us to assess whether the U.S. media are supporting or subverting democratic elections.

Party identification

In terms of party identification (also called partisan identification or "party ID"), it is important to consider the relevance of attachment to political parties suggested by *The American Voter* more than 40 years ago, in the context of more recent American elections. This is relatively easy to do, as there is a regular U.S. poll called the National Election Survey (NES) which asks people – among other things – how they arrived at their vote choice. Respondents are asked a range of questions, both on sociological attributes such as education and income as well as their level of interest in politics and a feeling of attachment to a political party.

In the U.S. the number of respondents who claim an affiliation to the Democratic Party (weak or strong) dropped from 57 percent in 1952 to 49 percent in 2002, according to the NES data. At the same time, identification with the Republican Party rose from 34 percent to 43 percent within the same timeframe. Those who did not identify with either party peaked in the mid-1970s at about 18 percent, but fell sharply to 8 percent by 2002. This suggests that party affiliation remains a powerful force in U.S. politics, and one that is moving in favor of the Republican Party. From the 1950s to the present, the Republican Party has become steadily more inclusive and liberal in its policies, while the Democrats have worked at shedding their image of "tax-and-spend" liberals. The Republican Party remains more conservative on social policy, although it is difficult to characterize the party nationally as there is no central party definition or discipline as in other countries. Rather, U.S. political parties are essentially a reflection of the policies of their candidates, rather than having candidates that carry out a central policy.

Paid political advertising

Advertising is a pervasive and expensive feature of U.S. elections. Spending on election campaigns has increased at a furious pace in the U.S., up fourfold from a relatively modest $171 million in the 1976 presidential campaign. In 2004, Bush alone spent $367 million and Democratic contender John Kerry was not far behind with $326 million, mostly on advertising. Candidates for U.S. Congress collectively spent well over a billion dollars. In 2000, the average winning candidate for the U.S. Senate spent $7.4 million, while the average winning candidate for the U.S. House of Representatives spent $849,000.[1] At the same time, as the U.S. State Department points out, parties and interest groups are playing a greater role in direct voter communication. While there have been attempts to rein in contributions to campaigns to avoid the undue influence of groups or individuals on policy, these efforts so far have been relatively ineffectual. Most of this money is spent on airtime for political advertising, which means a financial boost for the U.S. media during election times. It also means a heavy dose of propaganda for television viewers. As noted above, campaign advertising has become increasingly negative.

Television campaign coverage

Another new element of bias emerged in the 2004 presidential race, when it was clear that Fox News was biased in favor of President Bush and the Republicans.[2] This was a significant departure from American news tradition, in which the major television networks had generally attempted to remain relatively unbiased in their political coverage and framing. At the same time, Fox rocketed to the top of the ratings for news. As Bush won re-election by a narrow margin, this suggests that the influence of a popular news show may have made a very important difference. However, while Americans reported a relatively high level of interest in the 2004 campaign, they did not always like what they saw. In a survey of 1,209 people by the Pew Research Center for the People and the Press (2004b), 72 percent of the respondents said there was more mud-slinging or negative campaigning in that election compared with previous campaigns. That is more than double the percentage who complained about a negative campaign in a similar survey by Pew after the 2000 election.

The internet and the campaign

Another major change in 2004 was that the internet became a major source of campaign information for American voters for the first time in a presidential election, according to the Pew survey (Pew, 2004b). In the 2004 campaign, 21 percent of American voters relied on the internet for most of their election news, nearly double the 11 percent who said they relied on it in the 2000 presidential election. In addition, 41 percent of voters reported that they received at least some of their campaign news online. Unsurprisingly, it was the youngest voters who relied most on the Web for campaign information. Six out of every ten voters under the age of 30 reported using the internet as a news source in the campaign, compared with just 15 percent of voters aged 65 or older (Pew Research Center, 2004). The role of the internet in U.S. politics will be discussed in more depth in Chapter 8.

Key points about U.S. elections and the mass media

- Party identification – although lower than it was decades ago – is still very important in determining voter choice, reducing the role of the mass media to influence elections results. However, the media can be a critical factor in close U.S. elections.
- U.S. elections keep getting more expensive, mostly due to the cost of television advertising, although evidence suggests that it can be relatively hard to attract voters in this way.
- Campaigns, especially paid ads, have become more negative in recent elections.
- By 2004, a major U.S. television network (Fox) had become measurably biased for the Republican Party and incumbent George Bush.
- The internet plays an increasing role in U.S. elections, especially for younger Americans.

Elections and media in the United Kingdom

5.4 While the U.K. has prided itself on a less media-driven political sphere than that of the U.S., some scholars have shown concern that British politics have become "Americanized." Kavanagh (1996) has pointed to several features of British political campaigns that could be said to parallel U.S. elections, including a reliance on modern communications as well as a growing emphasis on media strategy and tactics. These new tactics include tailoring the campaign to fit the format of television, a new priority on political marketing within British parties, and an increase in negative campaigning. These notions of "Americanization" were brought to a very different political system and media market. As discussed in Chapter 2, Britain's media are dominated by the publicly funded British Broadcasting Corporation. Not only does the BBC accept no paid advertising at all, commercial television is banned from broadcasting paid political ads in the U.K.. As a result, the bulk of the paid campaign advertising is via posters (which create news stories if they are particularly provocative or interesting) or door-to-door campaigning. British parties also release political manifestos and party platforms, especially via their websites. News outlets cover the release of the manifestoes, publicize the various policies promoted by parties, and attempt to analyze them. Compared with U.S. election coverage, there is far more discussion about party policy than about individual candidate characteristics.

Although British members of parliament are elected in electoral districts across the country, this is where the similarity to the U.S. system ends.[3] While candidates for Congress and the U.S. presidency ultimately are selected via elections, British candidates are selected from within the political parties. As a result, the political parties have wide-ranging control over the candidates and the ability to use party discipline to direct the behavior of their candidates inside and outside Parliament. British political parties have central manifestos that outline clearly to the voter what they will attempt to do if elected into office – and parties can be held accountable for broken promises. In many electoral districts, the candidates who stand are strangers to the area. Nor do the British elect a separate head of state. Instead, the party that receives the largest percentage of the vote forms a government and appoints a set of ministers, including the prime minister.[4] Two political parties, the Conservative Party and the Labour Party, have alternated in power for the past several decades in the U.K.. While other parties have gained majorities in various constituencies, none has been able to amass enough votes to challenge the hegemony of the two major parties, although the Scottish National Party won the largest number of votes in the 2007 Scottish Parliamentary elections. Elections to the Parliament at Westminster are held at least once every five years and are called by the sitting government – usually about every four years. The most recent general election was in May 2005.

As in the U.S., the two main political parties in the U.K. have drawn closer to each other on economic and social policies. Once the avowed party of the working class, Labour transformed its image in the 1990s and seized power from the Conservatives in 1997, after almost 20 years of Conservative rule. The central issues in understanding the media and elections in the U.K. are the role of party identification in Britain; the role of public television and the tabloids in covering elections; how parties use their free broadcast slots for their party election broadcasts (PEBs); and whether the internet has approached the same impact in elections in the U.K. as it has in the U.S..

Party identification

As in the U.S., party identification remains an important indicator of voter choice. In the 2001 elections, for example, 79 percent of those who voted for the Labour Party also claimed Labour Party identification and 83 percent of the Conservative voters claimed they were Conservative Party supporters.[5] Social class still matters in the elections, although the same survey suggested that this correlation is not as strong as that of party identification. That being said, the Labour Party in particular is a very different party from the working-class champions that persisted until the 1990s. There are a handful of smaller parties in the U.K., mostly linked to regional and ethnic identity (such as Sinn Fein in Northern Ireland and the Scottish National Party).

Public television and tabloids in elections

True to their strong political allegiances, the British tabloids have the same slanted reporting during elections. One of the most interesting cases is that of the *Sun*, generally a more Conservative, albeit working-class newspaper. Owned by Rupert Murdoch's company News International Newspapers Ltd, the *Sun* switched allegiance from the Conservatives in 1997 and backed New Labour for its millions of readers. In point of fact, it is hard to determine if the *Sun* led or followed in this case, as the Conservatives had hit a critical low point in both popularity and the ability to implement effective policy. An analysis of the British Election Survey results by John Curtice (1998) concluded that while some people may have been persuaded to vote Labour by the *Sun*, the effect of this persuasion was probably balanced by those who were persuaded to vote for the Conservatives by other tabloid newspapers. British television news, particularly on the BBC, adheres to a careful model of balanced reporting on political parties that focuses much more on policy than personality than the U.S. television news (Oates and Williams, 2006).

Party election broadcasts

In Britain, political parties are given a handful of free slots of up to five minutes each on national television during the month-long election campaign. The distribution of the slots is based on the success of the parties in the previous election. In 2005, Labour and the Conservatives each received five slots and the Liberal Democrats received four slots. Many people watch the party election broadcasts; in 2001, 62 percent of those surveyed had seen a party election broadcast. Margaret Scammell and Ana Langer (2004) argue that while these broadcasts tend to be unexciting, they are an important part of the campaign rituals that reinforce political engagement and voting. The spots allow parties to bring up issues and set the political agenda without the burden of heavy fund-raising (or the implied obligations to the funders). The length of the slot at five minutes is quite awkward from an advertising point of view, far too long to project a quick, attractive image of a party and far too short for in-depth programming. In fact, parties have lobbied for more frequent, shorter slots and tend not to use the entire time. In 2005, Labour, the Conservatives, and the Liberal Democrats aired spots of 3:58, 2:57, and 2:50 minutes respectively.[6] In 1997, the Labour Party pioneered a particularly effective technique, essentially stringing together quite short spots to build up into a longer slot. That way, as people impatiently flipped back and forth to see if the slot was yet over, they often could pick up a short burst of a relatively effective message. In the elections in 2001 and 2005, the successful Labour Party focused more on feel-good issues and images, while the Conservatives often highlighted problems.[7]

The internet and British elections

What evidence is there to suggest that the internet is achieving a particular prominence in the British campaign? While the 2001 General Election was dubbed the "first internet election" (Ward and Gibson, 2003: 188), online campaigning did not reach the same influence and popularity as in the 2000 U.S. elections. In a study of candidate and local constituency party websites, Ward and Gibson found that use of the internet was "patchy," with political websites providing little more than "static online leaflets" (ibid.: 188). They judged the overall impact of the internet on the election as "minimal" – but at the same time pointed out that parties had some good reasons for failing to embrace all the features of the internet in the campaign. The reasons included concerns that the internet does not mobilize the average voter; the problems of drawing a reasonable number of voters to the website; the cost of designing and maintaining a sophisticated website; and fears that journalists might trawl websites to find and report on deviations from the national party platform (ibid.: 201–2). These problems are underlined by disquiet and even dislike on the part of some British citizens who believe that the internet can form a barrier, rather than a bridge, between common people and their elected representatives (Lusoli et al., 2005).

Overall, have British elections become Americanized in their media use? Certainly, it is clear that British parties are relying more on image than in earlier elections, although a prominent leader has long been a key feature of modern British politics (from Winston Churchill to Margaret Thatcher). While discussions of personalities and scandals are fed, in particular, by the tabloid newspaper culture, policy discussions remain at the forefront of British politics. In the 2001 elections, respondents to the national British Election Survey were overwhelmingly concerned about the National Health Service – and this was an issue that played a prominent role in the campaign. The nature of the British system in which a single party takes over the legislature and the executive, makes it far more difficult for parties to evade political promises that are printed in party manifestoes. At times, it might seem that British election campaign coverage parallels U.S. coverage, with a focus on leaders over ideas, the sharp sound-bite over the thoughtful speech, and a gleeful presentation of the trivia of the campaign trail. Yet, British campaign coverage remains centered on parties rather than leaders.

Kavanagh himself pointed out that the stronger structure of British political parties makes it unlikely that British elections will become Americanized – aside from the fact that British parties cannot buy advertising, they lack the funds for really expensive campaigns. Moreover, British politicians continue to attach more importance to policy and national party programs than do their U.S. counterparts. Ralph Negrine and Stylianos Papthanassopoulos (1996) suggest that it is not so much "Americanization" as "modernization" that best describes the changes in British campaign techniques, as the modern media can outstrip modern parties in terms of communicating with the voters. While some might fret that British parties are now more media-savvy, others would argue that a broader dissemination of the message via the mass media is a boon to democracy.

Key points about British elections and the mass media

- Party identification remains important in British elections, although the link between social class and voter choice is weaker than in the past.
- British parties maintain control over who runs in elections and have a highly centralized campaign policy.
- The BBC is committed to equal coverage for political parties in elections.
- There is no paid political advertising in Britain, but there is free time for parties on television called party election broadcasts (PEBs).
- The internet appears to play less of a role in British elections than in the U.S..
- The nature of strong, centralized British political parties will mitigate against British elections becoming too "Americanized," i.e., with even more spin and less focus on issues.

Elections and the media in Russia

5.5 It is clear from the discussion above that the shape and content of a political campaign depends a great deal on the nature of political parties and the mass media – as well as on the rules about media coverage in the campaign. One of the major differences in the U.S. and U.K. systems, apart from differences in party structures, is the law that bans paid political advertising from television in the latter. In Russia, the differences in political parties and the media systems – as well as legal constraints – have led to a system in which neither political parties nor the mass media serve the interests of the electorate. This is despite the fact that the 1993 Russian Constitution encouraged the growth of political parties in the design of the new state after the collapse of the Communist regime in 1991.

Political parties were to play an important role in the 1995 elections for the lower house of parliament, called the Duma. Half of the 450 seats were to be elected through national party lists, in which any party that received more than 5 percent of the popular vote nationwide would be allocated a proportion of the 225 party-list seats. The other 225 seats were to be elected via single-member districts, and candidates could run either with party affiliation or as independents. In fact, Russian President Boris Yeltsin (first elected while Russia was still part of the Soviet Union) was confident that the public would support pro-market, pro-Western parties that were sympathetic to his own presidential agenda. All parties were given ample opportunity to air their views: free air time on state-run television channels, free space in state-run newspapers, the ability to buy large amounts of paid advertising, and the change to get equal coverage on the nightly news. Individual candidates also had some free time and space in the local media.

In fact, Yeltsin and his advisers badly misjudged the outcome of the election. The Russian voters did support pro-market parties and candidates to a degree, but the most popular party proved to be a nationalistic, xenophobic party called (ironically) the Liberal Democratic Party of Russia. This party garnered the largest amount of party-list votes despite getting negative coverage on state television. The Communist Party of the Russian Federation also proved popular, despite the collapse of the Communist regime just two years earlier and almost no television coverage of their 1993 campaign. By the time of the 1995 parliamentary elections, pro-government parties that were more nationalistic and socialist in tone had emerged to take on these challenges. The news coverage, particularly on the prime state-run Channel 1, remained strongly biased in favor of pro-government parties. These parties also enjoyed massive amounts of advertising time and well-polished productions on free-time slots. While all of the parties were offered free-time slots under the law, only a few parties had enough money to use marketing and production tools to produce attractive advertising. The bias in the media as well as the government support of pro-state parties continued through each parliamentary election in 1995, 1999, and 2003 (Oates, 2006).

This bias has subverted the electoral system, which looks free and fair on paper, into a tool for supporting President Vladimir Putin's regime at the expense of democracy. The key factors to consider as to why this has happened are a lack of party identification as parties fail to survive (including a dearth of meaningful party platforms or ideology); the failure of the media to provide adequate and unbiased information to the voters; the Kremlin's unfair tactics that have subverted a democratic party system; and excessive mud-slinging and dirty tricks in campaigns. It should be noted that unlike in the U.S. and the U.K., neither parties nor voters have made effective use of the internet.

Failed parties, slippery party identification

The relative weakness of political parties and control of the media by the Russian elite has meant that the media (particularly television) have played an active role in subverting political parties. Parties are supposed to aggregate the interests of the masses so that their political preferences are represented at local, regional, and national levels. While this works differently according to locality, there are mechanisms for accountability in countries such as the U.S. and Britain. Although incumbents tend to be re-elected, there is a regular transfer of power between parties and candidates in democratic systems. In Russia, political parties have come to function much more as mere marketing vehicles rather than as organizations that offer people a say, even if quite indirect, in the leadership of the country. While many Russian parties were tiny and unprofessional, a handful of serious political grass-roots movements did emerge from 1993 onwards. In particular, the Communist Party of the Russian Federation had coherent policy statements, ideology, and consistent leadership.

The Kremlin and the "broadcast" party

Many factors have made it difficult for strong political party organizations to emerge in Russia. There was little tradition of grass-roots activism, there was virtually no funding, there was no experience on the part of citizens in running non-Communist organizations, and there was a woefully inadequate communications infrastructure. The lack of co-ordination and co-operation among parties led to a large number of tiny, ineffective organizations. In fact, 43 separate parties ran in the 1995 Duma elections, an impossible number for a rational, informed campaign. At the same time there was a dearth of party-building capacity, those already in power were forming their own political vehicles from above. Thus, a new pro-government "party" was created for each parliamentary election, garnered votes, and supported the Kremlin (at least for a time). These parties were distinguished by having government ministers as candidates; an excessive amount of positive coverage on state-run television; huge resources of finance and workers (actually on the state payroll) to carry out their campaigns; and very vague policy statements. Such parties do not last from one election to the next; rather, a new pro-government party has been created for each parliamentary election from 1993 to 2003. The general ideology of these parties moved further toward the center and away from pro-Western or liberal ideas over time (Oates, 2006). While other groups tried to form the same sort of "broadcast" parties (i.e., parties that were little more than a reflection of their paid time, free spots, and news coverage), the Kremlin came to dominate via these electoral vehicles. By 2003, the Kremlin "broadcast" party of United Russia won almost half the seats in the Duma with its simple slogan of "Together with the President."

Unfair media tactics

The Russian media have been biased in every election, although that bias has varied in strength and tone over the years (European Institute for the Media, 1994, 1995a, 1995b, 2000a, 2000b; Oates, 2006; OSCE/ODHIR, 2004). Arguably the worst media bias took place in the 1996 presidential elections as a wide group of media outlets conspired to hide the truth about an ailing Yeltsin from the electorate. Yeltsin, who was suffering from serious health problems including life-threatening heart disease, was deeply unpopular just before the elections of the summer of 1996. The relatively new commercial television station NTV had gained a great deal of popularity and credibility by late 1995. The Communist Party had enjoyed a renaissance in the 1995 Duma elections, winning the most seats in the party-list race. The Communist Party leader, Gennady Zyuganov, was a credible presidential candidate who could challenge the ailing and unpopular Yeltsin. Yet, Zyuganov had little chance to put across his case for the nation, as the news on all the main television channels hid Yeltsin's infirmity and gave the Communists insufficient coverage. As a result, even though Yeltsin's popularity had sunk to single digits in the beginning of 1996, he was able to win the presidential elections in June of the same year. While part of his victory was due to a lack of alternatives as well as the fear of the return of Communist rule, much must be attributed to the vigorous – and untruthful – campaign that permeated all of the major media in 1996.[8]

In 1999, a series of abusive attacks appeared against parties and candidates, particularly on Sunday night political talk shows. These included accusations against popular Moscow Mayor Yuri Luzhkov, who was challenging the Kremlin administration for national power by creating a major political party. Luzhkov, who later sued for slander and won, was accused of corruption, assesination plots, and planning violent demonstations (European Institute for the Media, 2000a:37) as well as possibly being involved in the contract killing of an American entrepreneur in the capital city. These shows were both incredibly unfair as well as very popular with the viewers. This type of *"kompromat"* (slang for "compromising materials" in Russian) remains a facet of Russian elections, although no longer used as overtly. Other tactics include hiring firms to find "black PR" or any negative material that can be used against a candidate in a planted newspaper article or news report.

Media as lapdogs instead of watchdogs

Well over a decade after the collapse of the Soviet Union, it is clear that a healthy electoral democracy has not emerged in Russia. What has been the role of Russian journalists in party politics? As discussed in earlier chapters, Russian journalists do not play a role of either watchdog or even broadcaster of general information. Rather, journalists and their media outlets take sides in political struggles. Over time, it has become harder to challenge the hegemony of the Russian president and his Kremlin allies. Thus, although earlier Russian elections featured messages from a wide spectrum of political views, by the 2003 parliamentary elections and the 2004 presidential election, there was little variation or meaningful political debate in the campaigns. By 2003, pro-government parties managed to win half the seats in the Duma and Putin won his 2004 re-election bid by a landslide.

Key points about Russian elections and the mass media

- There is virtually no partisan identification in Russia as most parties do not last more than a single election and successful presidential candidates have run without party affiliation.
- It is clear that Kremlin-backed parties appropriate state resources to run expensive election campaigns.
- The media have been biased in support of their favored candidates (instead of covering the campaign as news). This is particularly true on state-run Channel 1 television.
- Images and vague statements have replaced policy statements or ideology in election battles. Media-driven "broadcast" parties have subverted the development of parties with grass-roots.

- Russian elections, particularly in 1999, have been noted for mud-slinging and dirty tricks.
- Unlike in the U.S. or the U.K., the internet plays little role in Russian election campaigns.

Chapter summary

It should be said that election campaigns can produce some unexpected news – and some unexpected results. In Ukraine's "Orange Revolution", protestors were mobilized by media reports – especially on the internet – of election fraud and dirty tricks in the country's 2004 presidential elections. Eventually, after widespread and credible media reports that the opposition had poisoned opposition candidate Victor Yushenko, a new election was called and Yushenko was elected in early 2005. At other times, there are rather startling surprises within established systems. While many had written off American voters as uninterested in debates, the Bush/Kerry debates in 2004 attracted enormous interest. Sixty-nine percent of respondents to a survey by the Pew Research Center for the People and the Press (2004a) said they watched the September 30 debate, which is a huge audience for an election event. More to the point, the debates sparked a public discussion about issues in the campaign in a way that is rarely seen in American politics. As both the campaign trail and the media themselves offer so many twists and turns, it is hard to predict the precise role of parties, candidates, the mass media, and the voters in any system.

The experience of Western countries suggests that while different campaign rules about parties and the media have led to somewhat unique campaign traditions, the heavy reliance on broadcast image may have "Americanized" campaigns in Britain to a degree. At the same time, many voters in the U.S. and Britain remain relatively unmotivated by election campaigns, as many are anchored in fixed party preferences that endure for decades, despite the noise and drama of election campaigns. In the U.S. system, the news bias of a major television news source as well as the surge in use of the internet, which can provide information to voters in more personalized ways, are important points to ponder within the broader understanding of relatively fixed political preferences on the part of American voters. British parties – and hence British voters – remain more focused on issues during election campaigns.

In the past decade in Russia, both political parties and the media have increasingly failed to act in the interests of the electorate, choosing instead to serve mostly as vehicles for a small group of elites to strengthen their hold on power. The media could have played a more pivotal role in this post-Soviet regime, as Russian voters have had no chance to develop long-term political preferences to any post-Soviet party and have remained more open to media cues than their Western counterparts. As a result, Russian voters are more

Table 5.1   Comparison of British, U.S., and Russian national elections and the media

Attributes	United States	United Kingdom	Russia
Party system	Two-party system, Democrats and Republican.	Multi-party system, although Labour and Conservatives dominate. Smaller parties of note: nationalist parties including the Scottish National Party and Plaid Cymru in Wales; the Liberal Democrats	Multi-party system, but dominated by pro-Kremlin forces.
Executive	Elected separately. Non-incumbent must run in primaries to win party nomination.	Head of leading party in parliamentary elections appoints prime minister.	Elected separately. Winners have rejected party affiliation.
Political system	"Balance of Power" – Congress makes and passes legislation. Executive can approve or veto, Congress can override veto with a large enough vote.	Formed by majority party (rarely a coalition) in Parliament	1993 Constitution favors the president. Parliament has ability to complain, put things on agenda, challenge president to a limited degree. President can dissolve a recalcitrant parliament.
National electoral system	Senators (100 total) elected 2 for each state by popular vote; members of House of Representatives (435 total) elected within states in single-member districts by popular vote. President elected indirectly by popular vote (= electoral college).	646 Members of Parliament elected by popular vote in single-member district.	450 members of lower house of parliament (Duma). From 2007, all parties winning more than 7 percent of the national vote will fill the seats. Previously, half were elected via popular vote in 225 single-member districts.
Timing of elections and term limits	Election Day fixed on first Tuesday of November annually. Representatives must run every 2 years; senators every 6 years; president every 4 years. President can only serve two terms.	Must be held every 5 years, can be called earlier. No term limit for prime minister.	Presidential election now every 4 years in Spring. Lower house of parliament (Duma) now every December 4th. Upper House of Parliament no longer elected, now appointed.
Campaign rules	Candidates can buy ads in any media outlet. Extensive use of paid	Parties cannot buy advertising time, but get free time on	Candidates can buy ads in any media outlet. Also, all

Table 5.1   (Continued)

Attributes	United States	United Kingdom	Russia
	television ads. No time limit on campaigns. Presidential primary schedules make presidential campaign very long and costly. Ballot scandal in 2000 called into question the reliability of voting system.	major networks in proportion to their electoral strength (PEBs). Official campaign lasts roughly a month.	parties receive an equal amount of free time on major state networks. Official campaign lasts roughly a month.
Media trends	Increasingly expensive as candidates spend more and more on ads. Increasingly negative, particularly the Bush campaign of 2004.	Some evidence of "Americanization" but strong central parties and presence of public television keep campaign focused more on issues relevant to the public.	The media, particularly the powerful Channel 1, subverted to the needs of the Kremlin. Little fairness, objectivity, or balance in election coverage across media outlets.

dependent on political messages and information in the mass media, which in turn have become increasingly biased and influenced by elites. This has led to a rise of "broadcast parties," elite-dominated organizations that pose as political parties on the airwaves in order to win votes, yet ignore public preferences in the long term. Thus, while there are campaign effects that can be measured (albeit with caution) in established democracies, the Russian case suggests that media can subvert elections and stall democracy in societies that are struggling with democratic development.

Study questions

1   What does the existence of party identification mean for the role of the mass media in elections?
2   Does paid political advertising undermine or support democracy? In particular, does negative advertising or spreading bad news about competitors help to win an election?
3   How does the role of television in elections vary between the U.S., the U.K., and Russia?
4   How important are the mass media in determining the winner in elections? Discuss this as it relates to the U.S., the U.K., and Russia.
5   Which has more power in the electoral arena: political parties or the mass media?

Reading guide

Three of the classics of American voting behavior, which are important for understanding the relative role of the media in voter choice, are Berelson et al. (1954), Campbell et al. (1960), and Nie et al. (1979). For an overview of the central ideas in U.S. electoral studies by scholars, see Niemi and Weisberg (1993). For an early analysis of the party identification model in Britain, see Butler and Stokes (1969). A book that combines the notions of voting behavior and media influence in a recent British election is *On Message* by Norris et al. (1999). For Russian voting behavior, see White et al. (1997) and Colton (2001). For an overview of the media's impact on political parties and elections in Russia, see Oates (2006). For some insider accounts on the behavior of journalists and the mass media during election campaigns, see Kurtz (1998) for the U.S. system; Franklin (2004) and Mandelson and Liddle (2004) for the British system. Detailed accounts of how the media performed in Russian elections from 1993 to 2000 can be found in the European Institute for the Media reports. In terms of the role of the internet in elections, see Davis and Owen (1998). For information relating to internet use in the 2004 elections, see reports by the Pew Internet and American Life Project, as well as Owen (2006). For British politics and the internet, see Lusoli, Ward and Gibson (2006). An overview of Russian political parties and the internet in recent elections can be found in March (2006).

Internet resources

http://www.umich.edu/~nes/   The National Election Survey (U.S.), located at the University of Michigan, provides access to in-depth data about U.S. voting behavior.

http://www.data-archive.ac.uk/   The U.K. Data Archive, hosted by the University of Essex, is a gateway to data and studies about British politics, including electoral studies.

http://www.ssees.ucl.ac.uk/russia.htm   This is the website of the University College London School of Slavonic and East European Studies, which includes a range of weblinks for Russian election resources and beyond.

http://people-press.org/   The Pew Research Center for the People and the Press provides information on U.S. elections, attitudes, and the media in detailed, but comprehensible reports (free access).

http://www.annenbergpublicpolicycenter.org/naes/   The Annenburg Public Policy Center of the University of Pennsylvania runs the National Annenburg Election Study. It provides information on a large survey during the 2004 and 2008 U.S. elections, with a particular focus on media impact and use.

http://www.crest.ox.ac.uk/   The Center for Research into Elections and Social Trends (CREST) is an Economic & Social Research Council Research Center based jointly at the National Center for Social Research in London and at the Department of Sociology, University of Oxford. In particular, the working paper series has scholarly papers on elections, party identification and other British election issues (http://www.crest.ox.ac.uk/papers.htm).

www.ifes.org The International Foundation for Electoral Studies is a non-governmental organization that provides technical assistance to strengthen transitional democracies and has worked in more than 100 countries. The information on the website is useful for those who are interested in attempts to create "free and fair" electoral systems (including media coverage).

http://www.osce.org/odihr/ The Office for Democratic Institutions and Human Rights, a part of the Organization for Security and Co-operation in Europe (OSCE), monitors election fairness, including media performance, and provides reports online (including on Russia).

Notes

1 All campaign-spending figures are from the U.S. Department of State, reported at http://usinfo.state.gov/products/pubs/election04/campaign$.htm.
2 Research in the Department of Communications, University of Florida, directed by Lynda Lee Kaid, Sarah Oates, and Monica Postelnicu. Also see Morris (2005).
3 There are variations for elections that take place at the national (e.g., Scotland, Wales, and Northern Ireland), regional and local level, but they will not be discussed here.
4 The Queen is not involved in elections and, in fact, members of the Royal Family abstain from voting because it is deemed inappropriate for them to be involved in party politics.
5 According to the British Election Survey, available via the U.K. Data Archive at www.data-archive.ac.uk. This is based on 1,636 respondents surveyed just after the May 2001 British parliamentary elections.
6 According to the BBC; see http://news.bbc.co.uk/nolavconsole/ukfs_news/hi/mini_site/election_2005/party_election_broadcast/nb_rm_default.stm
7 Author's research.
8 There was also evidence of some vote fraud, although this was thought to be relatively minor.

References

Ansolabehere, S. and Iyengar, S. (1995) *Going Negative: How Attack Ads Shrink and Polarize the Electorate.* New York: Free Press.

Berelson, B.R., Lazarsfeld, P. and McPhee, W. (1954) *Voting: a Study of Opinion Formation in a Presidential Campaign.* Chicago: Chicago University Press.

Bimber, B. and Davis, R. (2003) *Campaigning Online: The Internet in U.S. Elections.* Oxford and New York: Oxford University Press.

Butler, D. and Stokes, D. (1969) *Political Change in Britain: Forces Shaping Electoral Choice.* London: Macmillan.

Campbell, A., Converse, P., Miller, W.E., and Stokes, D.E. (1960) *The American Voter.* Chicago: University of Chicago Press.

Carmines, E.G. and Stimson, J. (1980) "The Two Faces of Issue Voting." *American Political Science Review* 74 (1): 78–91.

Colton, T.J. (2001). *Transitional Citizens: Voters and What Influences Them in the New Russia.* Cambridge, MA: Harvard University Press.

Crewe, I., Gosschalk, B., and Bartle, J. (1998) *Political Communication: Why Labour Won the General Election of 1997*. London: Cass.

Curtice, J. (1998) "Was it the *Sun* wot won it again? The influence of newspapers in the 1997 election campaign". Working Paper No. 75 (September). Department of Sociology, University of Oxford: Centre for Research into Elections and Social Trends (CREST).

Davis, R. and Owen, D. (1998) *New Media and American Politics*. New York and Oxford: Oxford University Press.

Downs, A. (1957) *An Economic Theory of Democracy*. New York: Harper & Row.

European Institute for the Media (1994) *The Russian Parliamentary Elections: Monitoring of the Election Coverage of the Russian Mass Media*. Düsseldorf: European Institute for the Media. Available online at http://www.media-politics.com/eimreports.htm.

European Institute for the Media (1996a) *Monitoring the Media Coverage of the 1995 Russian Parliamentary Elections*. Düsseldorf: Germany: The European Institute for the Media. Available online at http://www.media-politics.com/eimreports.htm.

European Institute for the Media (1996b) *Monitoring the Media Coverage of the 1996 Russian Presidential Elections*. Düsseldorf, Germany: The European Institute for the Media. Available online at http://www.media-politics.com/eimreports.htm.

European Institute for the Media (2000a) *Monitoring the Media Coverage of the December 1999 Parliamentary Elections in Russia: Final Report*. Düsseldorf: European Institute for the Media. Available online at http://www.media-politics.com/eimreports.htm.

European Institute for the Media (2000b) *Monitoring the Media Coverage of the March 2000 Presidential Elections in Russia (Final Report)*. Düsseldorf: European Institute for the Media. Available online at http://www.media-politics.com/eimreports.htm.

Farrell, D.M. and Schmitt-Beck, R. (eds.) (2002) *Do Political Campaigns Matter?* London: Routledge.

Franklin, B. (2004) *Packaging Politics: Political Communication in Britain's Media Democracy*. London: Hodder Arnold.

Groeling, T. and Kernell, S. (1998) "Is Network News Coverage of the President Biased?" *Journal of Politics* 60 (4): 1063–87.

Holbrook, T.M. (1996) *Do Campaigns Matter?* London: Sage.

Ireland, E. and Nash, P.T. (2001) *Winning Campaigns Online: Strategies for Candidates and Causes*, 2nd edn. Bethesda, MD: Science Writers Press.

Kaid, L.L. and Holtz-Bacha, C. (eds.) (1995) *Political Advertising in Western Democracies: Parties and Candidates on Television*. London: Sage.

Kaid, L.L. and Johnston, A. (2001) *Videostyle in Presidential Campaigns: Style and Content of Televised Political Advertising*. Westport, CT: Praeger/Greenwood.

Kavanagh, D. (1995) *Election Campaigning: The New Marketing of Politics*. Oxford: Blackwell Publishers.

Kinder, D.R. and Kiewit, R. (1979) "Economic Discontent and Political Behavior: The Role of Personal Grievances and Collective Economic Judgments in Congressional Voting." *American Journal of Political Science* 23 (3): 495–517.

Kurtz, H. (1998) *Spin Cycle: Inside the Clinton Propaganda Machine*. London: Pan Macmillan.

Lusoli, W., Ward, S. and Gibson, R. (2005) "(Re)connecting Politics? Parliament, the Public and the internet." *Parliamentary Affairs* 59 (1): 24–42.

Mandelson, P. and Liddle, R. (2004) *The Blair Revolution Revisited*. London: Politico's Publishing.

March, L. (2006) "Virtual Parties in a Virtual World: Russian Parties and the Political Internet." In Oates, S., Owen, D., and Gibson, R. (eds.) *Politics and the Internet: Citizens, Voters and Activists*. London: Routledge.

Miller, W.L. (1991) *Media and Voters: The Audience, Content and Influence of Press and Television at the 1987 General Election.* Oxford: Clarendon Press.

Miller, W.E. and Shanks, J.M. (1996) *The New American Voter.* Cambridge, MA: Harvard University Press.

Morris, J.S. (2005) "The Fox News Factor." *The Harvard International Journal of Press/Politics* 10 (3): 56–79.

Negrine, R. and Papathanassopoulos, S. (1996) *The "Americanization" of Political Communication: A Critique.* The Harvard International Journal of Press/Politics 1(2): 45–62.

Nie, N., Verba, S. and Petrocik, J. (1979) *The Changing American Voter,* 2nd edn. Cambridge, MA: Harvard University Press.

Niemi, R.G. and Norris, P. (eds.) (2002) *Comparing Democracies: Elections and Voting in Global Perspective.* Cambridge and New York: Cambridge University Press.

Niemi, R.G. and Weisberg, H.F. (eds.) (1993) *Classics in Voting Behavior.* Washington, DC: Congressional Quarterly Press.

Norris, P. (2000) *A Virtuous Circle: Political Communication in Postindustrial Societies.* London: Sage.

Norris, P., Curtice, J., Sanders, D., Scammell, M., and Semetko, H. (1999) *On Message: Communicating the Campaign.* London: Sage.

Oates, S. (2006) *Television, Democracy and Elections in Russia.* London: Routledge.

Oates, S. and Williams, A. (2006) "Comparative Aspects of Terrorism Coverage: Television and Voters in the 2004 US and 2005 British Elections". Paper presented at the Annual Meeting of the American Political Science Association, Philadelphia, Pennsylvania.

Organization for Security and Co-operation in Europe/Office for Democratic Institutions and Human Rights (OSCE/ODIHR) (2004) *Russian Federation Elections to the State Duma 7 December 2003 OSCE/ODIHR Election Observation Mission Report.* Warsaw: Office for Democratic Institutions and Human Rights. Available online at http://www.osce.org/item/ 8051.html.

Owen, D. (2006) "The internet and Youth Civic Engagement in the U.S." In Oates, S., Owen, D., and Gibson, R. *The Internet and Politics: Citizens, Voters and Activists.* London: Routledge.

Patterson, T.F. (1994) *Out of Order.* New York: Vintage.

Pew Research Center for the People and the Press (2004a) *Debate Coverage Viewed Favourably: News Audiences Differ on Horse Race.* Washington, DC: Pew Research Center for the People and the Press. Available online at http://people-press.org/reports/ display.php3? ReportID=228.

Pew Research Center for the People and the Press (2004b) *Voters Liked Campaign 2004, But Too Much "Mud-Slinging".* Washington, DC: Pew Research Center for the People and the Press. Available online at http://people-press.org/reports/display.php3?ReportID=233.

Scammell, M. (1995) *Designer Politics: How Elections are Won.* London: Macmillan.

Scammell, M. and Langer, A.I. (2004) "Political Advertising in the U.K.: Avoiding Disbelief, Inviting Boredom." Paper delivered at the Annual Meeting of the American Political Science Association, Chicago, Illinois.

Semetko, H.A., Blumer, J.G., Gurevitch, M., and Weaver, D. (1991) *The Formation of Campaign Agendas: A Comparative Analysis of Party and Media Roles in Recent American and British Elections.* Hillsdale, NJ: Lawrence Erlbaum Associates.

Ward, S. and Gibson, R., (2003) "Online and On Message?: Candidate Websites in the 2001 General Election". *The British Journal of Politics and International Relations* 5 (2): 188–205.

White, S., Rose, R., and McAllister, I. (1997) *How Russia Votes.* Chatham, NJ: Chatham House Publishing Inc.

Media and War

⑥

Central issues

- How has the relationship between the military and the media changed from Vietnam to the present?
- What is the range of elements that affect how journalists in particular countries cover conflicts?
- Should journalists practice self-censorship during wars?
- What does the audience expect from war coverage?
- Is the coverage of wars fundamentally different in democratic and non-democratic media systems?
- What are the acceptable limits of censorship during a conflict?

Introduction

6.1 The coverage of war has developed quite distinctly from gritty film from the battlefields of Vietnam in the 1970s to the upbeat, "feel-good" stories of soldiers "liberating" Iraq in 2005. The overall content and tone of the media have shifted from reporting the difficult fighting on the battle-field to a self-censoring media in service of the military and the state. This chapter analyzes the change in war reporting from Vietnam as the first "tele-vision war" to the invasion of Iraq by the U.S. after the terrorist attacks of 9/11. While the Vietnam War offered better access to reporters and more crit-icism of the government than the current system, the notion of an antagonis-tic media that destroyed the military's chances in the long war in Southeast Asia is somewhat of a myth. While it is clear that the U.S. military learned important lessons about media management from the Vietnam experience, dif-ferent wars offer both varying opportunities and challenges to the military, government, and journalists alike in terms of telling the story. Overall, how-ever, it is clear that journalists, audiences, and political elites across the globe now expect war coverage that is more patriotic than objective or balanced.

What has led to these clear changes in the coverage of warfare? On the one hand, technological developments in weapons and communications have transformed both how wars are conducted and how they are reported. Other important factors include the nature and number of countries involved in the conflict; the distance of the conflict from the home country; the length of the clash; and the general mood of the public as their army goes to war (see Table 6.1 for a full list). In addition, conflicts are framed and reported within a broader framework of international relations, meaning that there have been changes in the definition of "friends" and "enemies" in the huge political shift brought about particularly by the collapse of the Soviet system in 1991. All of the fac-tors about the conflict and the political arena aside, war coverage also is shaped by the organization and structure of the media system of the country at war. As will be discussed below, the advent of major U.S. cable networks such as CNN and Fox have meant significant changes in the way in which wars have been reported. Another key factor is whether there is dissent among the political elites or the media organizations on how war should be reported – an important factor in the coverage of Vietnam as well as in the first Chechen War in Russia (1994–6).

This chapter will trace the developments that have led to a marked decrease in openness and freedom of information in the coverage of international con-flicts. The chapter starts with a discussion of the media in Vietnam. The analy-sis then focuses on how the British pioneered principles of military media control in the Falklands War, taming journalists with a pool system, self-censorship, and the type of appeals to nationalism that came to predominate by the first Gulf War in 1991. The chapter will include a discussion of the U.S. media's coverage of the wars in Iraq. It will contrast the notion of a "con-trolled" free media during war with that of the complete news blackout and resulting increase in human rights violations in Chechnya. What emerges from this analysis is that the events and level of violence of the conflict itself do not necessarily dictate coverage. Rather, an important element to understanding the nature of war coverage is insight into the way in which the states involved choose to frame the conflict.

Table 6.1   Factors affecting war coverage in democratic systems

Factor	Vietnam	Falklands	Gulf Wars
Global political situation	Cold War.	Cold War, but conflict didn't involve Communist countries.	Very end of Cold War; post-Cold War.
Framing of conflict by elites	At first unified, eventually split. President Johnson abandoned war effort.	Unified, both main political parties in favor of invasion.	Unified, both main political parties in favor of invasion.
Military information management	Little. Journalists facilitated in work by transport, support by military.	Heavy. Only small pool of reporters taken to location, little access to battlefield, little access to communications, censorship, threats, appeals to nationalism.	Heavy. Moves from pool system to embedding in second war. Little access to battlefield, threats of being cut off from further information, appeals to nationalism.
Location of conflict	Remote.	Relatively remote	Relatively remote to Americans, yet significant in terms of oil economy.
Length of conflict	Long.	Short.	Mixed. First war, only 3 months; second war from 2003 to present.
Media system most influential in framing conflict	U.S.: libertarian.	British: social responsibility in broadcast, heavy control by government sources via lobby system. Libertarian press sector very patriotic.	U.S.: libertarian but functioning under "patriotic" model. British coverage under social responsibility system.
Journalist self-perception	From supporters of military to questioning of U.S. presence.	Patriots, with attempts to deviate questioned by government.	Patriots for U.S., more questioning for U.K..
New media outlet	Growth of television news.	No major changes.	First war: CNN and coming of age of 24-hour rolling news. Second war: Fox News as patriotic media outlet

A common theme throughout the coverage of all wars is the classic dilemma for journalists of their responsibility to disseminate information to the public that conflicts with concerns for national security. While concerns over national security are often raised by governments, it is the journalists who have a much more difficult situation when covering wars. They face significant barriers to their central task of reporting. First, there are grave logistical difficulties in war reporting. Not only is it dangerous to report from a battlefield, but journalists can either be killed by the enemy or put other lives at risk by impeding the operations of their own military. While technology has solved many of the problems of filing stories – even live broadcasts – from remote areas, logistics still remain difficult. It is often hard to obtain even basic information, i.e., to know which side has lost or won or whether a city has been captured, in the "fog of war" on the battlefield. Military personnel are trained not to talk to reporters for security reasons; meanwhile, reporters cannot or will not interview soldiers on the other side for logistical reasons, patriotic concerns, or both. As a result, reporters become extremely dependent on information from their own military in covering a war. On one level, journalists must rely on the military for personal protection if they are near or on the battlefield. More importantly, they are almost completely reliant on them for any meaningful information and the ability to interview troops. Those reporters who choose to act "unilaterally" and go unescorted to the battlefields face being wounded or even killed by one side or the other. In the second Iraq war (2003 to the present), 95 of the 102 journalists who have been killed while working were not "embedded" with the troops.[1]

Finally, reporters are also citizens of particular nations. They realize that their coverage of a conflict can affect the outcome of the battle, from revealing strategic information to undermining public support for the war by focusing on the harsh realities of conflict. Journalists and their media organizations are forced to make difficult choices in conflict reporting. Can journalists reconcile the need to cover the story with both the demands of the military for secrecy and the call of patriotism from themselves, their editors, their publications, and their audience? Evidence from more recent conflicts suggests that the media are now effectively deployed in support of their military. At the same time, audiences are relatively accepting of war-time censorship and positive framing of the conflict. As a result, there is less accountability about both the conduct and the justification for war from the governments themselves. This can mean that governments, once effective "news management" of conflicts is established, are free to wage wars that go largely unreported in a realistic way.

The Vietnam War: the first television war

6.2 The Vietnam War must be understood within the context of world politics at the time of the conflict. The catalyst for the U.S. involvement in the war was the assassination of the U.S.-backed leader of Vietnam in 1963. A year later, the U.S. Congress passed the Gulf of Tonkin resolution after

North Vietnamese battleships allegedly fired on U.S. ships. Underlying the conflict over a mostly unmodernized country halfway around the world from the U.S. was the fear of Soviet influence in Asia. By 1965, the U.S. had deployed more than 200,000 soldiers to fight the North Vietnamese or "Vietcong." Troop levels eventually swelled to more than half a million. Much of the fighting was in dense, difficult jungle in guerrilla warfare situations.

At the same time, the political climate at home was shifting radically, as unrest over race and other issues swept through the U.S. in the late 1960s. The conflict remained in an uneasy political no-man's land, as the U.S. hesitated to deploy its full arsenal of weapons and troops. Resistance to both the mandatory draft for young men, as well as the war in general, hardened in the U.S. as the war dragged on. The war effort was essentially abandoned in 1973 and the last U.S. troops retreated in disarray from the Vietnamese capital of Saigon in 1975. North Vietnamese troops had won the war by 1975, although the new country never became a Soviet satellite in the same way as Eastern European countries.

Initially, the coverage of Vietnam was similar to that of earlier conflicts, although the advent of satellite transmission allowed journalists to report on the war with more immediacy. This is one reason Vietnam has been dubbed the first "television war." Another reason for this label is that footage from Vietnam was a familiar part of the evening news broadcast to Americans for more than a decade as television ownership increased dramatically. Journalists were allowed to travel extensively with the troops and, perhaps most crucially, were given transport and support by the U.S. military. Although Vietnam is often referred to as a war in which journalists were quick to underline the harsh realities of conflict, in fact the initial coverage of Vietnam was far more "patriotic" than focused on the ugly side of a guerrilla war (Hallin, 1986; Hoskins, 2004; Carruthers, 2000). According to a study by Hallin, the news coverage did not become critical until sections of the Washington elite had turned against the war. In addition to emerging fissures in the support for the war among the elite and the public, the length and nature of the war made bad news virtually inevitable. The draft made the Vietnam war a personal issue for young men in America. It became more and more difficult to frame the war as a positive extension of U.S. foreign policy as the number of soldiers killed and injured increased.

The brutalities of war – often never seen or merely framed as an unfortunate exception to the conduct of war – became prominent in the wake of the My Lai massacre in 1968. In this incident, eventually brought to light in 1969, about 500 Vietnamese in a small village believed to harbor the Vietcong were massacred by U.S. soldiers. Although there had been evidence that enemy soldiers had been in the village, those killed included babies, women, and elderly people who merely lived in the area. Coverage of the Vietnam War does not show that reporters and the media are naturally antagonistic to military operations if allowed to cover a war relatively freely. Rather, the coverage suggests that the length of the conflict, the moral justification for the violence, well-documented atrocities (it was an Army photographer rather than a journalist who took pictures of those massacred at My Lai) as well as a growth in anti-war sentiment among elites and the public all contributed to the change in tone of the coverage. It is not as simple as a "Vietnam syndrome" in which the mass media were allied against the military and turned the public against the war. Rather, the media came to reflect a growing sentiment held by many politicians, much of the public, and many of the soldiers as well. All of these groups started to perceive the war as wrong and a waste of American lives.

In his research of Vietnam coverage, Hallin (1986: 44) found that in the wake of the 1968 surprise attack by the North Vietnamese (the Tet offensive) there were ten times as many negative references to the democratic credentials of the U.S.-sponsored government in South Vietnam as there were positive references. At the same time, Hallin found there were almost six times as many negative references to the morale of U.S. troops as there were positive references. Thus, negative attitudes about the war were not necessarily generated by the media. However, they were echoed and amplified by the media, no doubt leading to support for the peace movement. In fact, President Lyndon B. Johnson himself came to feel that the war was unwinnable when famous CBS news anchor Walter Cronkite openly criticized the conflict. Hence, one can accept a limited definition of the "Vietnam Syndrome" that underlines the ability of the media to legitimize a public movement or criticize a government, even over the sensitive issue of war.

Key points about the Vietnam War and the media

- Reporters had relatively free access to the battlefield as well as newer technology that allowed them to send back moving images much more quickly than in previous wars, helping to make Vietnam the first "television war" as more Americans acquired television sets.
- Studies show coverage of the war was not particularly negative until after some elites had turned against the war.
- Sweeping social changes, including resistance to the draft, undermined support in the U.S. for the lengthy Vietnam War.
- The military and the government came to believe in the "Vietnam Syndrome" – that critical media coverage undermined support for the war and military operation – although this is not justified by studies of the actual coverage.

The Falklands War: the patriotic media model

6.3 The Falklands War in 1982 was a tiny conflict in comparison with the major U.S. troop deployment in Vietnam. However, this small war arguably rewrote the rules of engagement between journalists and the military. The Falklands are a group of small islands off the coast of Argentina in South America. Home to a few thousand residents, they are a territory of the U.K.. In 1982, the military dictatorship of Argentina – which had long claimed sovereignty over the islands – invaded and occupied the territory. The British government, led by prime minister Margaret Thatcher and the Conservative Party, responded swiftly with warships. The one-sided war lasted just three months as Britain reasserted sovereignty of the islands, leaving 655 dead on the Argentinian side and 255 slain on the British side. In direct contrast to the transport and support offered to journalists during the Vietnam War, the Thatcher government initially barred journalists from traveling with the troops at all. Giving way to pressure from journalists, the government eventually allowed a handful to travel with the troops, although access to both the battlefield and communication equipment remained severely limited (Harris, 1983).

The British government and military approached the news management of the Falklands crisis with a clear strategy: restrict access to the battlefield; control the ability of journalists to file their stories; censor any stories that they deemed unpatriotic; and encourage an atmosphere in which criticism of the justification or conduct of the Falklands War was unpatriotic and un-British (Philo, 1995). The British government was able to carry out the first three steps, in particular because the location was so remote that it was essentially impossible to reach the battlefield except by military transport. In addition, the only way to communicate internationally for journalists at the time was via the communication system on the military vessels. While the Thatcher government technically lacked direct control over either the public British Broadcasting Corporation or the print media, there was formidable pressure brought to bear on these organizations to toe the patriotic line. Given these constraints, the media coverage of the war was somewhat predictable.

The Glasgow Media Group (1995) identified three central elements to the news management of the Falklands War. First, there were the limits discussed above imposed by the British Ministry of Defense in the form of direct censorship and controls on journalists. The ministry itself selected the small number of journalists who were allowed to travel with the troopships to the southern Atlantic Ocean. The restrictions on reporting extended to delays in releasing pictures, as the government was concerned that graphic images could erode support for the war. News reports were directly censored during the Falklands War. The BBC complained that they were not allowed to show pictures of body bags or use the phrase "horribly burnt" to describe wounds.

The second element of control outlined by the Glasgow Media Group relates to the British "Lobby" system of journalism, which discourages aggressive challenges to the government (for more detail about the Lobby system, please see Chapter 4). If British journalists challenge their sources or release embargoed information, they are subject to being banned from contact with all top government sources. This makes it difficult for individual journalists or media outlets to challenge the government because they could lose their access to virtually the only source of information. At the same time, the British government at the time of the war had become more proactive about disseminating information, depending on public relations specialists rather than civil servants as they had in the past for dealing with the media (Glasgow Media Group, 1995). While previous British governments had focused on restricting the flow of information, the emphasis now switched to the double strategy of limiting access to damaging information while managing the flow of news to support the British cause. This critical addition of the second step became very apparent in the U.S. military media management in the Gulf Wars. In addition, the notion of allowing reporters access to the battlefield only in special groups or "pools" developed in the Falklands War. The pool system, which forces reporters to cooperate closely with the military in order to gain relatively safe access to a war zone, is very useful for controlling journalists and has been used in more recent conflicts such as the Gulf Wars.

The final, and arguably most important, element contributing to the patriotic level of news that emerged from the Falklands War was the motivation of the journalists and the media outlets themselves. While broadcasters in particular were careful not to offend the government, they also were concerned about the public tolerance for graphic footage from the war zone. They were prepared to self-censor on both the basis of taste and the perceived public mood. While there is a tradition in British broadcasting of balance and discussing issues from different sides, the BBC quickly found that this tradition was out of place in the "patriotic" reporting of the Falklands. The BBC did feature the views of some politicians opposed to the Falklands War on its prestigious *Panorama* news program. This broadcast was heavily criticized by the Thatcher government, Parliament, and by the *Sun* newspaper, which branded it "Traitorama." Both the chairman of the BBC Board of Governors and the BBC director-general were sharply criticized for the program at a meeting of Conservative Party members of parliament. The Glasgow Media Group (1995) argues that the reaction to the *Panorama* report had consequences for the general coverage of the Falklands War on the BBC. Internal memos in the BBC showed that the public broadcaster was more cautious in its coverage and those that didn't agree with the war were marginalized. In addition, pressure from the government led to the banning of interviews of the relatives of those who had been killed in the war. The general climate of patriotism made it difficult or even politically dangerous for those not completely in favor of the war to speak out in the media. In addition, there was little serious coverage of some peaceful plans to resolve the situation, including through the United Nations. Commercial television also pursued the "patriotic" line in the Falklands War, according to the Glasgow Media Group.

While it might be tempting to see the media response to the Falklands War as solely a result of better media strategy by the military, there are several factors that contributed to a particularly "jingoistic" or patriotic coverage of the war. One of the most important factors was the short length of the war, with less than three months from start to finish. Not only did journalists barely have time to travel to the conflict (if they were lucky enough to be part of the small press pool), but there was virtually no time for them to establish sources outside of the military. There was little moral argument in supporting the cause of Argentinians, thrust into the war by a military dictatorship eager to cling to power. The islanders themselves, although small in number, generally wished to remain a British territory. Few moral questions were raised by the British response to the Argentinian invasion of the Falklands. Some moral questions, however, were raised by the way in which the British tabloids chose to glorify the death of the badly-outgunned Argentinian soldiers. When the British military sank the Argentinian warship *Belgrano*, the *Sun* newspaper published a huge and arguably tasteless headline reading "Gotcha" (May 4, 1982).

In the wake of the Falklands War, there was criticism of journalists (often by their own profession) that the war coverage had been overblown and overly dramatic (Harris, 1983). As journalists themselves are quick to point out, the coverage of conflict is a particularly alluring, yet difficult task. Once at the front, it can become enormously difficult to get any information or resist the temptation to present one small corner of a large conflict as very significant. At the same time, it is important to avoid perceiving the coverage of the Vietnam War and the Falklands War as diametrically opposed. The Falklands War was extremely brief and not part of a global ideological struggle. If one compares the early, relatively optimistic reports from Vietnam with those of the Falklands War, it is clear that the length of the war also makes a significant difference to the nature of the coverage. It cannot be denied, however, that the British government's media management of the Falklands War represented a qualitatively different approach to conflict media management than the media strategy employed by the U.S. government in Vietnam.

Key points about the Falklands War and the media

- In a short, one-sided conflict, the British government showed how to deploy the media in support of a military operation, serving as a lesson in how to overcome the perceived "Vietnam Syndrome."
- The British government controlled the mass media through an intensification of its regular Lobby system at home, allowing only a few reporters to go with the troops, and censoring reports from the front.
- Both public and commercial media outlets favored reports strongly supportive of the military action, which did not reflect some reservations about the invasion on the part of the public.
- The fact that the Falklands War was a short, distant, and a very one-sided conflict made it relatively easy for the British Ministry of Defense to control the nature of reporting on the war.

The Gulf Wars: distance, control, and patriotism

6.4
The involvement of the U.S. military (as well as the British and other countries) in the Gulf is defined particularly by two conflicts in the late twentieth and early twenty-first centuries. The conflict known as the first Gulf War started in 1990, after the regime of Iraqi leader Saddam Hussein invaded neighboring Kuwait on the pretext of illegal oil drilling at the border. A joint force, led by the American military, invaded the country with heavy reliance on aerial bombing that began in January 1991. The Iraqi forces, badly outnumbered and overwhelmed by superior firepower, surrendered within weeks of the start of the aerial bombardment. Although Hussein was roundly condemned by the international community, he continued to rule Iraq. The second Gulf War was launched by the U.S. (with support from international allies such as the U.K.) in response to the reported threat of weapons of mass destruction held by Hussein, in an atmosphere heightened by fears of American security in the wake of 9/11 and the U.S. "war on terror." This section will discuss how military media management has developed through both of these conflicts.

Media management in the first Gulf War

Douglas Kellner's (1992) analysis of U.S. media coverage of the first Gulf War found that television stressed the inevitability of war and favored military solutions over diplomatic efforts or sanctions. War coverage was dominated by pro-war commentators, although there were some political commentators who questioned whether U.S. interests in the region were sufficient to justify military action. Much as in the Vietnam coverage, the media tended to reflect opinions held by elites rather than question the military action on behalf of the public. A study by the media group Fairness and Accuracy in Reporting (FAIR) found that out of almost 48 hours of coverage in the six months leading up to the 1991 invasion, only 29 minutes (1 percent of the coverage) dealt with opposition to military action. While it is true that there was relatively strong support for the first Gulf War, the coverage still was one-sided in favor of the invasion. Thus, alternatives to military action were not discussed or presented to viewers. It could be argued that the public weren't interested in any options or these choices were not presented by the political elites, but it is clear that (as in the Falklands War) considerations of whether war was the right solution to the threat of a corrupt regime were not part of the public discourse.

Robert Ivie (1980) found very similar rhetoric, with an emphasis on savagery as the American justification for war, for how the U.S. government justifies war in conflicts ranging from the War of 1812 to Vietnam. George Cheney (1993) found ample evidence of this in his study of the coverage of the first Gulf War, in which Saddam Hussein was found to be "merciless," "evil," "savage," threatening," "brutal," and "another Hitler." This was linked with what analysts perceived as the rhetoric for an irresistible momentum toward war, framing it as inevitable while the U.S. had "gone the extra mile for peace" and "Saddam" was forcing the hand of the U.S..[2] Cheney also found that both politicians and the media equated support for the troops with support for the war, a link that made it difficult to criticize foreign policy without criticizing the soldiers themselves. Emphasis on the technical superiority and advancement of weapons systems predominated over a discussion of policy – in the decision to go to war, the conduct of the war, and reconstruction options for post-war Iraq.

During the first Gulf War itself, a pool system worked well at limiting access to the troops. In this system, selected journalists only were allowed access to the front and to troops in a group. The pool system reinforced and exacerbated competition among journalists, making it enormously difficult to break the military's monopoly on access to the battlefield, soldiers, and information in general. According to a report on the pool system in *The New York Times*, "the military tightly controlled both access to and content of the news in one of the most thoroughgoing exercises in news management and manufacture of public opinion in U.S. history." The dissent of a large number of U.S. troops was kept quiet. Reporters critical of the war were denied interviews as well as pool access. In addition, all reports and videos were screened and subject to censorship by the military (Miller, 2004).

Concern on the part of the military about war reporting would be deemed prudent. It would be irrational to expect the military to value freedom of speech over national security at a time of war. Kellner, however, suggests that it was not just censorship on the part of the military that limited the coverage of dissent or opposing views during the first Gulf War. Rather, the media themselves were unwilling to show dissent or opposing views not only because of the fear of the government reaction to this coverage, but also because the media did not want to be seen to be out of touch with perceived public opinion. Failing to catch the public mood would have an adverse effect on public approval and ratings. This is similar to the support of the Falklands War by commercial news broadcaster ITV in the U.K. almost a decade before. In Britain, the only newspaper to oppose the 1991 Gulf War was the liberal *Guardian*, leaving the tabloids and even broadsheets to lurid headlines (such as "Go Get Him Boys" in the *Daily Star* on January 16, 1991, and "BASTARDS OF BAGHDAD" in the *Sun* on January 22, 1991.

The first Gulf War provides an example of the synergy between major news events (such as war) and changes in the media sphere. CNN, which was founded in 1980 as the first all-news network, was well positioned to provide extensive coverage of the first Gulf War. High viewer interest in the war and the more entrepreneurial approach to coverage – CNN left reporters in Baghdad during the bombing – arguably provided new ways of covering a conflict (Smith, 1992). However, it was not without controversy, as CNN correspondent Peter Arnett rather bitterly notes in an essay about his experience in interviewing an enemy leader during the war as well as remaining to experience the U.S. bombardment (Arnett, 1992). However, CNN coverage of the first Gulf War consolidated and improved the reputation of the network (in much the same way that the second Gulf War has helped to contribute to the popularity of Fox News).

One of the most intriguing questions is whether the public are convinced that war is a good idea by the politicians or by the media – or whether the tide of nationalism and patriotism at the idea of a war has a powerful emotive force of its own. Philo and McLaughlin (1995) argue that while most people in Britain in 1990 had no particular knowledge of the politics of the Middle East or the desire to go to war with Iraq, a majority of the population quickly become convinced that the war was "necessary" and "morally justified." Philo and McLaughlin (1995: 146) argue that "this change in public belief resulted from a very successful campaign of mass persuasion by politicians, the media and others in favor of military action" and that "voices against this were drowned by the chorus for war." On the other hand, the media may have had less of a role in this groundswell of support than a general need by the public to support their government in war without particularly questioning the rationale for that war.

Key points about the first Gulf War and the media

- In the first Gulf War, the U.S. military deployed two central communication strategies: (i) allowing only a few chosen reporters access to the front via a pool system and (ii) distributing compelling details and video footage via its briefings.
- The war was framed as "video war," remote from battlefield carnage.
- There was little coverage of opposition to the war.
- Journalists and media outlets were influenced by feelings of patriotism and nationalism.

Media management in the second Gulf War

The media management of the second Gulf War, launched in 2003, shows an important development in the relationship among the military, the media, and the audience. While this conflict has essentially the same type of media controls as found in the first Gulf War, this war adds the key element of "embedding" journalists with the troops themselves. This would appear to give journalists enormous latitude, unprecedented since Vietnam, in reporting from the front lines as they are allowed to travel, eat, sleep, and observe military action with the troops. In practice, however, embedding tends to tip the scales in favor of creating positive propaganda rather than meaningful information about the war. There are several constraints on the journalists involved from acting as mere gatherers of information. In the first place, journalists cannot reveal sensitive information without putting the soldiers – and by association themselves, and any supporting crew – at risk. Rather than an occasionally independent or critical stance taken by war correspondents at the end of the Vietnam War, embedded journalists run the risk of identifying too strongly with the troops. The reports that are sent in by the correspondents tend to exaggerate the importance of one small segment of the army, as opposed to giving viewers a balanced approach to the war. Finally, these segments – compelling, personal, and focused on individuals – may create a sense of the conflict as a sort of soap opera or war adventure film, divorced from either the larger principles at stake or the humanity of the "enemy." Ironically, this "personalization" of the war tends to further alienate viewers from the civilians or the "enemies" on the other side. For example, live coverage of the opening days of the second Gulf War as a Fox News correspondent rolled out with the troops on tanks to the battlefield is compelling and dynamic television. While it provided viewers with a front-row seat at a tank battle, did it leave them better informed about the overall conflict? It would seem that the concept of embedding, despite the opportunities it may provide, has great potential to further distort coverage of military action.

It must be said that the second Gulf War has provided very different challenges to conflict media management as well as to Western audiences. The rationale for the attacks was different, as Iraqi forces had not (as in 1991) invaded another country and there was no United Nations resolution to send in troops. It is clear that public anger in the U.S. over the 9/11 attacks provided powerful emotive force to rationalize the invasion, led by the U.S. and joined by some allies. Hussein, who had remained in power in Iraq after the 1991 war, was resurrected as a personal target (and eventually captured, tried, and executed). In the U.K., Prime Minister Tony Blair had a much more difficult time than President Bush from both the media and the public in justifying Britain's involvement in the attack. Blair based the decision on what he called compelling evidence of weapons of mass destruction under the control of a lawless renegade regime. Not only was U.S. and world opinion more divided about the war, but the military operation was not the "surgical" air war as it was presented in 1991. Rather, the war has consisted to a great degree of an extended, difficult ground war with unclear boundaries. The death toll of soldiers has been much higher. In addition, the reputation of the U.S. military was badly damaged by the release of photographs (starting in 2004) showing prisoners being abused by U.S. troops at the Abu Ghraib prison.

Despite these issues, the post-9/11 climate in the U.S. has made audiences often willing to place concerns with security issues over concerns over human rights. As a part of the general insecurity that Americans feel, the justification for the second Gulf War can be loosely framed within a general need to make the world more secure within the frame of the "war on terror." This was a point underlined by President Bush in his successful 2004 re-election campaign, as he linked the war in Iraq with protection against terrorist acts in the U.S..[3] Although there has been significant opposition to the second Gulf War, diffuse concerns about possible international injustices were overwhelmed in the 2004 campaign by fears about personal security on the part of Americans. In a series of ten focus groups just after the November 2004 elections, Republicans and Democrats alike cited a great deal of concern with safety and security (Oates and Postelnicu, 2005). Although they often questioned Bush's decision to invade Iraq, the progress of the war, and the death of American soldiers there, they were quick to view Bush as more decisive and "stronger" in protecting Americans than Democratic contender John Kerry. The second Gulf War might be unpopular with a segment of the U.S. population, but Bush enjoyed particular prestige as his role as president also meant that he was serving as commander-in-chief of all U.S. armed forces.

If the first Gulf War was a critical event for the development of CNN, the second Gulf War has proved an important watershed for Fox News. As noted in earlier chapters, Fox News is unusual for being the first major U.S. television network to have a marked conservative, Republican slant. Although news in general became more patriotic in the wake of 9/11, Fox has a particular emphasis on patriotism and nationalism. As such, the framing of war fits well into the overall themes and coverage style of the station. At the same time, this type of coverage has proved enormously popular with Americans and has helped propel Fox News to become the most popular cable news network. This suggests two important elements of war coverage. First, it can provide an important boost to a media outlet. In addition, the popularity of Fox suggests that the channel strikes a deep chord with its audience, one that responds to news that favors patriotism over objectivity or balance. Media researchers have known for decades that most the people prefer media outlets that parallel their own outlook. Fox has a particularly healthy relationship with this audience. At the same time, it shows other networks – which must compete fiercely for a dwindling audience – that patriotism sells.

On a final note about the current Gulf War, it is interesting to speculate how a compulsory draft into the military would affect public opinion. Although young people are reputed to be relatively apolitical (a notion that is challenged by some social scientists), a shift in the conflict from an abstract principle of patriotism to being obliged to fight in the war could have a considerable impact on public opinion. Young men are currently required to register for the possibility of military service in the U.S., but there are no plans to revive the draft, despite difficulties in recruitment for the U.S. military.

Key points about the second Gulf War and the media

- The new strategy of "embedding" reporters with troops, leading to the further inclusion of the media with the military mission, does not contribute to more meaningful news about conflict.
- The post-9/11 patriotic mood makes questioning of the war – either tactics or justification for the conflict – unacceptable to many audiences.
- The second Gulf War fits well into the news agenda of Fox News and shows that patriotic approaches to war coverage can find broad resonance with the U.S. audience.

Chechnya and censorship

6.5
The Russian case provides a clear example of how changes in the media environment and the political situation led to very different coverage between the first Chechen War (1994–6) and the second Chechen War (1999 to the present). While the presence of an entrepreneurial commercial television station in the mid-1990s fostered more balanced coverage of the conflict, virtually completely censorship has dominated in the current Chechen war. In order to understand this, it is necessary to discuss both some military and media history. Chechnya had long been one of the least assimilated areas of the Soviet empire, although it never achieved the status of an independent nation as was the case for Lithuania, Latvia, and Estonia. Despite the "Sovietization" of their region, the Chechen people overwhelmingly rejected both Soviet atheism and the Russian language. Throughout the 72 years of Soviet rule, Chechens maintained their Islamic identity as well as their Chechen language, even in the face of mass repression under Soviet dictator Josef Stalin. In 1994, Russia sent its troops into Chechnya, a part of Southern Russia that had declared independence from the Russian Federation. The Russian government contended that military intervention was necessary to re-establish order in the region, where organized crime was widespread. The peak of the first war, which was fought between ill-trained Russian troops and a fairly unified Chechen guerrilla force, coincided with the advent of the first major commercial television station in Russia (NTV). While state-run television sanitized the conflict and presented the native population as keen for Russian rule, the commercial NTV news teams displayed a very different picture of Chechnya to the Russian public. The NTV news programs challenged the Russian military's contentions, interviewing Chechens more realistically and showing the Russian military's widespread failures. NTV's coverage of the war no doubt contributed to its unpopularity and the Russians withdrew in 1996 after negotiating a shaky peace arrangement. The Russian military and government showed relatively poor control of both information and the battlefield in the first Chechen war. The NTV reporters were able to travel with the Chechen soldiers, which gave them almost unprecedented scope to report a war in modern times as some journalists could use contacts on both sides of the conflict.

In a few years, however, the situation and the war coverage both changed significantly. After a series of terrorist attacks (mostly in Moscow) attributed to Chechen rebels and a Chechen incursion into a neighboring region, Russian forces returned to Chechnya in 1999. The war continues, but there is little information available. Not only is the Russian military more effective at controlling information, but the Chechen forces no longer provide safe haven for journalists. It has become one of the most dangerous places in the world, in which journalists in particular are at grave risk of being kidnapped and murdered. At the same time, President Putin has consolidated his political position and – unlike his predecessor Boris Yeltsin – does not tolerate criticism in the central media in important policy areas. In the wake of the forced ownership changes at NTV in 2001, the news on this commercial television station no longer reports on the Chechen War in the same manner. Rather, by 2004 the coverage was only a shadow of its on-the-ground reporting in 1995. Hence, while it is the same country and the same combatants locked in essentially the same conflict, the news given to the general public is quite different.

The Russian public remains quite divided over the best course of action in Chechnya, but there is little information for them to consider about what really happens in this southern corner of their nation. Anna Politkovskaya, one of the few journalists to continue to report authoritatively on the war for a liberal newspaper in Moscow, was assassinated outside her own home in 2006. However, focus groups suggest that Russians remain relatively content with a "patriotic" frame, aware that there is little hope of a useful or beneficial outcome to the war (Oates and Postelnicu, 2005). Although they know there is little real information from the conflict, anger over terrorist attacks and resignation over the difficulty of the situations have made them more accepting of sanitized government reports (or no real information at all) about Chechnya.

Chapter summary

Does it matter that Americans prefer Fox News war coverage to more objective or balanced reports on the second Gulf War? On the one hand, there is the notion in both the libertarian and social responsibility systems of the media that journalists should inform rather than indoctrinate. The roles are supposed to be slightly different in each system, with the libertarian system providing the greatest range of news to the audience. Yet, this isn't what happens during war reporting. Rather, the libertarian system of the U.S. has a very narrow range of views, particularly when it comes to reporting on the international system or the political context of a conflict. It is too simplistic to say that U.S. citizens are simply duped by their media systems. In focus groups and opinion surveys, they show concern about international security. However, it would appear that what the American audience seeks in war coverage is more about reassurance than challenging facts – an echo of what Russians seek for news on Chechnya. As the popularity of the Fox Network suggests, the audience is looking for a simplified story line that consistently supports "their" soldiers and, to a slightly lesser degree, the nation's purpose. Many analysts argue that this creates an environment in which leaders have too much latitude to pursue a war and there is little ability to rationally discuss options to war. However, it would appear that a "patriotic" model of the news media comes into play, in which the audience expects a limited range of nationalistic images at the same time as rejecting or avoiding information that challenges their patriotic vision of their nation.

How can you define this "patriotic" model of the news media? There are several distinct elements that emerge from a study of how modern wars are

Table 6.2   The patriotic model of war coverage

1	Media do not question the rationale for war.
2	No discussion of foreign policy options to war.
3	No elite dissent over war is reflected in the media.
4	No public dissent over war is reflected in the media.
5	Reliance on nationalistic images, framing of troops as heroes, framing of foreign leaders as demons.
6	Little to no information from civilians of country under attack.
7	Heavy reliance on military information.
8	Journalists provide propaganda rather than useful information from the front.
9	Media feed on patriotic fervor of its audience.
10	Media that do not follow the general trend of coverage are seen as traitors.
11	Logic of war coverage overwhelms the typical journalistic practices (i.e., of a libertarian or social-responsibility system).

Source: Author's research.

covered in the U.S., the U.K., and Russia (see Table 6.2). These factors include the fact that the media do not question the rationale for war and there is no real discussion about options to the war. No serious elite disagreement or public protest over the war is reported in the media. The coverage itself relies heavily on nationalistic images, dividing the combatants into "heroes" and "demons" (although it is the foreign leaders rather than the foreign soldiers that are particularly demonized). There is little attention to the plight of the civilians in the country under attack or a meaningful discussion of their political views. There is a strong reliance on information from the military, including video supplied by the military. The audience expects patriotism from its media and the media support this fervor – for nationalistic or commercial reasons. Journalists become a propaganda wing of the military rather than independent observers. War is reported as something outside of normal politics. Media outlets and journalists who do not follow this general news line are perceived as traitors rather than respected as following the tenets of responsible journalism.

On the one hand, it would appear that the military, the media, and the public are colluding to ignore the ugly reality of war. However, the "patriotic" model of war reporting makes a great deal of sense; if a war were reported fully, it would be far harder to maintain support for the conflict. Hence, much like the way in which voters in democracies will accept the election of a rival leader, it would appear that populations often tolerate a sanitized or even glamorized version of a war as a palatable story line. Just as many would perceive war as removed from politics as usual, so war reporting must follow a particular logic that has more to do with power than with democratic principles. It is interesting to note that the level of adherence to the "patriotic" model of war coverage varies a great deal among conflicts as well as among countries. However, it would appear that this "patriotic model" of the news media tends to overwhelm the way in which the media operate in peacetime within certain countries. The British media, fueled by a government scandal about the possible "sexing up" of the weapons of mass destruction dossier in the run-up to the second Iraq War, have produced more critical war coverage. This is at odds with the way in which the British media covered either the Falklands War or the first Gulf War. Certainly, the second Gulf War has been longer and provided more time for this sort of reflection. Yet, the social responsibility model and its need to build societal consensus would seem to mitigate against more openness in conflict coverage. In fact, in terms of war coverage, it should be noted that this "patriotic" model would appear to more relevant in understanding the nature of the coverage – and the audience's response to it – than in-depth knowledge about the particular media system at peace. The patriotic model of conflict coverage also could suggest that more coverage of the war will not necessarily lead to more information; rather, embedding and some of the live battle coverage on Fox turns war into more of a spectacle than a political event.

Even though there is compelling evidence that the media present quite limited, biased information in conflicts, leaders often express frustration with the lack of the commitment of the media – public or commercial – to the state's cause. Laura Roselle (2006) examined the conflict media management of Vietnam by the U.S. president as well as attempts by Soviet leaders to control the information flow about the Soviet invasion of Afghanistan (1979–89). In both cases, leaders felt enormous frustration with attempting to frame the story in a way that would support their military actions, speak to the national identity of the time, and foster their own political agendas. Just as journalists feel constrained by a range of factors in covering wars, leaders struggle with how to balance the needs of policy and public information.

In addition, evidence suggests that journalists themselves make relatively little difference in the coverage of war. There are several reasons for this, which can be seen throughout the conflicts listed above. Even in times of peace, there is evidence that the media tend to reinforce, rather than challenge the views of the elites. The media themselves are unlikely to lead change, but rather have a tendency to follow changes among elites and – sometimes – among the general public. This inclination is even more pronounced during wars (even though critics often charge the media with being liberal). Criticism of Vietnam in the media only became apparent after there were sharp divisions among the elite. Arguably, the media reinforced these divisions and sparked a much broader discussion about U.S. involvement in Vietnam. At other times, detailed and balanced coverage of military conflicts is frustrated by a long list of obstacles. These hindrances include difficulty in gaining access to the battlefield; modern warfare such as bombing raids that are impossible to cover without military access; military control on information; as well as the fear of being denied access to additional information if a journalist challenges the military or government too directly. Overlying these problems is a far greater barrier to balanced or objective coverage of a war: the public often prefer sanitized coverage from the front. If the media highlight – or even report on – the death of civilians or some of the more gruesome aspects of the conflict, they can alienate viewers and readers.

What the Russian media coverage of the second Chechen War does show is that there is indeed a difference between the "patriotic" model of war coverage and the suppression of war coverage altogether. There is worrying evidence that there is widespread abuse of Chechen civilians (and captured Russian soldiers) in the conflict, but news about their fate is intermittent and mostly limited to websites as opposed to the mainstream media. While coverage of the Falklands War and the Gulf Wars has been criticized for overdependence on military information, excessive patriotism, and a lack of sensitivity to the broader issues, there has been access to information. Audiences are making choices, even if these are limited choices. Although it is most likely to occur after the fact, there also has been discussion about both military and policy decisions made during the war. This has included concerns that the U.S. forces killed soldiers that were trying to surrender in the first Gulf War as they fled along the Basra Road, as well as the international scandal about abuses at the Abu Ghraib prison under U.S. occupation in Iraq. While there is concern that the "fog of war" hides human rights abuses on a staggering scale, the coverage in the U.S. and British media has a least given an opaque view of the situation. In terms of Chechnya, there is virtually no meaningful information from the region, leaving the military without even the restraining presence of a tame and patriotic press corps. It would suggest that the type of war coverage generated in a repressive regime such as Russia is, in fact, qualitatively different from the jingoistic and incomplete reports in democratic media systems. It also begs the question of what happens in the many conflicts in repressive regimes around the globe where camera crews and correspondents never even come close.

Table 6.3   Models of war coverage

War	Model
Vietnam	Relatively free movement of journalists provided by military. Initially patriotic, eventually critical of the war. Presented in political context. Information on enemy. Coverage evolves over several years. Myth of "Vietnam Syndrome" emerges.
Falklands	Journalists controlled by military. Difficult to file stories. Information censored; media outlets often opt for patriotism over balance. Very short war, no evolution in coverage. Pool system developed.
Gulf War I	Journalists controlled by military in pool system. Journalists and media outlets self-censor due to patriotism and fears of losing military access. Cable News Network (CNN) provides more balanced coverage, important evolution of 24-hour rolling news.
Gulf War II	Journalists become part of military information system via embedding system. Journalists and media outlets self-censor due to patriotism and fears of losing military access. British media more balanced, questioning. Fox News shows popularity of patriotic (as opposed to balanced) coverage.

Study questions

1 What is the "Vietnam Syndrome" and why is it based more on myth than on reality?
2 Why was the Falklands War important in terms of developing methods of media management in conflicts?
3 What methods of military media management were imported from the Falklands War to the first Gulf War?
4 How does the "embedding" system in the second Gulf War affect the way that journalists report on wars?
5 Why is there a difference in the way the Russian media covered the first Chechen War (1994–6) and the current Chechen War?
6 What is meant by the "patriotic" model of war coverage?

Reading guide

For a thoughtful overview that blends facts and ideas about war coverage, see Susan Carruthers' book *The Media at War: Communication and Conflict in the 20th Century* (2000). Hoskin's 2004 book covers the more general theme of war, media, and memory over different conflicts. Hallin's book (1986) debunking the myth of the Vietnam syndrome is a classic in the field. *Gotcha!* by Richard Harris (1983) is a British journalist's discussion of the coverage in the Falklands War, providing a wealth of insider detail for those interested in media and politics in conflict. The Glasgow Media Group provides a social science perspective on the Gulf War in Chapters 5 and 6 of Philo (1995). For the first Gulf War, the edited volume by Hedrick Smith (1992) provides first-hand accounts of those who covered the first Gulf War as the Harris volume does for the Falklands War. Philip Taylor (1993) discusses the first Gulf War from a political communication point of view. For some rare field reporting from Chechnya, see Anna Politkovskaya's *A Small Corner of Hell: Dispatches from Chechnya* (2007).

Internet resources

www.fair.org   Fairness and Accuracy in Reporting (FAIR), a U.S. media watch group, has been offering "criticism of media bias and censorship" since 1986. The website has a section on war coverage at http://www.fair.org/index.php?page=7&issue_area_id=26

www.cpj.org   The Committee to Protect Journalists is an NGO with a particular focus on the dangers to journalists during war. In particular, see its report on the fate of the more than 100 journalists killed in the second Gulf War at http://www.cpj.org/Briefings/Iraq/Iraq_danger.html.

http://www.pbs.org/wgbh/pages/frontline/gulf/   This project of the Public Broadcasting Service in the U.S. provides a range of information on the first Gulf War.

http://www.pbs.org/wgbh/amex/vietnam/series/index.html   This website discusses *Vietnam: A Television History*, a documentary series that was produced for U.S. public television as part of the American Experience series. The website also offers the program for sale, which can provide a good research and learning aid.

http://www.lib.berkeley.edu/MRC/pacificaviet/   This is the Social Activism Sound Recording project of Pacifica Radio and the University of California (Berkeley), including anti-Vietnam War protests in the San Francisco area and beyond.

Notes

1   In addition, most of them (80) were Iraqi. These figures were compiled by the Committee to Project Journalists; see the report on their website at http://www.cpj.org/Briefings/Iraq/Iraq_danger.html.
2   Hussein was routinely referred to by his first name in much of both the U.S. and world media, which clearly separated him from the sort of respect usually given to world leaders (even of repressive regimes). He was executed in Iraq in 2006.
3   According to research by the author and Lynda Lee Kaid at the University of Florida, which included coding news items in the two-month electoral campaign just before the 2004 U.S. presidential elections. This research was funded by the British Economic and Social Research Council. For further details on the study, see Oates (2006) and Oates and Postelnicu (2005).

References

Arnett, P. (1992) "Why I Stayed Behind." In Smith, H. (ed.) *The Media and the Gulf War: The Press and Democracy in Wartime* (pp. 308–14). Washington, DC: Seven Locks Press.

Carruthers, S. (2000) *The Media at War: Communication and Conflict in the 20th Century.* New York: St. Martin's Press.

Cheney, G. (1993) "We're Talking War: Symbols, Strategies and Images." In Greenberg, B. and Gantz, W. (eds.) *Desert Storm and the Mass Media* (pp. 61–73). Cresskill, NJ: Hampton Press.

Glasgow Media Group (1995) "The Falklands War: Making Good News." In Philo, G. (ed.) *Glasgow Media Group Reader, Vol. II: Industry, Economy, War and Politics* (pp. 76–101). London: Routledge.

Hallin, D.C. (1986) *The "Uncensored War": The Media and Vietnam.* New York: Oxford University Press.

Harris, R. (1983) *Gotcha! The Media, the Government and the Falklands Crisis.* London: Faber.

Hoskins, A. (2004) *Televising War: From Vietnam to Iraq.* London: Continuum.

Ivie, R. (1980) "Images of Savagery in American Justifications for War." *Communication Monographs* 47 (2): 279–94.

Kellner, D. (1992) *The Persian Gulf TV War.* Boulder, Co: Westview Press.

Miller, D. (2004) *Tell Me Lies: Propaganda and Media Distortion in the Attack on Iraq.* London: Pluto.

Oates, S. (2006) "Comparing the Politics of Fear: The Role of Terrorism News in Elections Campaigns in Russia, the United States and Britain." *International Relations* 20 (4): 425–37.

Oates, S. and Postelnicu, M. (2005) "Citizen or Comrade? Terrorist Threat in Election Campaigns in Russia and the U.S." Paper presented at the Annual Meeting of the American Political Science Association Meeting, Washington, DC. Available online at http://webzoom.freewebs.com/saoates/oates%20postelnicu%20apsa%202005.pdf

Philo, G. (ed.) (1995) *Glasgow Media Group Reader, Vol. II: Industry, Economy, War and Politics.* London: Routledge.

Philo, G. and McLaughlin, G. (1995) "The British Media and the Gulf War." In Philo, G. (ed.) *Glasgow Media Group Reader, Vol. II: Industry, Economy, War and Politics,* (pp. 146–58). London: Routledge.

Politkovskaya, A. (2007) *A Small Corner of Hell: Dispatches from Chechnya.* Chicago: University of Chicago Press.

Roselle, L. (2006) *Media and the Politics of Failure: Great Powers, Communication Strategies, and Military Defeats.* New York: Palgrave Macmillan.

Smith, H. (ed.) (1992) *The Media and the Gulf War.* Washington, DC: Seven Locks Press.

Taylor, P.M. (1993) *War and the Media: Propaganda and Persuasion in the Gulf War.* Manchester: Manchester University Press.

Media and Terrorism

7

Central points

- The relationship between terrorists and the media is more complex than the idea that the media foster terrorists by giving them the "oxygen of publicity."
- The difference between a "freedom fighter" and a "terrorist" is often defined by the media.
- It is difficult to find a single model to describe the interaction between the media and terrorists because the political situations that spawn terrorism are so different.
- Like war reporting, coverage of terrorism tends to focus on the immediate news rather than delve into the causes of political violence.
- The media can exacerbate the political situation by either demonizing particular political forces or failing to include them in political dialogue.
- Evidence from the U.K. suggests that terrorism can be alleviated, to a degree, by the encouragement of dialogue between entrenched enemies via the media.

Introduction

7.1 British prime minister Margaret Thatcher once accused the media of giving terrorists the "oxygen of publicity" and allowing them to thrive in Northern Ireland. In the minds of many political leaders, if the media simply stopped reporting on terrorist events, terrorists would stop killing innocent people. After all, terrorists do claim that they perpetuate violence against innocent civilians only in order to make their political views heard. If there is no publicity surrounding the event, then there is theoretically no point to the terrorism. Unsurprisingly, it is not that simple. This chapter describes and analyzes the relationship between terrorists and the media in different countries. At the center of the discussion are several important issues that have been raised by the media coverage of terrorists in the U.K., the U.S., Russia, and beyond. First, there is no single, universal definition of terrorist that fits all cultures. In some parts of the world, particularly in places such as Palestine and the former white regime in South Africa, the line between 'terrorist" and "politician" becomes particularly blurred. There is a different range of tolerance and expectation in the coverage of terrorist events across time and among different countries. Studies of war coverage have revealed some clear influences of specific conflicts (see Chapter 6). Yet, it is difficult to find comparative elements of terrorism coverage to help us understand the relationship between terrorism and the media in a meaningful way. However, two clear points emerge. First, the media make an enormous difference in the key definition of terrorist acts of violence as either *criminal* or *political* in nature. In addition, the media generally do not provide analysis or background to terrorist events, making it difficult to either understand the roots of the conflict or work toward a solution.

In the case of defining terrorism as criminal, the media do in some ways deprive terrorists of a critical element of the "oxygen" of media coverage. Although the media report on the acts of terrorism, they tend not talk about the political aims of the terrorists. In this sense, terrorists are reduced to mere murderers. However, while this does deprive the terrorists of a political voice, it does not rob them of their power to create fear and intimidation. In fact, people may become more distressed and upset at terrorist acts if they are divorced from any notion of political or civil control. As such, terrorism becomes a random act for which there is no solution except to demonize the group involved and increase security within society at the expense of civil liberties. Ironically, this process of demonization can amplify the alleged power of the terrorist group and its influence, as has been seen in the case of Al-Qaeda.

Hewitt (1992) is one of the few social scientists to highlight the unevenness in coverage of terrorist groups by country. For example, the German media have "exaggerated the dangers of terrorism and supported government countermeasures wholeheartedly" (ibid.: 174). In Italy, coverage of terrorism changed significantly in 1970s, as a tolerance for the Red Brigade as a type of modern Robin Hood gave way to "virtually unanimous" condemnation of terrorism in wake of escalating violence (ibid.: 174–5). Hewitt cites bias and unfairness in the coverage of terrorists in democratic countries, particularly by the British media in Northern Ireland. He recognizes the tendency in North America and Britain for the media to ignore the social causes and goals of terrorism (ibid.: 177), a finding echoed by others (such as Philo and Berry, 2004). Hewitt also found that "terrorist" was not necessarily a negative term for all audiences, being positive for Palestinians in reference to the Palestinian Liberation Organization and only relatively negative for blacks in South Africa in terms of the African National Congress. Most of the research cited by Hewitt suggests that the level of support respondents in various countries felt for terrorists was much more closely linked to their own proximity to terrorist attacks rather than media coverage of terrorism. Although Hewitt wrote this chapter almost a decade before 9/11 and the spate of terrorist attacks in Russia, the point he makes is salient to the present situation: the public respond more intensely and more emotively when terrorism ceases to be abstract and becomes concrete. The media coverage shifts as well, moving away from any analytical look at the political situation and focusing much more on the violence, the possible retribution for the terrorists, and the prevention of subsequent attacks.

It is clear from this discussion that the media face a very difficult task in the coverage of terrorism. Realistically, they cannot ignore terrorist events. Under the libertarian model, media consumers would expect to be given information on the tragedy. Even under the social responsibility model, which calls for restraint in terms of news that can destabilize or upset the population, terrorism cannot be ignored. The media face choices about how much to reveal about any victims, how to report without impeding rescue operations, which information cannot be released because it would hinder police investigation, and whether speculations about future attacks might cause panic. These were dilemmas encountered, in particular, during major terrorist events such as 9/11, the July 7 bombing of the London transport system in 2005, and the siege of the Beslan school in Southern Russia in 2004 (all discussed below). Unlike the variations found in the reporting of different wars, the coverage of contemporary terrorist attacks tends to be very similar across countries and over time. The news media focus on twin themes of patriotism and reassurance. Terrorist groups are demonized. There is an emphasis on the response by the police and the military. Despite a large volume of coverage, there is very little analysis of the background and causes of the terrorist act itself.

Despite the difficulties and dangers posed by terrorism coverage, there are ways in which the media can work to defuse terrorism, particularly in the longer term. The traditional view of the relationship between media and terrorism has been the dangerously symbiotic relationship of the two (Wilkinson, 1997). The terrorists receive publicity for their attacks while the media attract viewers and readers with the coverage. Yet, the interaction between the media and terrorists is not always a bleak reinforcement of the power of lawlessness to disrupt a society. In the case of Northern Ireland, politicians chose to use of form of "megaphone diplomacy" (Sparre, 2001) to moot ideas about possible reconciliation between the two entrenched enemies of Catholic Nationalists and Protestant Unionists. Although the British government had sworn not to negotiate with terrorists, ideas for reconciliation were discussed by political leaders in newspaper columns. The deadlock was ended and eventually led to the peace process in the mid-1990s. Although this process is still ongoing, the level of violence has subsided and dialogue has increased between the two sides of the conflict. It should be noted, however, that it was the choice of the politicians to use the newspapers rather than a proactive move by journalists to lead the dialogue for reconciliation themselves.

Far more common is evidence that the media exacerbate the divisions in the society that lead some to turn to political violence. There is a qualitative difference between complaints that the media ignore certain groups and trivialize politics and the notion that the media work to promote a political line at the expense of a sizable minority or even dispossessed majority of the population. Most groups who can consider themselves marginalized in certain societies – including anti-globalization groups, British socialists, African Americans, senior citizens, etc. – do not routinely turn to violence as a means of gaining publicity for their causes. States consider terrorists to be acting outside the bounds of civil society by targeting innocent people. In turn, terrorist groups consider states to be acting outside the bounds of civil society by not incorporating their political demands into the state structure. Sometimes, such as with the African National Congress in South Africa, groups that are labeled terrorists by the regime are, in fact, expressing the political will of a broad segment of the population. In other countries, the situation is even more confusing. In Israel, the majority of the Israeli press consider Palestinian suicide bombers to be murderers, while to many Palestinians the suicide bombers are martyrs for a political cause. The two sides in the conflict within the same territory simply do not share a political reality (Philo and Berry, 2004). Yet, how much are the media to blame for the long-standing conflict between Israel and Palestine? It raises the question of whether the media can really function as peacemakers between two deeply embedded sides in a conflict. Some, such as Wolfsfeld (2004), argue that the media framing of a peace process can be critical to its success – and that the media can nurture a destructive cycle of mistrust and hatred.

The following sections will look at four case studies in terrorism. First, the chapter will consider the case of the Northern Ireland and the British media, a long conflict that challenged the boundaries between political expression and national security in the U.K. A switch in government media policy would appear to have helped bring an eventual reduction in terrorist violence in the region. The chapter will then discuss the media framing of terrorism in the wake of 9/11 in the U.S. This coverage is then compared with the media reaction to the July 7, 2005 bombings of the London transport system. Finally, the chapter will reflect on terrorism coverage in the more authoritarian media system in Russia. What emerges is that while any attempt at media "framing" tends to be overwhelmed by the drama of terrorist events, the long-term media coverage of terrorism appears to be a critical factor in any attempt to lessen the impact of terrorism on a society.

Domestic terrorism: Northern Ireland and the British media

7.2 One of the longest case studies of terrorism and the mass media comes from Northern Ireland. While the Republic of Ireland became an independent country from the U.K. in early twentieth century, six counties in the north of the country remained under British rule. Although Irish nationalist feelings were relatively high in the territory, there was a sufficient majority of Protestants who identified with being British rather than Irish to make a case for keeping the territory as part of the U.K. This was enormously controversial, particularly to the many Catholics living in Northern Ireland, who identified much more strongly with being Irish than being British. This minority, referred to as Nationalists, continued to feel that they were being denied the right of an Irish Catholic homeland as well as full civil rights in a British state. Those people who identified with being British, primarily Protestants, were known as Unionists. The problems were exacerbated by anti-Catholic discrimination in the governance of Northern Ireland.

Several terrorist groups evolved, most notably the Irish Republic Army (IRA), which staged bombings in the U.K. (although violence in Northern Ireland itself claimed more lives). Terrorist tactics also emerged on the part of the Unionists. Minority Catholic groups claimed that terrorist response was the only viable response to the repression by the British state (including what they termed the "occupation" of the territory by the British Army). Terrorists received support from some segments of the community as well as from supporters abroad. The British official policy was not to negotiate with the IRA or other groups that employed terrorism as part of a communications strategy, defining their violence as criminal rather than political in nature. Violence waxed and waned, with no real progress toward reconciliation until political elites started working on a peace process in the mid-1990s. Northern Ireland now has a National Assembly and more self-rule, but the issue of Unionist versus Nationalist still pervades the political, cultural, and social spheres in the nation.

There are two important elements to the reporting of terrorism in Northern Ireland. On one level, the British media had no choice but to report on the terrorist attacks, particularly as they often took place across the sea in England itself. Reporting on the acts of violence was one issue. Another related and far more important concern over the long term was the framing of the conflict itself. The British media had a nationalist interest in portraying the conflict as the protection of innocent civilians against Irish-Catholic terrorists. On the other hand, many in Northern Ireland as well those outside of Britain saw the Irish-Catholic population as oppressed by the British regime, perceiving the IRA and others more as "freedom fighters" than as "terrorists." Society was so deeply divided in places, with social cleavages reinforced by different religions, separate neighbourhoods in many cities, separate schools, and even a different interpretation of the very history of the region. With so little common ground, it would be essentially impossible for the media to build on a non-existent sense of unity or common purpose. In fact, many analysts perceived the media coverage of Northern Ireland as an intense propaganda war in which there was a struggle between Nationalists who wanted to unite with Ireland on one side and the British government on the other. The most powerful argument that the government could use to encourage coverage of the Unionists as legitimate and the Loyalists as "terrorists" would be a range of security laws, including the Official Secrets Acts, the Prevention of Terrorism Act (1974), the Emergency Provisions Act (1978), and the Police and Criminal Evidence Act (1984). The D Notices or British Ministry of Defense edicts could be used to justify censorship of coverage of particular acts as well. The government argued that that broadcasters could not claim there was a public interest in discussing terrorism in Northern Ireland in an analytical, in-depth, or personalized way. While it was politically difficult for the British government to engage in direct censorship (although it had that right in certain situations), the *threat* of censorship could be effective at limiting coverage of groups linked to terrorism.

As a result, covering Northern Ireland in anything beyond the most basic reporting was very difficult, particularly for broadcasters (Miller, 1995). Between 1959 and 1993, more than 100 programs on Northern Ireland were banned, censored, or delayed. The question became to what degree could the British media, particularly with the BBC's policy of balance, give voice to the political views of those on the Catholic/Loyalist side? After a series of IRA attacks in the early 1980s, the British Conservative government decreed a policy of banning the speech of any known terrorist group on television. Analysis by Miller showed that this had the effect of both reducing the amount of coverage of the Nationalist positions and, occasionally, reducing the coverage of Northern Ireland to the level of farce as some broadcasts used voice-overs to get around the ban. More seriously, the Conservative government's hard line on coverage of terrorist groups in the late 1980s and early 1990s led to a dearth of discussion of one of the most serious issues in British society. Even thought-provoking news analysis programs, very much a part of the BBC tradition, were discouraged. It is also worrying that the tactics of the police and the military were left relatively uncovered, arguably leading to abuses of power and further erosion of the possibility of the reconciliation between the two sides in Northern Ireland.

The situation appeared to be hopeless. However, public opinion surveys consistently showed that a sizeable portion of the Northern Irish population wanted peace restored to their territory and a resumption of normal political, civil life. The level of terrorism was not steady over the history of Northern Ireland, rising and falling over time. In the mid-1990s, the British government chose to pursue a more aggressive policy of reconciliation, most notably by abandoning its long-standing policy of not negotiating with terrorist-linked organizations such as the IRA. The initial signaling to both elites and the general population was through a series of newspaper columns in the Northern Irish press. This has been dubbed "megaphone diplomacy" by Sparre (2001). Eventually, a peace agreement was signed, an Assembly was restored, and normal elections were held. Although the peace process is still volatile and the Assembly has often been unable to work together, many analysts argue there has been a critical, positive change in Northern Irish politics.

A series of columns in the Northern Irish press did not bring about a fundamental change in politics. This change was initiated by the British government and political will in Northern Ireland and the British government for change. A "hard line" on terrorist activity over decades was unable to stop terrorist activity in Northern Ireland. However, it could be argued that once the media were allowed to reflect upon possible solutions, that this served as an important element of the peace process. Both the interpretations of history and the path for the future remain contested in Northern Ireland. But denying terrorists the "oxygen" of publicity did not appear to work well and no longer is part of the government media strategy in Northern Ireland. Northern Ireland serves as an example of how the media might be able to serve as a catalyst for change when political elites and journalists alike abandon entrenched positions of demonization.

Key points about Northern Ireland, terrorism, and the media

- The divisions between Nationalists and Loyalists in Northern Ireland were so severe that it was difficult to find common ground.
- Until the mid-1990s, the British media mirrored the government's policy of framing Irish terrorists as criminals.
- The government used a range of tactics, including the broadcasting ban and pressure on broadcasters, to control coverage of Northern Ireland.
- The government's switch in media policy to "megaphone diplomacy" in the mid-1990s arguably helped to bring about a reduction in violence and some semblance of normal political life in Northern Ireland.

Terrorist shock: 9/11 and the U.S. media

7.3 It would be difficult to think of a more stark contrast in the notion of terrorism between Northern Ireland and the events of 9/11. While Northern Ireland was an evolving domestic issue over centuries for Britain, a single day in 2001 changed the relevance of terrorism for Americans. On September 11, 2001, suicide bombers allied with the Al-Qaeda terrorist group hijacked four airliners in order to crash them into targets in the U.S. Two struck the World Trade Center in New York City and another hit the Pentagon just outside Washington, DC. Another crashed in a field in Pennsylvania, although tapes suggest that the terrorists were attempting to steer this plane into the White House or the U.S. Capitol. Almost 3,000 people died in the attacks, most of them in New York City (National Commission on Terrorist Attacks Upon the U.S., 2004). The attacks caused widespread panic and disruption, particularly as all air traffic was abruptly canceled or recalled. According to the U.S. government report on 9/11, "what ensued was a hurried attempt to improvise a defense by civilians who had never handled a hijacked aircraft that attempted to disappear, and by a military unprepared for the transformation of commercial aircraft into weapons of mass destruction." While terrorist acts were not unprecedented in the U.S., the scale and method of the attack were particularly shocking for the American public.

Just as the domestic security forces had no precedent for this type of attack, the news media also were faced with a completely new and alien situation. Unsurprisingly, television followed what Graber (2005) has termed the "crisis" method of coverage. Given the enormous interest generated by the story, all television stations with news content immediately switched to live, blanket coverage of the events. There was no existing frame for the story – as there are with events such as elections, natural disasters, or even riots – hence the initial coverage was as confusing and chaotic as the events themselves. The first plane hit one tower of the World Trade Center at 8.46 a.m., the second hit just 17 minutes later. In another half hour, the third plane hit the Pentagon. The final place crashed into a field in southern Pennsylvania at 10.03 a.m. It was clear that the events themselves were controlling the news coverage, to a degree that has been unprecedented before or since. To viewers watching the coverage, it would appear that the consistent laws of a functioning, safe society were unravelling as planes literally fell out of the skies to kill innocent civilians. As Graber points out, a side-effect of crisis coverage is a barrage of unmediated information, much of it incorrect, uninformed, or merely inchoate, as broadcasters rush to get information on the air.

It should be noted that the breaking television news did not rush to identify the terrorists as a particular group. In the 1995 bombing of the Oklahoma City federal building, early news reports attributed the bombing to Muslim extremists. This led to hate crimes against Arab-Americans, even though it quickly emerged that the bombers were a group of white Americans. The media were faced with a number of enormous challenges on the day of 9/11: first, how to simply get the facts in a timely manner in such a chaotic situation that spanned two major U.S. cities; second, how to relay useful safety information to the populace; and third, how to reassure traumatized citizens. Although the U.S. media rely on a libertarian rather than social-responsibility system, they are competent at performing all three of these roles. Asking it to perform all of these roles simultaneously was an enormous challenge.

How did the U.S. media perform? McDonald and Lawrence (2004) analyzed the prime-time news broadcasts from ABC, NBC, and CNN in the three days after 9/11. They found that although the networks devoted a great deal of time to the attacks – even canceling advertisements – the additional time did not lead to more meaningful political and historical context for the attack. Rather, the coverage followed a style similar to that of crime reporting, a script that elevates the drama of the situation while suggesting a satisfying retribution by society. It was clear that Americans were receiving important emotional support and gratification from television in this time of crisis. However, McDonald and Lawrence concluded that the way in which the emotional content outweighed the informational content in the wake of 9/11 did not necessarily serve the public's long-term interest or the ability of the media to mediate the threat of terrorism. The television coverage did not analyze why certain groups would resort to terrorist tactics against the U.S. or whether terrorists had a meaningful base of political support. Nor did the news coverage discuss what policy choices may have led to the terrorist attacks or what policy choices could address the problem. Rather, the news discourse focused on finding whom was to blame for the attacks and how much proof of this blame would be required before the U.S. could retaliate. The inevitability of violent retaliation was never questioned or discussed. This is particularly worrying in that the news coverage encouraged Americans to think of all "terrorists" in the same way, when in fact terrorists are as diverse as the causes, people, or nations they purport to represent.

All of this was nothing new for terrorism coverage in the U.S. A study by Shanto Iyengar (1991) of television news coverage of terrorism in the late 1980s found that 74 percent of all news stories on terrorism consisted of live reports on some specific terrorist act, group, victim, or event. Only 26 percent of the reports discussed terrorism as a general political problem (ibid.: 27). By 9/11, there had been several terrorist attacks involving Americans, most notably the 1995 Oklahoma City bombings (which killed more than 100 people, including children at a daycare center). Yet, the 9/11 attacks were a "new brand" of terrorism, according to 9/11 report by the National Commission. Hutcheson et al. (2004) found that prominent U.S. news magazines were functioning not as watchdogs, but more as cheerleaders for the government in the wake of 9/11. They analyzed five weeks of *Time* and *Newsweek* after 9/11 and found that journalists closely paralleled the way in which government and military officials were emphasizing "core American values" in the wake of the attacks. At the same time, the journalists echoed the twin themes of U.S. strength and the demonization of the "enemy." As Hutcheson et al. point out, it is not surprising that journalists at these news magazines, which reflect the U.S. world view in general, would feel personally compelled to be extremely patriotic immediately after 9/11. In addition, the media rely heavily on government officials as sources, and politicians were united in a nationalistic outlook in the wake of the attacks. Hence, there was little dissension to report. At the same time, the readers were no doubt seeking an unquestioning, pro-American type of coverage. As a result, there was relatively little discussion in the media about the passage of the U.S. Patriots Act, even though it restricts some aspects of civil liberty. In a more normal political climate, there would be more political debate and discussion about both going to war and legislation that curtails some individual rights in the name of national security.

For Robert Entman (2003), the coverage of 9/11 shows how President Bush was able to lead media coverage in an almost unprecedented fashion. The U.S. president normally does have a great deal of power to set the news agenda, although presidents themselves are quick to point out that it is not easy to direct the attention or emphasis of the news media in a unified way. However, President Bush and his administration were able to perpetuate the appropriate media response to 9/11 as a war with Afghanistan and Iraq. Entman sees this as proof of the "cascading activation" model, in that interpretive frames of the news start at the top level and flow downward. It then becomes difficult – particularly if there are no meaningful elite divisions also flowing downwards – for the media to resist these particular frames. Although an outlet as respected as *The New York Times* tried to shift the focus of concern over terrorism support from Afghanistan to Saudi Arabia, this did not become a meaningful part of the possible response to 9/11, according to Entman. Rather, President Bush's initial frame for the attacks overwhelmingly dominated the news, using "familiar enemies" for the "war on terror."

This research suggests that the media responded to the 9/11 attacks using a model not unlike the "patriotic" approach to war coverage discussed in Chapter 6. There was a great deal of news from the scenes of the attack, with myriad stories of human tragedy. There was some discussion of the gaps in domestic security and surveillance that allowed the attacks to proceed. There was little attempt, however, to examine whether the 9/11 attacks were part of a broader political movement and a result of U.S. foreign policy. Rather, they were framed as the act of a group of extremists, who were aided and abetted by rogue regimes in places such as Afghanistan and Iraq. On one level, this reassured the American people that the "criminals" would be "punished." On the other hand, it left unanswered many questions about future insecurity in an uncertain world. It also speaks to a broader issue in coverage of foreign affairs by U.S. media outlets. In general, there is a cycle of disinterest in foreign news, which can be confusing and alienating to U.S. news consumers. As a result, U.S. media outlets cover little foreign news and the audience remains uninformed. However, in a complex world with shifting alliances, this makes it difficult for readers and viewers to understand the causes (or possible solutions) to international conflict, including terrorism.

U.S. media consumers were not slow to pick up on these issues. In a series of ten focus groups just after the 2004 U.S. presidential elections, respondents often said they felt they were getting little in-depth information from news reports about terrorism.[1] One focus-group participant in Washington, DC, said that terrorist reports – particularly the different threat levels that are reported as colors – were becoming as banal and meaningless as weather reports. Overall, the focus-group respondents particularly disliked the changes in threat status via this color system, saying that it only make them anxious without providing them with more information. They felt there was no discussion on how to resolve the threat of future terrorism. As another participant in DC put it, the media "do a very good job of explaining all the ways that we're not safe." Overall, there were increased feelings of helplessness, dread, and sometimes fear that the world was simply a more dangerous place for Americans – and that there was little that could be done about. As a student in Missouri said:

> Like, you know, why are the terrorists blowing themselves up and killing people, you know? I mean, they are not doing it just because they hate Americans and they want to be spiteful. There's a reason behind what's happening, you know?

Key points about 9/11 and the media

- The events of 9/11 offered an unprecedented challenge to the media, particularly television, in the U.S.
- Media responded to 9/11 with news coverage that was highly patriotic, as opposed to analytical or reflective.
- Studies suggest that the media closely followed and did not question the agenda of President Bush, particularly the decision to invade Afghanistan and Iraq as part of the "war on terror."
- Media outlets chose to pursue patriotic coverage for a range of reasons, including the patriotic feelings of journalists and perceived expectations of the audience:
- U.S. citizens in focus groups found terrorism coverage that reported on the threat, but did not provide useful information, upsetting.

The London transport bombings and the British media

7.4 While the U.S. reaction to 9/11 was shock, the British reaction to the bombings on the London transport system on July 7, 2005 could be described more as confirmation of a long-standing fear. On this summer morning, four young men who described themselves as devout Muslims carried bombs they had crafted in a Leeds apartment into central London. They detonated three bombs on Underground trains and one on a bus near an underground station during the morning rush hour in London. The explosions killed 52 people, in addition to the four bombers, and hundreds were injured. The bombings led to widespread disruption in one of the world's largest cities. This was the deadliest act of terrorism in the country since the bombing of Pan Am Flight 103 over Scotland that killed 270 people in 1988. Two weeks after the July 7, bombings in 2005, a further four explosions took place on the London Underground and on a London bus. However, the bombs apparently failed to explode properly and no one was killed. Suspects were later arrested for the July 21 bombings.

Commercial, public, and international media outlets immediately began covering the events. Roger Mosey, head of BBC television news, reported that 30 million people tuned into BBC news on the day of the bombings.[2] The BBC and other broadcasters suspended normal coverage to bring breaking news from London. One of the comments about the BBC coverage – which at first reported a power surge on the Underground – was that it was slower to report the terrorist attacks than other networks. Mosey defended the network's coverage, saying that other news sources inflated the number of casualties: "That isn't the way the BBC operates, so on very rare occasions our information will be "later" than some of our rivals: accuracy is more important than speed, though we want to achieve both." The BBC also struggled to make sure that the live video from the scene would not be unduly distressing or disturbing. Mosey said one sequence shown on live television was perhaps inappropriate, but for the most part the broadcaster was able to stay within the bounds. The comments by Mosey underline the challenges that television producers – and not just those at public stations – have in managing news about terrorism.

The major difference between the coverage of the July 7 London bombings and that of 9/11 was in the domestic focus. The British media have long experience in domestic terrorism because of Northern Ireland. Although the political situation has changed considerably, an act of terrorism in London was not unprecedented. While the 9/11 coverage often focused on the surprise and shock of the event, the coverage of the London bombings put the event in a familiar context in a number of ways. First, London has considered itself a terrorist target for decades. In addition, there had been numerous threats to London – and particularly to the Underground – discussed especially in the wake of 9/11 and Britain's involvement in the second Gulf War. Issues surrounding the perceived cultural isolation of British Muslims had been discussed in the media as well. As a central part of the coverage, the BBC and other media outlets examined the reasons behind the attack. Although a government report into the attacks eventually concluded that the extent of Al-Qaeda involvement was unclear, it was clear that all four bombers had an interest in fundamentalist Islam (House of Commons, 2006). One of the bombers left a suicide tape, claiming he was directed by Al-Qaeda, although this would appear to be more in the sense of inspiration rather than practical support. Coverage after the discovery that the bombers had been British Muslims fostered media-led discussions about the reasons for minorities feeling isolated in British culture.

In addition, there are compelling aspects of media culture that led to different coverage of 9/11 and the 2005 London bombings (Barnett et al., 2007). In a study that compared coverage of 9/11 and the London 2005 bombings on CNN and the BBC, researchers found that the BBC provided more deliberate, if less speedy and sensationalist, coverage in the London bombings:

> The [BBC] failed to give an accurate picture of the chaos, carnage and violence that (briefly) gripped London. Yet, in failing in this regard, it succeeded in another. It rapidly moved to put the event in perspective focused more on analysis and less on the events of the terrorist attack. (Ibid.: 19)

Comparison of the coverage in the hours after terrorist attacks found the BBC deliberately avoided the more gruesome images and mentions of injuries, as well as provided more public service information than CNN. In addition, the public service broadcaster avoided political criticism immediately after the event (ibid.).

For the British public and the British media, the July 2005 bombings brought up a separate set of issues from those in 9/11. Although tragic (albeit on a smaller scale), the bombings could be discussed and understood in a context familiar to the media audience. In discussions in focus groups immediately after the bombings, most respondents claimed they were not surprised by the bombings, feeling that London was an inevitable target.[3] Hence, although the public seemed resigned, the bombings did not significantly change their feeling of security or their perception of the world. As a result, the tragedy had far fewer political consequences. There remained a robust debate about mandatory national identification cards – a controversial security measure proposed by the current British Labour government – after the 2005 bombings.

Key points about the 2005 London transport bombings and the media

- The British media were relatively well prepared to deal with terrorist events in the capital city of London.
- The audience was less traumatized and shocked by the events than the U.S. audience for 9/11.
- There was not a sustained "patriotic" response on the part of British media outlets in the wake of the London 2005 bombings.

The framing of Chechen terrorism in Russia: Beslan

7.5 An important theme of this book is the difference between how events are covered in the media systems of liberal democracies and how they are handled by the media in less free systems. This allows us to analyze how much coverage is affected by the structure and openness of a media system, and how much is dictated by the nature of the events themselves. What emerges from a study of Russian news coverage of terrorist events, particularly the siege of the Beslan school in August 2004, is that complete demonization of an enemy leads to further hatred within a society. These intense feelings can then be deployed in support of the leaders' policies, including the continued war in Chechnya. It is natural that there is little sympathy for brutal terrorists, particularly those that attack children at a school. However, arguably the Russian coverage of the Beslan siege only further fanned the flames of hatred and underlined the power of terrorists to damage civil society.

The Beslan school siege in September 2004 was the most violent and disturbing in a series of terrorist attacks carried out by Chechen rebels, or at least attributed to them. During Soviet times, terrorism did not have the same political implications as in a less controlled state. Unlike Western governments that were concerned with public opinion, the Soviet regime had more latitude to dispatch terrorists with violence. In addition, there was so little tolerance for dissent, so much repression in Soviet society, and such strict control on movement, that it was much more difficult to organize a terrorist organization. As a result, there were few terrorist attacks in the Soviet era (1917–91). Soon after the collapse of the Soviet regime, however, some of the political battles turned violent and terrorism was one weapon used, particularly in the Chechen war. The first major Chechen terrorist action, the hijacking of a plane flying from Southern Russia to Turkey, took place just weeks after the break-up of the Soviet Union in August 1991.

Chechnya, which is a district in Southern Russia, declared independence from the Russian Federation in 1991. As discussed in Chapter 6, the Chechen province and Russia have been openly at war from 1994–6 and again from 1999 to the present. Those who favor Chechen independence point to the enforced annexation of the region into Russia (even before Soviet times) and the cultural distinctiveness of the predominantly Muslim region. Although part of the Russian argument for fighting the Chechen independence movement has been to maintain country boundaries and discourage a general break-up of Russia along ethnic lines, there is also the issue of security for the Russian state. At the end of the Soviet regime and in the more chaotic days of the young Russian state, Chechnya was considered a lawless region that fostered organized crime and a lack of civil society. Underlying the conflict is racism and apprehension for the ethnic Russians who had settled in the area, particularly in the capital city of Grozny, as well as concern for the security of the oil pipeline that runs through the region.

In some ways, the Chechen situation shares characteristics with the relationship of Northern Ireland within the U.K. There is both an ethnic and a religious element to the conflict. Unlike the situation of Northern Ireland, however, there is no pretence of normal civil society or politics in Chechnya. Although one can argue that media coverage of Northern Ireland has been flawed, biased, or incomplete, meaningful media coverage of Chechnya is now virtually non-existent. There is no chance for the media to build any sort of common ground. Instead, the Russian media aggressively pursue a policy of demonization of the Chechens, an approach which found favor with respondents in focus groups in Russia in 2004 (Oates, 2005). By the same token, it would appear that the Russian media give Chechen terrorists an immense amount of "oxygen," turning them into a byword for fear and terror among the populace. Even the shadow of this fear can be used to inculcate support for repressive measures against the region, although public opinion polls show somewhat mixed opinions among Russians about continuing the war in Chechnya.

By the time of the Beslan hostage siege in 2004, terrorism coverage had evolved several distinct characteristics. As in the West, media outlets found that terrorist events made compelling television. However, unlike the terrorist attacks discussed above, these terrorist events were often hostage situations. For example, Chechen rebels dressed as Russian soldiers invaded the small town of Budyonnovsk in Southern Russia in June 1995, taking about 1,800 people hostage at a local hospital. The Chechens, led by Shamil Basayev, demanded the withdrawal of Russian troops from Chechnya. After negotiations with Russian prime minister Viktor Chernomydrin, and fighting in which about 130 people were killed and hundreds wounded, the terrorists retreated safely back to Chechnya. They used some hostages as human shields (Mosnews, 2005). The situation was broadcast live on Russian television. While arguably Chernomyrdin emerged relatively well from the situation, it gave enormous attention to the Chechen cause.

The Russian government tolerance for media coverage in hostage situations was sorely tested by another Chechen attack, this time on a crowded Moscow theater showing a popular musical in October 2002. Terrorists supporting Chechen independence took more than 900 hostages and demanded the withdrawal of Russian troops from Chechnya. Some hostages were released, but several were shot by the terrorists. The siege lasted two and half days, until Russian special forces gassed the theater, killing 42 terrorists and 171 civilians. The use of the gas was controversial, although options were limited in dealing with terrorists armed with suicide bombs. What became more controversial was the fact that the Russian special forces would not release the name of the gas, making it impossible to give effective emergency treatment to the victims affected by the gas. (This relates more to the inability of the Russian military to give information in general.) Chechen rebel leader Basayev claimed responsibility for the attack. In a move that challenged the boundary between the public's right to know and journalistic sensationalism, a Moscow television station broadcast from within the theater building during the siege. The broadcasts were blocked by the Russian government. In addition, the government censored coverage on another television station and a radio station – as well as publicly criticized a newspaper for its coverage. In November 2003, the lower house of the Russian parliament speedily approved broad new restrictions on media coverage of terrorism.

This law was in effect for the next major hostage situation. Although Moscow was hit by a deadly bombing in its subway system in the spring of 2004, this did not garner the worldwide attention of the Beslan school siege that began on September 1, 2004. Terrorists took hostage hundreds of children and adults (who were visiting the school as part of a traditional school celebration) at a school in this Russian town in the North Ossetia region near Chechnya. Conditions in the school gym, where the hostages were held, were grim as the terrorists wired bombs and refused to give the children food or water. Relatives outside the school and local law enforcement – most of whom had relatives inside the school – became increasingly desperate as the stand-off continued. Gunfire broke out on the third day of the stand-off. Many of the hostages were killed when the terrorists' bombs were detonated. Overall, an estimated 344 hostages, more than half of them children, were killed and hundreds were wounded. Once again, Basayev claimed responsibility for the terrorist attack. Unlike many other Russian terrorist attacks, the Beslan school siege drew worldwide attention. The involvement of a school and the emotive saga of parents and children separated – or trapped together in a hostage situation – gripped the attention of the world.

President Putin, among other Russian leaders, has remained frustrated that the horror of the Beslan school siege did not highlight Chechen atrocities – or the purported links of Basayev to Al-Qaeda. When compared with Bush's ability to create a following for a "war on terror" with a very broad remit to rationalize U.S. foreign invasions, Putin and his administration seem unable to translate genuine fear and disgust over Chechen terrorism into international support for Russia's war with the Chechens. Part of this is no doubt due to evidence that Basayev and his supporters are far more interested in an independent Chechnya than a pan-Islamic movement. However, although Putin enjoys a more controlled media environment than Bush, it is clear that his government must struggle with three key barriers to effective media "spin" on terrorist events: hostage situations that are more difficult to control in terms of the media; the fact that Russians have a more detailed understanding of the Chechen issue than Americans do of Middle East or extremist Islam; and poor media management tactics that owe more to Soviet repression than twenty-first century "spin."

It was unlikely that the media management of a school siege and hostage situation in a town in a remote district from Moscow was likely to be well organized. However, according to journalists, there was no media management except for an attempt to claim that the number of hostages was lower than that cited by the local residents. In addition, foreign media quickly arrived to cover the story, which meant that the Kremlin could not rely completely on its formal and informal controls on its own television and other media. There was little fear that the international media would give a sympathetic portrayal of the Chechen terrorist cause, particularly as attitudes about terrorists had hardened in the international media since 9/11. Rather, the Russian security forces had never worked in a way that usefully incorporated the media into a terrorist or war situation (such as pool reporting or embedding in the Gulf Wars). As such, the coverage was very much unfiltered and unedited. What emerged was the suffering of the hostages and their families – and the tragic confrontation on the third day that ended with the death of so many. The coverage underlined the helplessness of the families and even the security services, while emphasizing the ability of a small band of armed terrorists to inculcate fear on a mass level.

Russian journalists complained that the Russian government made it enormously difficult to cover the incident. It is clear that the Russian government's media management style was to prevent journalists from gaining information on the ground. To that end, journalists reported in a document to the Organization for Security and Co-operation in Europe that they were unable to get any official statements during the siege (Haraszti, 2004).[4] In addition, when officials did release a figure for the hostages, it was suspiciously low. The report gives evidence that it was not simply poor management, but actual lies and deliberate inaccuracies that were given to the journalists at the scene of Beslan. Anna Politkovskaya, a Russian journalist who wrote extensively on Chechnya for an opposition newspaper in Moscow, claimed she was poisoned by a cup of tea on her flight to the scene to keep her from reporting on the incident.[5] Ironically, the Russian government's refusal to co-operate with journalists meant that the harrowing pictures of the siege and hostages were essentially unmediated by any realistic reaction or reassurances from Russian forces on the ground.

If one thinks about the terrorist and the journalist as symbiotic, it is useful to ask what each gained from the other in the Beslan siege. The Chechen terrorists were able to further transmit images of power and fear to the general population, as well as underline their demand for an independent Chechnya. Journalists in both Russia and beyond had a compelling story that attracted the attention of viewers, listeners, and readers. But what was the effect of the coverage on the overall cause of the terrorists, which is an independent Chechnya? Arguably, the effect of the media coverage would be negative for the Chechen cause. The Beslan school siege gave the Russian government clear and compelling material for the continuing demonization of the Chechen people and to win the war in the Chechnya by any means necessary. The Chechen terrorists might win the attention in the battle, but they hurt their cause being discussed in a rational way. In addition, the Beslan school siege would reanimate for many the tragic terrorist events in the recent past, including 9/11, making it more difficult for Chechen rebels to gain status as civil society actors. Terrorists might argue that they must murder civilians in a political cause, but in the case of Chechnya it also feeds into how the Russian government frames and justifies its own violence in the region. While finding a specific country that is at fault in 9/11 is problematic, the links between Chechen terrorists and their country are clear in the minds of most Russian.

When thinking about the negligible political value of killing hundreds of adults and children in Beslan, it would appear that terrorism is much more criminal than political.

Key points about Russia, media, and terrorism

- The Russian military and government do not appear to have a media management plan for terrorist incidents, making it difficult for journalists to cover the events.
- The Russian public are comfortable with the continued demonization of Chechen terrorists, although there is not overwhelming support for the continuing war in Chechnya.
- It is difficult to see any positive international attention or "oxygen of publicity" that Chechen terrorists garnered with the Beslan school siege.

Chapter summary

This chapter started with some broad theories about the relationship between the media and terrorists, notably that the media provide critical "oxygen" to terrorists. Yet the actual review of media performance in various situations involving terrorism suggests that there are perhaps more differences than there are similarities in the journalistic coverage of anything called "terrorism." In the case of Northern Ireland, the coverage of terrorism has been embedded within centuries of conflict over Irish-Catholic versus British-Protestant interests. Although terrorist acts were labeled as criminal by the British media, they were perceived as political by much of the population in Northern Ireland (and abroad). As a result, it was not until there was a distinct change in government media policy and a willingness to place the terrorist acts within a political framework that the media could play a role in reconciliation in the regime.

On the other hand, there has been little attempt to place the horrific events of the single day of 9/11 into a realistic political context. Rather, the events have been used to justify a particular approach to international relations – including the invasion of two countries – on the part of the U.S. While respondents in ten focus groups in late 2004 could see that there was no obvious and direct link between Al-Qaeda and Iraq, the general climate of fear motivated many to support invasions in Iraq and Afghanistan. The British media were more successful in taking stock of the political motivation behind attacks on July 7, 2005 on the London transport systems. Arguably, this is due to the fact that the British media have much more experience in covering domestic terrorism.

The Russian media, on the other hand, have little opportunity or motivation to frame the actions of Chechen terrorists as political rather than criminal. Within the current Russian political context, it would be difficult to initiate serious questioning of the Russian policy in Chechnya without financial, legal, or other harassment from the government (although a handful of minor media outlets have questioned the war and Russian military actions there). Rather, there is little motivation for Russian media outlets from a political or a commercial perspective to discuss any political aspects of Chechen terrorist acts. Aside from the danger of alienating or angering the Kremlin, most of the Russian audience would not appreciate a sympathetic portrayal of Chechen terrorists. For them, demonization of Chechen terrorists is fair coverage. As a result, there is little impetus for anything beyond event-driven, sometimes sensationalist, coverage of terrorist events. As in the U.S., there is little reflection on the deeper political associations, roots, or causes – with the same problem of little reflection on anything but military solutions to the problem of terrorism. As a result, it would seem that coverage of terrorism is better explained by the political context in which it takes place, rather than any particular international model or understanding of the media/terrorist relationship. In each country, there can be a different approach to government media management of terrorist incidents, a different reaction from journalists, and a different set of reactions from the public.

Study questions

1 Discuss the "oxygen of publicity" and whether this is a useful way to describe the media/terrorist relationship.
2 Did the deployment of "megaphone diplomacy" help bring peace to Northern Ireland?
3 What characterized the coverage of 9/11 in the U.S. media?
4 Why is British coverage of a post 9/11 world somewhat different from U.S. coverage?
5 What does Russian coverage of terrorist events suggest about the importance of government media management tactics?

Internet resources

http://www.start.umd.edu/   National Consortium for the Study of Terrorism and Responses to Terrorism (START) is a project of the Department of Homeland Security's Science and Technology Directorate. It brings together and archives working research by social sciences relating to the origins, dynamics, and impacts on terrorism.

http://www.rand.org/research_areas/terrorism/   This website has terrorism resources from the RAND Corporation, a non-profit research institute on social issues.

http://www.osce.org/documents/rfm/2004/09/3586_en.pdf   This is a report (in English) on the experience of Russian journalists covering the Beslan school siege in 2004. It provides a particularly good insight into the challenges faced by Russian journalists, both in crises and in their profession in general.

Notes

1 These focus groups were conducted under a grant from the British Economic and Social Research Council on "Framing Terrorist Threat in U.S. and Russian Elections." The author worked with Lynda Lee Kaid (University of Florida), Mitchell McKinnon (University of Missouri), and John Tedesco (Virginia Tech) in carrying out the U.S. focus groups. For more detail, see Oates and Williams, 2006.
2 See http://media.guardian.co.uk/site/story/0,14173,1527063,00.html, an article entitled "Accuracy and Honesty" written by Mosey a week after the event and published in the *Guardian*'s Media section on July 13, 2005.
3 These focus groups were held as part of a research project, "The Framing of Terrorism in British Elections," also funded by the British Economic and Social Research Council. The project held 17 focus groups in London and Scotland in the summer of 2005.
4 This report is available online in English at http://www.osce.org/documents/rfm/2004/09/3586_en.pdf.
5 Politkovskaya was later assassinated by an unknown gunman in 2006.

References

Barnett, B., Reynolds, A., Roselle, L. and Oates, S. (2007) "Journalism and Terrorism across the Atlantic: A Qualitative Content Analysis of CNN and BBC Coverage of 9/11 and 7/7." Paper presented at the International Communication Division of the Association for Education in Journalism and Mass Communication Annual Convention, Washington, DC.

Bucy, E.P. (2003) "Emotion, Presidential Communication, and Traumatic News: Processing the World Trade Center Attacks." *The Harvard International Journal of Press/Politics* 8 (4): 76–96.

Entman, R.M. (2003) "Cascading Activation: Contesting the White House's Frame after 9/11." *Political Communication* 20 (4): 415–32.

Graber, D. (2005) *Mass Media and American Politics*, 7th edn. Washington, DC: Congressional Quarterly Books.

Haraszti, M. (2004) *Report on Russian Media Coverage of the Beslan Tragedy: Access to Information and Journalists' Working Conditions*. Organization for Security and Co-operation in Europe (OSCE). Available online in English at http://www.osce.org/documents/rfm/2004/09/3586_en.pdf.

Hewitt, C. (1992) "Public's Perspective," In Paletz, D.L. and Schmid, A.P. (eds.) *Terrorism and the Media*. London: Sage.

House of Commons (2006) *Report of the Official Account of the Bombings in London on 7th July, 2005*. London: The Stationery Office.

Hutcheson, J., Domke, D., Billeaudeaux, A., and Garland, P. (2004) "U.S. National Identity, Political Elites, and a Patriotic Press Following September 11." *Political Communication* 21 (4): 27–50.

Iyengar, S. (1991) *Is Anyone Responsible? How Television Frames Political Issues*. Chicago: University of Chicago Press.

McDonald, I.R. and Lawrence, R.G. (2004) "Filling the 24×7 News Hole: Television News Coverage Following September 11th." Paper presented at the Annual Meeting of the American Political Science Association, Chicago, Illinois.

Miller, D. (1995) "The Media and Northern Ireland: Censorship, Information Management and the Broadcasting Ban." In Philo, G. (ed.) *Glasgow Media Group Reader, Vol. II: Industry, Economy, War and Politics*. London: Routledge.

Mosnews.Com. (2005) "Russia Remembers Victims of Basayev Raid on Budyonnovsk." Available online in English at http://www.mosnews.com/news/2005/06/14/budyonnovskanniv.shtml.

National Commission on Terrorist Attacks Upon the U.S. (2004) *9–11 Commission Report.* Washington, DC: National Commission on Terrorist Attacks. Available online at http://www.9–11commission.gov/.

Norris, P., Kern, M. and Just, M., (eds.) (2003) *Framing Terrorism: The News Media, the Government and the Public.* London: Routledge.

Oates, S. (2005) "Framing Fear: Findings from a Study of Election News and Terrorist Threat in Russia." *Europe-Asia Studies* 58 (2): 281–90.

Oates, S. and Williams, A. (2006) "Comparative Aspects of Terrorism Coverage: Television and Voters in the 2004 U.S. and 2005 British Elections." Paper presented at the Political Communication Section Pre-Conference of the Annual Meeting of the American Political Science Association, Philadelphia, Pennsylvania. Available online at http://www.media-politics.com/publications.htm.

Philo, G. and Berry, M. (2004) *Bad News from Israel.* London: Pluto Press.

Sparre, K. (2001) "Megaphone Diplomacy in the Northern Irish Peace Process: Squaring the Circle by Talking to Terrorists through Journalists." *The Harvard International Journal of Press/Politics* 6 (1): 88–104.

Wilkinson, P. (1997) "The Media and Terrorism: A Reassessment." *Terrorism and Political Violence* 9 (2): 51–64.

Wolfsfeld, G. (2004) *Media and the Path to Peace.* New York: Cambridge University Press.

The Internet and Democracy

8

Central points

- The internet has not radically changed the fundamental relationship between rulers and citizens, but it has provided useful tools for activists to mobilize for specific political causes.
- The internet blurs traditional distinctions between news production and news consumption.
- Internet usage patterns and the concept of the "digital divide" are important in considering the effect of the internet on the political sphere.
- In analyzing the internet, it is important to look at its distinct elements, including web page content, email, forums, blogs, and podcasts.
- While it is hard to prove that the internet has a dominant role in politics, there is convincing evidence of the internet's ability to act as a catalyst in certain political situations.
- The internet has not replaced the traditional media, but the relationship between the traditional mass media and the internet is increasingly synergetic and symbiotic.

Introduction

8.1 The internet is a sphere that can involve virtually all levels of the political communication world simultaneously. At the same time, it can embrace the officials who are broadcasting their policies via websites, the mass media that are interpreting these messages on separate websites, as well as the citizens sitting at their computers and absorbing internet content. This can make it maddeningly difficult – as well as particularly intriguing – for social scientists trying to study the political impact of the internet. Just as with the traditional mass media, it is important to consider which level of analysis is under examination. For example, the study of the political messages broadcast by a party is distinct from a study of how the internet users are accessing, interpreting, or believing those messages. At any rate, it is impossible to understand the meaning or impact of a party website in a vacuum. How does the website relate to the overall party communication strategy? Is the information on the website different or unique from the party information in the traditional forms of the mass media? Is it targeted at a different audience? Does it attract a different audience? Perhaps most important of all, does it mobilize its internet audience in new and different ways from the traditional methods of political campaigning? Looking at this single example of how to structure the study of political party websites suggests that the study of the internet should be approached with particularly careful analysis.

It might be difficult for students to imagine a time before the internet. It is sometimes equally difficult for political communication scholars to figure out how to fit the internet into the study of media and politics. In the first place, the internet changes so quickly that it is hard to describe – much less analyze – in a meaningful way. In addition, academics often stand up to give a lecture on the internet to the class only to find that the students have practical knowledge of the online world that far outstrips their own. Younger individuals tend to undertake a far wider array of activities on the internet than their older peers. As a result, the experience of students on the internet can seem rather distant from what they are taught in political science. Fortunately, the past few years have seen a rapid expansion of internet studies, both incorporating the internet into existing political communication models as well as developing new methods of political analysis focusing on the internet itself.

There are some central issues in the study of the internet. One of the classic questions is whether the internet serves to *support* or *threaten* civil society. While this is within the larger quandary of whether media generally support or subvert civil society, there are particular features of the internet that make this question more complex. The internet has fundamentally different characteristics from the traditional mass media (such as television, radio, and print outlets). While traditional mass media transmit information to the recipient in essentially a one-way direction, users of the internet have a range of relationships with the online world. Sometimes internet users merely receive information, such as by clicking on news websites. However, internet users also exchange information as individuals via email, with instant messaging, or via forums and blogs (web logs that function as online diaries). They even become content producers in their own right by creating their own blogs or full websites.

With all the new possibilities for information delivery and creation, the internet should offer enhanced political communication within society. This chapter will discuss the "civic" side of the internet. It will analyze ways in which the internet functions as part of the democratic process in the U.S., the UK, and other countries. This will include an analysis of the central theories in internet studies in democracies, usage of the internet, and attitudes toward the internet. The chapter will include case studies that illustrate the ways in which governments, parties, social groups, and others have attempted to use the internet to build better societies and citizens. The central conclusion of this chapter is that the internet has not radically changed the fundamental relationship between rulers and citizens, but it has provided some useful tools for activists to mobilize for specific political causes. The internet has not replaced the traditional media, but the relationship between the traditional mass media and the internet is increasingly synergetic and symbiotic. As the internet is an international, rather than a national, phenomenon, this chapter will not divide into country studies as in the earlier chapters. Instead, the chapter will discuss central concepts in internet studies, with appropriate examples from the U.S., Britain, and beyond. The next chapter (Chapter 9) will discuss how the internet can be used to challenge civil society, including an examination of how some regimes limit access or how anti-state groups such as terrorists can employ the internet for their ends.

Central theories in internet studies

8.2 Many of the terms relating to the internet are used interchangeably, but it is important to point out that the "internet" and the "World Wide Web" is not the same thing. The internet (or "the net") refers to the vast, interconnected set of computer networks that span the globe. The World Wide Web (or "the Web") is a collection of documents, images, video, sound, and other resources often linked by hyperlinks and found via their internet address or Uniform Resource Locator (URL). The internet serves as the host of the World Wide Web and other services such as email. The internet has its origins in a U.S. defense communication system. From this text-based system used mostly for emails in the early 1990s, the Web has grown into an enormous, global information management, and commerce empire. According to the World Internet Usage survey, by 2007 there were 1.1 billion people connected to the internet, or approximately 17 percent of the world population (http://www. internetworldstats.com/stats.htm). The World Internet Usage survey estimates that the number of people online doubled in the seven years from 2000 to 2007.

It is important to try to fit the internet into the general model of studying political communication. As discussed in Chapter 1, there are three basic levels of analysis to study the mass media and politics – news production, content, and audience consumption. The internet can cause these levels to shift and react in dynamic ways. For example, someone in a chat room is both a consumer and producer of text as he or she reads messages and posts responses in rapid succession. Often, the boundary between traditional media outlets and the internet is unclear, as virtually all media outlets now distribute at least some of their content online. However, the internet offers significantly more than just a new distribution system for the mass media. It also provides:

- A low-cost (often virtually no-cost) ability to distribute information to a potentially limitless global audience;
- Potential freedom from editorial filter and controls;
- Relative freedom from national media control and an ability to build an international audience;
- An interactive environment in which people can easily cross from being news consumers to news producers.

What is on the internet? This is another frightening question to ask students, because they tend to know the most recent – and often the most controversial – sites online. The bulk of internet content remains relatively private, particularly in that the most popular use of the internet continues to be sending email (although younger users often prefer the interactivity of instant messaging). Parents, politicians, and others worry that this online world is mostly hidden from public view. However, there are constraints on the internet developing as a replacement for the traditional mass media and known patterns of socialization. First, much of the most popular internet content is produced by major publishers who have traditional media outlets (television, newspapers, etc.) and are regulated by the same standards. So while the method of delivery is different, the content is essentially the same. In addition to distribution, the traditional mass media now rely heavily on the internet for gathering information, further linking the online and traditional media. Finally, television remains as a very important social activity, including during critical times such as election campaigns.

According to the Pew Research Center for the People and the Press (2004), 86 percent of the U.S. public used television to gather information in the 2004 presidential election campaign.[1] Television remains a powerful shared experience that is not (or at least not yet) replicated on the internet. It should be noted, however, that television viewing itself is becoming more fragmented and individualized with the proliferation of broadcast offerings.

Alternative messages are merely a click of the mouse away on the internet. This allows groups in the news – and those generally not covered by the mainstream media – to broadcast information directly to individuals. The problem these groups have is in drawing attention to themselves. This is the notion of the "Googlearchy," a phrase that takes its name from the dominant search engine Google (www.google.com) and the word "hierarchy." Google uses a complex, secret algorithm to determine which pages are returned in internet searches. The higher your webpage is in the list, the higher you are in the Googlearchy. For most personal websites and blogs, they are so far down on the Googlearchy that it would be impossible to attract a reasonable audience. However, the internet provides an incredibly useful synergy for groups to take advantage of media attention. For example, if U.S. readers see a news story with comments from the American Association for Retired People (AARP) on the high cost of prescription drugs, they can then click on the AARP website to get more in-depth information and help. They may decide to join or support the organization in another way. Thus, there is a type of Web synergy with the traditional mass media. It is this particular mix of the traditional media directing people to specific spaces on the internet that provides new opportunity for social engagement.

There are several distinct categories of internet use including email, instant messaging, forums, blogs, chat rooms, and podcasts (see Table 8.1 for definitions). As the definitions in the table suggest, the format, extent of audience engagement, and political potential of these internet features all vary somewhat. In thinking about the interaction between the internet and politics, it is important to consider which function is under examination. Does posting information about global warming on a website cause people to become more concerned about the environment? Can you mobilize the masses via email? Do blogs really set the political agenda in some places in the U.S.? Can the British Conservative Party leader David Cameron actually attract younger voters through WebCameron with his regular podcasts (www.webcameron.org.uk)? These are the types of questions that are possible to study and try to answer – and are much more useful than labeling the internet as "good" or "evil."

On the subject of evil, however, it is important to address the fact that much internet content does not conform to the standards of restraint and even decency in the traditional mass media. Internet content is governed by national law in the same way that traditional media content is regulated, but it is impossible to police the internet in the same way. Much internet content is simply not visible to the majority of people and can be removed quite easily. In addition, while online content is produced in one location, it typically can be viewed globally. Hence, a country that outlaws pornography cannot stop a webmaster in another country from putting pornographic pictures or films on a webpage (although they can charge their own citizens with a crime if they are caught downloading it). The same features of the internet that make it a potential tool for democratization make it a conduit for amoral, illegal, or what many would call reprehensible, behavior. As the modern internet delivers both information and services, this means that the scope for illegal or immoral behavior increases. Anyone who thinks that the internet can be

Table 8.1   Key features of the internet

Term	Definition	Political significance
Internet or the net	Vast, interconnected set of networks that span the globe.	Useful to consider the various diverse components separately rather than try to make judgments about the internet as a single entity.
World Wide Web or the Web	Collection of documents, images, video, sound, and other resources often linked by hyperlinks and found via their internet address or Uniform Resource Locator (URL).	Useful to consider the various diverse components separately rather than try to make judgments about the Web as one entity.
Email	Electronic mail.	Allows users to engage in rapid, direct communication with little regard for distance/time differences. Constrained by ability to speak the same language.
Instant messaging	Electronic chat, users type in messages to each other in real time.	Creates a more intense, direct form of communication than email but not so useful for in-depth, abstract exchange of information. Constrained by ability to speak the same language and typing speed/ability.
Forum	Facility on the World Wide Web for holding discussions and posting user-generated content, typically moderated by an individual or a group.	Allows users to start new discussions and comment on on-going discussions. Some are moderated more strictly than others.
Blog (web log)	A website in which an individual or small group make entries in a journal style.	Tends to be an asymmetric relationship, with the blogger broadcasting information (although most blogs allow comments). The line between prominent bloggers and journalists is particularly thin in the U.S.
Chat room	Web space that allows people to instant message with a group of people at the same time.	Creates a more intense, direct form of communication than email but not so useful for in-depth, abstract exchange of information. Constrained by ability to speak the same language and typing speed/ability.
Podcasting	A collection of files (usually audio and video) residing at a unique web feed address.	Tends to be an asymmetric relationship, with the podcaster broadcasting information. Podcasting is proving particularly popular for U.S. candidates.

Source for definitions: Wikipedia

effectively policed or is constrained by some sort of moral code would be dissuaded by a few internet searches. While the potential of the internet for the destruction of civil society will be considered in more depth in the following chapter (Chapter 9), the "darker" side of the internet does not nullify the democratic potential of the internet. These two aspects of the internet exist simultaneously. There also is a clear trend in which attempts to operate outside the law on the internet often become part of the "civil web." For example, the music-sharing website Napster was started by a university student to trade (copyrighted) tracts of music. Eventually, the music industry sued the student and forced the closure of the website – but not before the idea of sharing music over the internet had taken hold. Napster now operates a popular, legal website to sell music downloads. In addition, the music industry itself changed the way it distributed its products.

History of internet studies: cyber-optimist, cyber-skeptic, or cyber-pessimist?

Scholars were at first quite enthusiastic about the potential of the internet to enhance civil society. While the mass media have faced much harsh criticism for their alleged undermining of civic society (Putnam, 2001), Pippa Norris in *A Virtuous Circle* (2000) suggests that the media truly serve a useful function in keeping citizens engaged and informed in democracies. The question of where the internet fits on this spectrum of opinion is still open for debate. Initially, much of the writing on the internet fitted into the "cyber-optimistic" school of thought, suggesting that the internet provided unique and exciting opportunities to improve society (Rheingold, 1995; Toffler and Toffler, 1995; Dyson, 1998). Many scholars saw the internet, with its ability to empower citizens to react to information quickly and mobilize with new digital technologies, as key to the renewal of direct democracy and citizen empowerment. The idea was that this new media would inevitably lead to the creation of a kind of decentralized public space that was free from the control of political elites. As a result, citizens would have the opportunity for more in-depth and direct involvement in their political fortunes. While some scholars did not expect a sort of online commons to revolutionize society, they did feel that the internet had potential for improving governance through online opportunities such as e-voting, government-sponsored chat rooms, or other political communication tools made possible by the new technology.

Some political scientists, known as cyber-skeptics, were unconvinced about the political potential of the internet. The internet, it was concluded, was neither the agent of the glorious revolution nor apocalypse now, but a reinforcer of the status quo (Bimber, 1998; Hill and Hughes, 1998; Davis and Owen, 1998; Norris, 2000). Indeed, the "cyber-pessimists" actually saw potential for great harm. This group perceived the capabilities of the internet as dangerous to democracy because of its potential to erode social capital and community ties (Wu and Weaver, 1996; Street, 1992; Lipow and Seyd, 1996; Etzioni and Etzioni, 1999; Galston, 2003). Cyber-pessimists often worry that if citizens are in front of their computer screens (or online via another method), they will be less likely to engage in the traditional community and political activity that is celebrated by Robert Putnam (2001) in *Bowling Alone*. Others also see in the internet a problematic potential to reduce the quality of political debate and discourse (Streck, 1999; Sunstein, 2001) as well as the accountability of the government (Wilhelm, 2000; Lessig, 1999; Adkeniz, 2000; Liberty, 1999; Elmer, 1997).

While cyber-optimism versus cyber-pessimism is one way to frame the internet debate, it is not particularly useful to students of political science. It is like asking whether television is "good" or "bad." This is such a broad question that it is impossible to measure and compare the effect of online communication on the political sphere. The central question about the internet is not about good and evil. Rather, social scientists should look at the specific role that the many elements of the internet can have in improving or damaging democracy. In order to do this, it is important to analyze who is producing the content on the internet, what this content looks like, and who is using the content. This parallels the three basic levels of analysis in the study of media and politics (news production, content, and audience) that are outlined in Chapter 1 and discussed throughout the text.

Key points about the central theories in internet studies

- It is impossible to analyze the political role of the internet as a single entity as the online world has distinctive features with different functions.
- The boundaries between the traditional mass media and the internet continue to break down as traditional mass media publish and broadcast information online.
- The central features of the internet include web page content, ermail, instant messaging, chat rooms, forums, blogs, and podcasts.
- While it can be difficult for groups to draw attraction to themselves in the sprawl of the online world, the internet provides useful tools for synergy for groups to amplify their political messages.
- The notion of "cyber-optimism," "cyber-skepticism," and "cyber-pessimism" are not particularly useful for contemporary internet studies.

Internet governance and control

8.3 The nature, structure, and content of the internet might suggest that is free from national and international control. In fact, the internet is both self-regulated and regulated by a series of controls at different levels of governance (Reilly, 2007). Caral (2004) defines three points at which the internet can be controlled and regulated: the physical, the code (or transport) layer, and the content layer. The physical layer refers to the actual equipment on which the internet operates, from the personal computer at home to the telecommunications network that hosts the internet servers. This is the layer most readily controlled by a national government. For example, governments typically regulate the telecommunications industry and can shut down parts of the telecommunication infrastructure (such as servers) that are hosting what that national government defines as illegal websites (pornographic, terrorist, money scams, invasion of privacy, libelous material, etc.). However, while national governments can control the technological infrastructure within their own countries – although much of this is more in the commercial sphere than under direct governmental control in many nations – they cannot stop these "illegal" websites from being hosted on physical locations outside of their borders. As there is no international body that has the power to police the entire internet, nations cannot enforce their own definition of illegal websites worldwide. While physical control can include limiting access to the internet by controlling access to computers themselves, this is enormously difficult in developed countries (although countries such as China are relatively good at tracking all computer use due to its massive policing infrastructure).

The internet is also controlled in the "code" or "transport" layer, i.e., the software that operates the system and links the servers together. No body of laws governs this physically intangible layer. Self-regulation dominates in the code layer, more by default than by design (Caral, 2004), with software standards that are global, cross-border, and pervasive. In particular, the code layer is overseen by a set of self-governing bodies, including the Internet Corporation for Assigned Names and Numbers (ICANN), the World Wide Web Consortium (W3C), and the Internet Engineering Task Force (IETF). Finally, the content layer is regulated by the well-established body of national laws, including those that govern the broadcast and print media, i.e., publication of obscene articles; distribution/possession of child pornography; transmission of grossly offensive, indecent, obscene, or menacing messages; and the piracy of copyrighted material. While all of this is regulated on a national level, the fragmented nature of the internet means that it is enormously difficult to police. However, countries such as China with a vast investment in policing resources, are relatively effective at controlling citizen access to off-limits areas of the internet (discussed in more detail in Chapter 9).

Internet users and usage

8.4 If the case of Napster shows how the internet has changed the way businesses deal with consumers, how can we assess the way the internet has changed how political institutions interact with citizens? The first thing to consider is *who* uses the internet and *how* they use it. Unsurprisingly, the 1.1 billion internet users are concentrated in the industrial world. The overall amount of use has grown enormously as Asian countries (particularly

China) have embraced the internet. In fact, the largest number of users (389 million) are in Asia, followed by 313 million in Europe, and 232 million in North America, according to World Internet Usage. It is important to think about those raw numbers in terms of the overall population. Although Asia has the highest numbers of users overall, North America has the largest percentage of its population online (almost 70 percent) followed by Australia and the surrounding regions (Oceania) at 54 percent. About 39 percent of the population of Europe is online, compared with only about 10 percent of the Asian population. Thus, penetration of the internet within various regions is not the same as the overall usage. Latin America and Africa have relatively low internet usage, with just 3.5 percent of the population online in the latter region.

It is this pattern of internet usage and penetration that is discussed under the term known as the "digital divide." If the internet really is a tool that can empower citizens, it is particularly worrying to reflect that access is overwhelmingly the privilege of the wealthiest citizens in the most advanced democracies (Norris, 2001). Even within countries, there are significant barriers to the poorest citizens having the same quality and ease of access to the internet, creating divisions of potential online empowerment not only between countries, but within them as well. Aside from the geographic divisions listed above, some of the most obvious "digital" divisions are:

- *Wealth:* Richer people are more likely to have the equipment and means to access the internet.
- *Education:* The more education a person has attained, the more likely he or she is to use the internet.
- *Technical:* Those who have better connections, such as fast broadband, can use a far broader range of internet facilities.
- *Age:* Younger people tend to use it more often and in a greater variety of ways than older people.
- *Time of adoption:* The longer you have been using the internet, the more likely you are to move from being just an internet content consumer to becoming an internet content producer.

The U.S. provides a good case study of how the internet is used in a well-wired society. By February 2006, almost three-quarters of U.S. adults (about 147 million people) were internet users, according to research by the Pew Internet & American Life Project (http://www.pewinternet.org/).[2] This was up from about 133 million people or about two-thirds of the U.S. adult population in January 2005. The percentage of people who had broadband connections at home increased markedly, from 29 percent in 2005 to 42 percent in 2006. As noted above, this is significant because the higher speed, constant availability, and better capacity of broadband encourage a far wider, more persistent use of the online world than the older dial-up connections. On one side of the U.S. "digital divide" are well-connected home users with equipment that can keep up with fast pace of Web offerings, according to the Pew study (Rainie et al., 2005). Not only are you far more likely to use the internet if you are a young American (84 percent of those aged 18 to 29 are online compared with just 26 percent of those aged 65 or older), but your children will engage you with the internet as well. According to the 2006 Pew study, 60 percent of American adults who do not have a child living at home go online, compared with 83 percent of parents of minor children. On the other side are roughly 65 million American adults (out of a total of about 220 million) who do not go online. Most of those have had some exposure to the internet, but they are not a regular presence in the online world.

Only one in five American adults report that they have never used the internet and that they do not live in an internet-connected household. In all the excitement about the potential of the internet, social scientists have tended to overlook that some individuals see the internet as either a worrying unknown – or even a detriment to society. When the Pew study asked people to talk about why they didn't use the internet, it became clear that there was a hard core of hostility to this type of mass medium. People said they would rather "do things in person" or communicate with others over the phone. Some even felt that computers were "ruining the world," that they might become "addicted" to it, or even that it was the "devil's work." Researchers have long articulated some negative aspects of the internet, such as the worry of spreading pornography, the possible exploitation of children through online contact with child molesters, and the ability of anti-social groups to spread hate speech and enlist disaffected citizens to their causes. However, most researchers have not considered that some people would reject the internet as a mass medium because of strongly held personal beliefs about the role of computers and technology in eroding civil society. At the same time, it is clear that these people are in the minority. While some Americans remain skeptical about the internet, the majority of American adults are engaging in a growing range of internet activities, although email remains a particular favorite. According to the Pew research, the most common activity for the U.S. internet user is sending email (52 percent of internet users on a typical day) and getting news (31 percent). After that, people are vaguer about their reasons for internet use, with 30 percent of them reporting that they go online daily for no particular reason.

There are a lower percentage of citizens online in Britain than in the U.S.. More significantly, it would appear the number of those choosing to go online has peaked. According to figures from the Oxford Internet Institute (www.oii.ox.ac.uk), about 60 percent of the British population was online by 2005, up only marginally from 2003. In addition, internet use by British citizens remains a relatively new phenomenon when compared to the U.S.. By 2005, 16 percent of British internet users had been online for a year or less, 17 percent for between one and two years, 42 percent for two to five years, and only 25 percent for more than five years. Most British university students today are in the last category, typically recalling that they first used the internet when they were about 11 or 12 at their school. This is contrast to many college-age Americans, who had internet in the home by the time they were young teenagers. As noted above, research indicates that the range of options people will use on the internet increases the longer they have been online. Since British users generally have been online for less time than their U.S. counterparts, it suggests that their use of the internet is less varied. This is reflected in the relatively slow appearance of British party political websites, which has lagged behind the rapid development of the political internet in the U.S.. Although significant government funding has been invested in developing the internet to improve British government service, research suggests that British citizens have their doubts about the ability of the online sphere to improve governance in the country. It also appears that uptake of regular internet use has stalled in Britain at about two-thirds of population, suggesting that Britain may never become a completely "wired" nation.

According to a 2005 Oxford Internet Institute (OII) survey, virtually everyone online in Britain uses email. In addition, 83 percent of users browse the internet for general information, 66 percent look for information about local events, 61 percent seek out news, 55 percent look at weather reports, 54 percent check the sporting news, and 42 percent have hunted for jobs. There is a less enthusiastic response to an expansion of the online political sphere, despite investment by national and local governments in their "e-governance" programs. According to the OII survey, only about 39 percent of British internet users have taken advantage of e-government resources, and this includes those who merely looked for information about the local government on web pages. About 20 percent have sought information for local government services, schools, or central government services. When it comes to taking action or making views known via the internet, British users seem particularly reluctant. Only 5 percent have ever sent an email to their local government representative and only 3 percent have emailed their Member of Parliament. Interestingly, use of the internet in Britain actually appears to expand the use of the traditional mass media in some ways. In the OII survey, 20 percent of the respondents said they read newspapers online that they didn't read in print. Mostly, internet users claim that their regular media use isn't affected by their time online – after all, not all of them are using the internet to find news – but some (28 percent) say the internet causes them to view less television, read fewer books (17 percent), or even read fewer newspapers or magazines (13 percent). While there is only a relatively small "digital divide" in terms of internet use between U.S. and British citizens, trust seems to be more of an issue in Britain. While government regulation of the internet has not been a major issue in the U.S. (except in terms of controlling suspected terrorist groups), 29 percent of British citizens felt that the government should regulate the internet. However, 27 percent also felt that the British government should not regulate the internet and the rest were undecided or just not sure.

Some research suggests that, although there is relatively wide usage of the internet, it remains a fairly passive experience for most. Jakob Linaa Jensen (2006) studied the use of the web-based E-Democracy project in Minnesota, set up to facilitate political discussion and activism. His study found that the users of the system were overwhelmingly those who were already politically engaged and active, using the E-Democracy system to further their activities. Linaa Jensen speculated that the internet can help to foster political "gladiators" who will use a range of tools – in both the online and offline worlds – in order to further their political involvement. The idea suggests that the bulk of the other citizens, including those going online regularly but remaining political uninvolved, function merely as political "spectators."

Key points about internet users and usage

- More than 1 billion people worldwide use the internet, but this is still less than 20 percent of the world's population and the users are mostly in developed nations.
- There is a "digital divide" of internet haves and have-nots both between countries (developed and less developed) and within countries themselves as richer, better educated, and younger people use the internet more.
- The U.S. has greater internet penetration than Britain, but there remains a core of people in both countries who avoid the online world.
- Many are enthusiastic about the democratizing potential of the internet, but others remain deeply skeptical.
- The longer you are online, the more likely you are to use a broader range of internet functions.

Internet content: from email to podcasts

8.5 On a typical day in January 2007, the Yahoo.com listing for most popular searches on its internet search engine tells an important story about how Americans use the Web. The seven most popular searches for the day were listed as: Super Bowl, Internal Revenue Service, Britney Spears, WWE (World Wrestling Entertainment), Beyoncé Knowles, Lindsay Lohan, and the NFL (National Football League). It is clear that Americans were using the internet to augment their seasonal interest in professional football as the biggest match of the year approached in late January. In addition, they were worrying about their taxes at the start of the New Year and amusing themselves by looking up some of their favorite celebrities. It is clear that the internet is not a completely alternative sphere, in that real-world events and people were the motivation for much of the use shown in this example. The question then remains whether the internet in the U.S. has added something distinctive to this relationship among the media audience, media content, and the people who produce that content.

When examining internet use, it is also important to think about what the internet might replace in the lives of citizens. For example, in some cases the internet does not merely augment information from the traditional mass media – it essentially replaces it. Clearly, though, the internet offers a range of possibilities to engage citizens in political life in many ways. In particular, the internet offers citizens in democracies the ability to become more involved in politics by:

- Attaining more in-depth information about particular topics with relative ease and at very low cost.
- Responding and providing feedback to news reports.
- Publishing their own views directly.
- Contacting, mobilizing, and organizing others for a cause.

What data are there to suggest that U.S. citizens are using the internet for any of the four civic tools listed above? In terms of news, there is evidence that the internet does not provide qualitatively different news for most Americans. The method of delivery varies, allowing the U.S. audience to narrow and tailor the news for their own interests. Thus, in a news broadcast the audience is obligated to sit through perhaps all of the news to reach an item of interest, while the internet audience can simply go immediately to areas of interest. There is concern that people will further ignore complicated topics such as economics and foreign policy to focus on less weighty issues.

The Pew Internet & American Life Project has found that Americans rely more and more heavily on the internet for information in elections. In a survey of 2,562 people after the U.S. elections in 2006, the organization found that 31 percent of the respondents used the internet during the campaign to get political information and to discuss the race via email. Although Pew surveys have found a consistent increase in internet use in U.S. elections from the time it was first measured in 1996, there was evidence of significant broadening of the type of use in 2006. A considerable group of internet users – almost a quarter of those who relied heavily on the internet in the election – actually became online political activists (at least to a degree) during the campaign. This means that they created political content, forwarded information, and rallied support for parties and candidates online. At the same time, the Pew project found that the more mainstream media organizations that distributed information online were drawing political material from blogs, online comedy sites, government websites, candidate web pages, and alternative political sites. This suggests a further blurring of lines between "mainstream" media and "alternative" media on the internet.

In thinking about the impact of the internet on politics in the U.S., it is important to consider the different internet functions discussed above (see Table 8.1). Which of these functions, ranging from email to podcasts, seems to have changed the political sphere in the U.S.? Studies about this are relatively rare, but becoming more common. Below is a summary of some useful studies that focus on particular functions of the internet.

Web page design

At first, scholars merely noted that certain organizations had websites. But it soon became clear that not all websites were created equal. While some groups merely listed basic facts, others started using features such as registration, surveys, downloadable documents – and eventually forums, blogs, and even podcasts. Internet scholars developed a way of measuring the number and type of features on particular websites (in particular, see Gibson and Ward, 2000). Some of the first studies compared party political websites and tracked the quick evolution from static web pages to the interactive ones that exist today (particularly on the U.S. internet). The Gibson and Ward scheme uses a system to score web pages based on the following features: information provision, resource generation, openness, participation, networking, and campaigning. The scholars collected this data on Australian, U.S., and British parties to find that U.S. parties used a broader range of features on party web pages to try to entice the voters. Many others have used the Gibson and Ward coding scheme in other countries, including March (2006) who employed it to measure Russian party websites and found that they had relatively few of the features of their Western counterparts. In another project, Scott Wright (2006) speculated about how much the design of particular Web portals mattered for getting citizens involved. In comparing two Web-based community tools sponsored by local government in Britain, Wright found evidence that various factors, such as a good design for citizen input, responsiveness to the online discussion by local officials, and the presence of a local issue (in this case foot-and-mouth disease affecting area livestock) all contributed to more effective use of e-governance initiatives. This type of research highlights that the internet is only one in a range of factors that can affect social capital and citizen involvement.

Email

While email is acknowledged as a very useful personal and business communication tool, can it be used to mobilize people for political causes? This is a question researched by Lusoli and Ward (2006) in a study of the Countryside Alliance in Great Britain. The alliance is concerned with issues about British rural life and livelihood, particularly in terms of preserving the ability to hunt and supporting farmers. The group staged a large "Liberty and Livelihood" march in London in 2002 to protest against the government ban on hunting with dogs and other issues. Lusoli and Ward examined the cyber-strategy of the group, including its website and email newsletter. The scholars were particularly keen to analyze a group that is popular with older Britons, who are relatively unlikely to go online. By using both an online survey and a more traditional postal questionnaire of the Alliance membership, the researchers found that the internet helped the organization to attract more members who were younger and in professional jobs. In addition, there was evidence that the internet deepened participation among the existing members by rallying them to march on London. However, a key finding was that sending information directly into members" inboxes via email played a very important role in mobilizing members to protest. Websites can be good for the initial recruitment and providing information, but it would appear that sending email is the critical element that can galvanize people into action for a particular event or cause.

Instant messaging, forums, and chat rooms

The older generation may regard casual conversation on the internet as just another way that younger people waste time. Scholars, however, are beginning to consider what this contact among a relatively broad range of individuals may mean in terms of social and political development. By analyzing data from a Pew project that examined the internet habits of U.S. families, Owen (2006) found that the younger generation embraced this type of internet communication at a far greater rate than older people. She also found evidence that this broader internet use did translate into political participation, as younger people used cyber-communication to both monitor politics and get involved in elections. In addition, young people were more confident about producing political content. Her findings counter fears by scholars such as Putnam (2001), who see the internet as a source of fragmentation rather than social engagement and cohesion.

Blogs and podcasting

A blog represents an important evolution in internet use, in which a member of the internet audience chooses to become an internet producer. Web companies such as myspace.com offer free web space to bloggers and the phenomenon has been particularly popular in the U.S.. However, it would be difficult to define most blogs as strictly political in nature. Most blogs are about relatively narrow personal issues and are often unrestrained by taste, political correctness, or even good grammar (this is perhaps why they are particularly popular). A listing on the top ten blogs on myspace.com for one day in January 2007 showed an eclectic range of soft-core pornography, a discussion of racism by a bikini-clad aspiring model, a discussion about reality television, and commentary by a student about annoying classmates in his college courses. These blogs could be considered trivial or just personal opinion, although at least one of them has overtly political content (the blog about racism). What these blogs do not have is a long-term focus on political discussion and engagement with a relatively large audience. There are influential political blogs in the U.S., often written by journalists or people with developed political knowledge. Among the top ten (as rated by the number of incoming web links) are Instapundit (www.instapundit.com), Michelle Malkin (www.michellemalkin.com), Daily Kos (www.dailykos.com), and Little Green Footballs (www.littlegreenfootballs.com).[3]

Blogs are often the way rumors or personal information reach critical mass and become part of the political agenda. Several political scandals originated in blog reports. For example, the sexual scandal involving White House intern Monica Lewinsky and President Bill Clinton was first reported in 1998 on a political blog called the Drudge Report. The line between blogs and journalism is often quite thin, with prominent bloggers writing for newspapers and newspaper reporters writing their own blogs. As in the case with email, it would appear that blogs have influence when they are linked to a particular event (or scandal). They provide another source of information, but do not replace the power or authority of television broadcasts or national newspaper reports. This view is confirmed by a study of 233 bloggers by the Pew Internet & American Life Project in 2006. Only one-third of these bloggers perceived this internet activity as a form of journalism, and only 11 percent said they focused mainly on government or politics in their online diaries. Rather, most of them were interested in working about two hours a week on their blogs to express their creativity and interests for themselves or a circle of friends. These "ordinary" bloggers, who make up the majority of those who create and maintain blogs, are not particularly political in nature. Although blogging has been cited as an emerging force in elections in the U.S., research by Stanyer (2006: 2) in the 2005 British election found political blogging was in its "infancy" in the UK. In a content analysis of more than 300 blogs and 1,300 posted messages, Stanyer found few people posting messages about the campaign – or even accessing blogs on a regular basis.

What about podcasting? As sites such as youtube.com show, virtually anyone can create and upload video content to the Web. When viewing a lot of the offerings, one often wonders why they bothered. However, there are times when the development of new forms of communication can create new voices with a political impact. For example, Channel 5 in the UK made a documentary in 2006 entitled *Shock Docs: Soldiers' Trophy Pics*. The documentary discussed how soldiers in the current Gulf War were taking video equipment – sometimes just cell phones – and making home movies of their battle scenes and experiences in the Gulf. The videos, some of them with shockingly brutal images, are then set to music and exchanged on various websites. As a result, a new type of unmediated war footage is available to a broad population. Are "trophy pic videos" a form of free speech or are they a form of tasteless exploitation of the enemy for entertainment value? In the film, the soldiers themselves are not completely sure, but they seem to feel that a memory or "trophy" of their time in conflict helps them to come to terms with the experience. Without the internet to spread the inexpensive clips – created and edited on personal computers – this type of coverage would never have reached the public view. Although these individual "war videos" cannot challenge the television framing of war in a patriotic or sanitized way, these personal war blogs provide very different graphics, narrative, and framing to one segment of the audience.

Key points about internet content

- While many perceive the use of chat rooms, forums, and email as personal, studies suggest this is one way young people in particular engage in the political sphere at the same time as they make personal contacts.
- The key features of the internet allow the medium to give users in-depth information with relative ease, respond to information, publish their own views directly, and mobilize others for causes.
- An active email campaign is more effective than a passive website posting in mobilizing support for a cause or event.
- While a handful of blogs have political influence in their own right, most blogs are more personal in nature.
- Podcasting – especially video distribution online – offers new and untested opportunities for the dissemination of powerful or disturbing material that can potentially challenge the political status quo.

Chapter summary

There is fairly compelling evidence that the internet news sphere remains mostly a place of "walled gardens," in which people use the online version of a trusted newspaper, radio station, or television network rather than searching for news randomly. While the delivery method is different – and offers the opportunity to tailor the news, respond via email, or even participate in forums sponsored by the media organization, it does not fundamentally change the relationship between the news organization and the audience. The news organization broadcasts the news and the audience consumes it, albeit in a slightly different manner. Although individuals now have the ability to link directly to alternative news sources, the overwhelming majority of the audience do not do so on a regular basis.

In looking ahead to the role of the internet in civil society, the Pew Center asked American citizens to speculate about what the internet would be like in 2020. Their respondents predicted that a low-cost global network will be thriving and creating new opportunities in a "flattening" world. However, almost half of the respondents (42 percent) worried about the ability of humans to control this rapidly evolving technology. They feared a group of tech "refuseniks" would emerge, people who avoided the internet or even those who were willing to revolt against the technological advances through violence and terror.

This projection revealed that Americans also have their reservations about the internet as simply a force for social participation and cohesion. If Americans have these reservations even with relatively enthusiastic use of the internet, it would suggest that the internet is unlikely to be a force for apocalyptic change worldwide.

Study questions

1 Identify and discuss some of the central challenges in studying the role of the internet in the political sphere.
2 What is "Googlearchy" and why is it significant?
3 Discuss the cyber-optimist versus cyber-pessimist debate and evaluate its usefulness in understanding the political role of the internet.
4 What is the digital divide and how does it suggest that the internet is not particularly "democratic"?
5 Define the key features of the internet and analyze the democratizing potential of each feature.
6 Why do some people avoid the online world?

Reading guide

One of the best books for an overview of the field of internet and politics is *Internet Politics* by Andrew Chadwick (2006). This volume outlines key texts and examples to give students and researchers a thorough overview of the field. For particular case studies and research design in internet studies, see Oates et al. (2006). The online journal *First Monday* at www.firstmonday.org provides scholarly articles on the internet. In the past few years, useful studies of the internet and politics have been appearing in journals relating to media and politics (including *Political Communication, European Journal of Communication,* and *Media, Culture and Society*).

Internet resources

www.opennetinitiative.net   The OpenNet Initiative is a collaborative partnership of four academic institutions: the Citizen Lab (www.citizenlab.org) at the Munk Center for International Studies, University of Toronto; the Berkman Center for Internet & Society (cyberlaw.harvard.edu) at Harvard Law School; the Advanced Network Research Group at the Cambridge Security Program (www.cambridge-security.net), University of Cambridge; and the Oxford Internet Institute (www.oii.ac.uk), Oxford University. All of these groups provide detailed analysis of the internet on their websites.

http://www.pewinternet.org/   The Pew Internet & American Life Project is a non-profit organization that produces reports exploring the impact of the internet on families; communities; work and home; daily life; education; health care; and civic and political life. The reports, based on extensive surveys, are available for free download. For the 2020 forecast, got to http://www.pewinternet.org/PPF/r/188/report_display.asp

Notes

1 This report is available online at http://people-press.org/reports/display.php3?Report ID=233.
2 This study is available online at http://www.pewinternet.org/PPF/r/150/report_display.asp.
3 According to rankings from The Truth Laid Bear website, as reported in Wikipedia, see http://en.wikipedia.org/wiki/Political_blog and the Truth Laid Bear website at http://truthlaid-bear.com.

References

Adkeniz, Y. (2000) "Policing the Internet: Concerns for Cyber-rights." In Gibson, R. and Ward, S. (eds.) *Reinvigorating Democracy? British Politics and the Internet* (pp. 169–88). Aldershot: Ashgate.

Bimber, B. (1998) "Toward an Empirical Map of Political Participation on the Internet." Paper presented at the Annual Meeting of the American Political Science Association, Boston, Massachusetts.

Caral, J. (2004) "Lessons from ICANN: Is Self-regulation of the Internet Fundamentally Flawed?" *International Journal of Law and Information Technology* 12 (1): 1–31.

Chadwick, A. (2006) *Internet Politics: States, Citizens, and New Communication Technologies*. Oxford: Oxford University Press.

Davis, R. and Owen, D. (1998) *New Media and American Politics*. Oxford: Oxford University Press.

Dyson, E. (1998) *Release 2.1 : A Design for Living in the Digital Age*. London: Penguin.

Elmer, G. (1997) "Spaces of Surveillance: Indexicality and Solicitation on the Internet." *Critical Studies in Mass Communication* 14 (2): 182–91.

Etzioni, A. and Etzioni, O. (1999) "Face-to-Face and Computer-Mediated Communities: A Comparative Analysis." Paper presented at Virtual Communities: Eighth Annual Conference on Computers, Freedom and Privacy, University of Texas, Austin.

Fox, S. (2005) *Digital Divisions: The Internet and Campaign 2004*. Washington, DC: Pew Internet and American Life Project. Available online at www.pewinternet.org.

Galston, W. (2003) "The Impact of the Internet on Civic Life: An Early Assessment." In Kamarck, E.C. and Nye, J.S. (eds.) *Governance.com: Democracy in the Information Age*. Washington, DC: Brookings Institution Press.

Gibson, R. and Ward, S. (2000) "A Proposed Methodology for Studying the Function and Effectiveness of Party and Candidate Websites." *Social Science Computer Review* 18 (3): 301–19.

Hill, K.A. and Hughes, J.E. (1998) *CyberPolitics: Citizen Activism in the Age of the Internet*. Oxford: Rowman & Littlefield.

Lessig, L. (1999) *Code and Other Laws of Cyberspace*. New York: Basic Books.

Liberty (ed.) (1999) *Liberating Cyberspace: Civil Liberties, Human Rights and the Internet*. London: Pluto Press and Liberty.

Linaa Jensen, J. (2006) "The Minnesota E-democracy Project: Mobilising the Mobilised?" In Oates, S., Owen, D., and Gibson, R.K. (eds.) *The Internet and Politics: Citizens, Activists and Voters* (pp. 39–58). London: Routledge.

Lipow, A. and Seyd, P. (1996) "The Politics of Anti-Partyism." *Parliamentary Affairs* 49 (2): 273–84.

Lusoli, W. and Ward, S. (2006) "Hunting Protestors: Mobilisation, Participation and Protest Online in the Countryside Alliance." In Oates, S., Owen, D., and Gibson, R.K. (eds.) *The Internet and Politics: Citizens, Activists and Voters* (pp. 59–79). London: Routledge.

March, L. (2006) "Virtual Parties in a Virtual World: The Use of the Internet by Russian Political Parties." In Oates, S., Owen, D., and Gibson, R.K. (eds.) *The Internet and Politics: Citizens, Activists and Voters* (pp. 137–62). London: Routledge.

Norris, P. (2000) *A Virtuous Circle: Political Communication in Postindustrial Societies.* Cambridge: Cambridge University Press.

Norris, P. (2001) *Digital Divide.* Cambridge: Cambridge University Press.

Oates, S., Owen, D., and Gibson, R.K. (eds.) (2006) *The Internet and Politics: Citizens, Activists and Voters.* London: Routledge.

Owen, D. (2006) "The Internet and Youth Civic Engagement in the United States." In Oates, S., Owen, D. and Gibson, R.K. (eds.) *The Internet and Politics: Citizens, Activists and Voters* (pp. 20–38). London: Routledge.

Pew Research Center for the People and the Press (2004) *Voters Liked Campaign 2004, But Too Much "Mud-Slinging."* Washington, DC: Pew Research Center for the People and the Press. Available online at http://people-press.org/reports/display.php3?ReportID=233.

Polat, R.K. (2005) "The Internet and Political Participation: Exploring the Explanatory Links." *European Journal of Communication* 20 (4): 435–59.

Putnam, R.D. (2001) *Bowling Alone: The Collapse and Revival of American Community.* New York: Simon & Schuster.

Rainie, L., Cornfield, M. and Horrigan, J. (2005) *The Internet and Campaign 2004.* Washington, DC: Pew Internet and American Life Project. Available online at http://www.pewinternet.org/PPF/r/150/report_display.asp.

Reilly, P. (2007) *Framing online communications of civil and uncivil groups in post-conflict Northern Ireland.* PhD dissertation. Glasgow: University of Glasgow.

Rheingold, H. (1995) *The Virtual Community: Finding Connection in a Computerised World.* London: Minerva.

Stanyer, J. (2006) "Levelling the Electoral Communication Playing Field? The Hype and Reality of Campaign Blogging." Paper presented at the Annual Meeting of the American Political Science Association, Philadelphia, Pennsylvania. Available online via the APSA meeting paper archive at http://64.112.226.77/one/apsa/apsa06/index.php?cmd=apsa06.

Streck, J. (1999) "Pulling the Plug on Electronic Town Meetings: Participatory Democracy and the Reality of Usenet." In Toulouse, C. and Luke, T. (eds.) *The Politics of Cyberspace* (pp. 18–47). Routledge: London.

Street, J. (1992) *Politics and Technology.* New York: Guildford Press.

Sunstein, C. (2001) *Republic.com.* Princeton, NJ: Princeton University Press.

Toffler, A. and Toffler, H. (1995) *Creating a New Civilization: The Politics of the Third Wave.* Atlanta: Turner Publications.

Ward, S. (eds.) *Reinvigorating Democracy?: British Politics and the Internet.* Aldershot: Ashgate.

Wilhelm, A.G. (2000) *Democracy in the Digital Age: Challenges to Political Life in Cyberspace.* New York: Routledge.

Wright, S. (2006) "Design Matters: the Political Efficacy of Government-run Discussion Boards." in Oates, S., Owen, D., and Gibson, R.K. (eds.) *The Internet and Politics: Citizens, Voters and Activists* (pp. 80–99). London: Routledge.

Wu, W. and Weaver, D. (1996) "On-line Democracy or On-line Demagoguery?: Public Opinion 'Polls' on the Internet." *Harvard International Journal of Press/Politics* 2 (4): 71–86.

The Internet and Protest 9

Central points

- The diffuse and decentralized nature of the internet offers opportunities for protestors in countries that lack freedom of speech.
- There is evidence that the internet can help protestors within countries disseminate information, but the internet itself is not generally powerful enough to create change when faced with organized state repression.
- The internet provides clear advantages to protestors attempting to organize internationally.
- There is little evidence that the internet empowers terrorists in a special way, although more study is needed.
- The internet does not appear to currently have the power to change the fundamental relationship between the political elites and the masses – but it could provide access to information to challenge repression within countries over a long period of time.

Introduction

9.1

Despite a lot of evidence to the contrary, people generally still believe in the power of information to change the world. U.S. presidential candidates spend hundreds of millions of dollars on political advertising in a single campaign. British citizens willingly pay an annual fee to support public broadcasting. The Russian government makes a huge effort to control all major media outlets within its borders. Yet, the studies of media and politics throughout this volume suggest that while words matter, they matter only within particular contexts. For example, an American presidential candidate challenging a popular incumbent is probably wasting a lot of money, because it is almost impossible to defeat a popular president. Political messages tend to matter most at times of crisis and change, reflecting and deepening rifts within society. The internet, as with other mass media, can play a role in these changes. This chapter will look at whether the particular features of the internet make it a more useful catalyst for protest than the traditional mass media.

There are several components of the internet that suggest it would be a useful tool for protestors. As discussed in the last chapter, the internet offers a quick, low-cost way to broadcast information globally. Although there are national and international constraints on internet usage, these often can be avoided – at least for a time. Thus, the internet can sometimes subvert the control of a repressive state. This is particularly important if protestors are seeking to build an international audience to help their cause, such as with the Chiapas revolt begun in the 1990s or in the case of the Chechen War. On the flip side of this is the concern that the particular features of the internet can facilitate the actions of geographically disparate groups for dangerous activities, including terrorism. Chapter 8 discussed how the internet could contribute to democracy, while this chapter is about how the internet can challenge what citizens perceive as a dearth of democracy and fair play. While in some ways these concepts overlap, the discussion below is about the attempt to use the internet as a *challenge* to existing regimes. In some examples, this is about groups that seek change within a state. In others, it is about the potential of the internet to build an international movement, even a terrorist organization. What these attempts have in common is the use of the internet not really to improve, but to fundamentally change, the political status quo. If the internet has this potential, it would make it a particularly important and unique political tool.

Bennett rejects doubts by some social scientists that the capacity of the internet to spark social action is weak: the internet "is implicated in the new global activism far beyond merely reducing the costs of communication, or transcending the geographical and temporal barriers associated with other communication media" (2003: 143). Rather, the internet can "facilitate the loosely structured networks, the weak identity ties, and the patterns of issue and demonstration organizing that define a new global protest politics." In particular, the online sphere allows for the low-cost ability to create permanent campaigns, the growth of broad networks despite relatively weak social and ideological ties, as well as the transformation of networks into social action. While Bennett acknowledges that this same pace and capacity make internet-based groups vulnerable to problems of control, decision-making, and collective identity, he builds a compelling case for the particular power of the internet to mobilize across traditional barriers and boundaries. His findings are supported by examples of social action that have been fostered by the internet, including anti-globalization protests, the Zapatista insurgency in Chiapas, MoveOn.org and others. Weinmann (2004: 6) suggests that terrorists use the internet in a similar fashion to civil society groups, namely for recruitment, networking, sharing information, and distributing propaganda to a potential global audience. Similarly, Tucker asserts that terrorists use information and communication technologies to re-organize themselves into decentralized networks, theoretically leaving them immune to decapitation by the authorities, as they are based on the idea of "leaderless resistance" (2000: 1). What is of particular concern to civil society is the way in which the internet may provide a "multiplier" effect for terrorists, allowing them to mine the entire virtual world for dispossessed citizens to join an international, anti-social cause. By the same token, the notion of "leaderless resistance" can aid groups seeking to challenge what they perceive as national or international repression through civic means, whether they view their cause as domestic or international. The studies and examples below will explore the success and failure of the internet to support forms of resistance, looking in turn at domestic protest, international movements, and terrorism online.

The internet and domestic protest

9.2 The non-centralized, inexpensive, and non-hierarchical features of the internet make it useful for disseminating information when the traditional mass media within a nation do not choose to cover a cause. In addition, the internet can broadcast this information to (potentially) an enormous global audience. As discussed in Chapter 8, studies into the internet's capacity to improve democracy suggest that the potential of the internet to craft social change and cohesion is perhaps overstated. However, there is evidence that specific causes and campaigns can be particularly successful when broadcast on the online world. For example, Britain's Countryside Alliance was able to better organize large protest marches in London in 2003 via a combination of traditional meetings and persuasive email missives (Lusoli and Ward, 2006). This research, however, examined the role of the internet in places that had relatively open media systems. Although many groups complain that they get little or biased coverage of their causes, the media system in democracies is not controlled by a repressive elite that practices censorship. In places such as China and Russia, however, the media environment is quite different. Rather than benign (or even malevolent) neglect, it is government policy to ban the mention of certain groups, protestors, or even ideas that challenge the central government's hold on power. As discussed in earlier chapters, Russian President Vladimir Putin does not tolerate criticism of his policies in key areas from either state-run or commercial television news in Russia.

Theoretically, the internet could serve as the medium for those who oppose Putin's monopoly on the central media. However, the problem isn't gaining a voice. There are outlets to express diverse opinion in Russia, including newspapers and radio stations, although the opposition views in the mass media are relatively rare. The challenge is in gaining the attention and trust of the audience. Part of the problem is the "digital divide" (Norris, 2001), in that Russians have relatively low access to the internet. More to the point, studies show that Russians overwhelmingly prefer and trust their central, state-run television stations to other types of media, including the internet (Oates, 2006). Although Russian internet sites offer a range of opinions, the Russian online sphere does not appear to act as a political catalyst (March, 2006). The greater range of information online can do little to empower Russian citizens. The government has eliminated realistic political opposition at the ballot box, so Russian citizens cannot vote the Kremlin's allies out of office. In the daily struggle to survive in difficult economic times, Russians have little ability to organize effective social movements. There are protest rallies in Moscow that go unreported or are "spun" to make the protestors appear essentially as anti-social deviants. In addition, there is little rule of law in a country that is plagued by an unwieldy civic code and a corrupt bureaucracy.

It would be unsurprising if the Russian government essentially chose to ignore the internet. As noted above, the internet in Russia has relatively little reach and public impact. In addition, an appearance of democratic dialogue and alternative viewpoints online suits the Russian government's preference for an appearance of media diversity coupled with systematic repression of major media outlets. In addition – as the discussion below about the Chinese method of controlling the internet will suggest – policing the online world can be expensive and difficult in an industrialized society. However, there are two particular cases that suggest the Russian government cannot be complacent about the role of the internet in their civic sphere. The first is the existence of pro-Chechen websites, which have served as one of the few sources of information from the Chechen side of the on-going wars (Thomas, n.d). In particular, the "Caucasus Center" site created by Chechen leader Movladi Udugov proved particularly popular and it was ranked 21st in popularity among all internet websites accessed from Moscow in 1999, according to Thomas.[1] He contrasted the popularity of this pro-Chechen website with one of the sites to counter the Chechen cause, which logged at only 357th in popularity in hits from Moscow. As Conway (2006) suggests in her study of Israelis who visit Palestinian websites, visiting the website of an "enemy" does not mean support of the enemy cause. Rather, people are seeking information, which is particularly relevant in Russia because there is little news about

Chechnya in the traditional mass media. However, it does give the "enemy" an opportunity to propagandize, a particular internet activity that Conway labels "cybercortical" warfare. Although the Russian government has made an effort to improve its media military strategy regarding Chechnya (Thomas, n.d.), the endemic violence and chaos in Chechnya makes regular reporting from the area impossible. As a result, the internet becomes an important source of information – and the Russian government becomes concerned that it also becomes a source of undermining their framing of the conflict.

The Chechen internet presence demonstrates that it is not easy for a single state to eliminate the internet existence of an enemy. The Russian military have widespread popular support for the war in Chechnya, but are poor at providing the type of "feel good" information and reporting found in the U.S. system (see Chapter 6 on the Media and War). As a result, Russian citizens hungry for information – particularly in a country in which there is mandatory military service and a reasonable chance that a young man will be sent to fight in Chechnya – will seek out information even from "enemy" websites. In addition, the case of the Chechen websites show that it takes international co-operation, often a struggle for the Russians in a complicated post-Cold War world, to eliminate the source of the sites. In September 1999, the Russian minister of internal affairs traded information on Osama Bin Laden in exchange for help from the U.S. Federal Bureau of Investigation in eliminating internet sites set up by Chechen supporters.[2] Russian hackers did shut down the Caucasus Center site in August 1999 (posting a picture of famous nineteenth-century Russian poet Mikhail Lermontov holding a Kalashnikov rifle on the site) (Thomas, n.d.). However, the Caucasus Center website was still running (in Russian, English, Arabic, Ukrainian, and Turkic) as of mid-2007, as were a number of other pro-Chechen and anti-Chechen websites. One of the more prominent pro-Chechen websites has been based in Malaysia, making it particular difficult for the Russians to shut it down (Thomas). While Chechen war coverage may be a distant, sanitized exercise in the Russian media (Oates, 2006) and virtually uncovered in the international mass media, it is very much unforgotten on the internet.

Another internet case study that would challenge the notion that the internet is powerless to change the direction of a post-Soviet regime is the online role in supporting the Orange Revolution in Ukraine in 2004 and 2005. The protests that led to the Orange Revolution were triggered by the 2004 Ukrainian presidential election, which was marked by unfair practices including biased coverage in state-funded television, voter intimidation, poisoning of the chief rival to the incumbent president, and electoral fraud. It became apparent that the run-off election between the popular, relatively pro-Western challenger Viktor Yushchenko and incumbent Viktor Yanukovych had been rigged in favor of Yanukovych, who had close ties to Russia. In a twist worthy of a spy novel, medical evidence confirmed that Yushchenko had been poisoned, made critically ill, and badly disfigured. While there had been political unrest and tensions in particular between pro-Russian and pro-Western forces in post-Soviet Ukraine, the protests surrounding the 2004 elections were on a more massive scale. They included large public demonstrations and strikes. Under intense national and international pressure, the Ukrainian government held the elections again, and Yushchenko won the post as president in January 2005.

Unlike in Russia, it would appear that information was translated into protest and political change in Ukraine. As media scholars know, that is an exciting – and relatively rare – event. However, it is important to theorize about why the media mattered in this particular case, and how it differed from the neighboring case of Russia. First, Ukrainian politics have been marked by less consensus than Russian politics since the collapse of the Soviet Union in 1991. This is partly because while Russia has essentially one major power base – the Moscow-centric Russian elite – Ukraine remains politically divided between a Ukrainian power base centered around the west of the country and the traditional Russian-dominated eastern half of the country. Attitudes toward Russia are very mixed as Ukrainian nationalists have long disliked Soviet/Russian rule. And while Russia and Ukraine have faced many of the same social problems in the wake of Communism's collapse, the economic and social dislocation in Ukraine has been even worse. Arguably, this has inculcated more radical attitudes on the part of the populace.

Historic and cultural differences aside, there also are key divergences in the post-Soviet media history between Russia and Ukraine, particularly in terms of the development of the internet. While the internet has been of seemingly little political importance in Russia, it has been much more politically prominent in Ukraine (Krasnoboka and Semetko, 2006). Krasnoboka and Semetko write that there is compelling evidence that the internet in Ukraine "sets a political agenda for the Ukrainian parliament, president and other mass media by running its own criminal, journalistic, legal and political investigations as well as by accusing top-level officials of illegalities and providing evidence to back up these accusations" (ibid.: 183). Krasnoboka and Semetko point out this is not a "miracle of democracy"; rather conditions in Ukraine and the peculiar history of the first online newspaper dramatically pointed the Ukrainian audience to the internet in 2000. The internet became a prominent catalyst for rebellion against the regime because "an appropriate combination of necessary conditions appeared almost simultaneously in Ukraine" (ibid.: 183).

Again, the tragic events surrounding the first online newspaper in Ukraine read more like a flamboyant spy novel than the sad case of murder and possible corruption at the highest levels that they represent in real life. The online newspaper *Ukrainska Pravda* [*Ukrainian Truth*] was co-founded by Ukrainian journalist Georgiy Gongadze in April 2000. Later that year, Gongadze was murdered and his headless corpse was found outside of the capital city of Kyiv. This marked the start of a political crisis in Ukraine, with the first wave of mass protest demonstrations in 2000 and 2001. While people were first concerned over the disappearance of Gongadze and the subsequent discovery of his corpse, the country was galvanized when the Socialist Party leader publicly accused Ukrainian President Leonid Kuchma and other top officials of plotting to silence Gongadze. This included an alleged tape recording of the two officials, the transcript of which was published internationally via a Dutch website. Krasnoboka and Semetko were particularly interested in how internet coverage of these events differed from coverage in the traditional mass media in Ukraine. They analyzed coverage on a television station, in a newspaper, and on a website from the period of the heaviest protests. Even though they deliberately did not select a particularly pro-presidential newspaper or television station, they still found much less bias on the internet. In particular, the internet coverage was careful to delineate the reasons for the protest and give the political context for them. At the same time, Ukrainian television was more events-driven in the coverage, which gave much less voice to the protestors. The newspaper coverage was markedly more Soviet in style, suggesting that the protestors were merely disrupting society rather than making legitimate political claims. The internet became a more prominent part of the political sphere due to its intimate connection with the Gongadze case and the ensuing protests. As such, the concept of the internet as an important, trusted, and authoritative source for dissent in Ukraine was consolidated. Although internet penetration is probably lower in Ukraine than in Russia (reliable statistics are hard to come by), the internet has an enhanced reputation as a political actor because of the Gongadze murder and subsequent events. This underlines the point that it would appear unlikely that the internet can generate political protest or social change on its own, but it can provide a powerful catalyst for change in certain situations.

So far, there is relatively little evidence of systematic government control of the internet in Russia and Ukraine, although there remain general worries about pressures on highly visible websites. States with non-democratic rule, however, do have elaborate and arguably effective ways of controlling public use of the internet. In 2005, Reporters Without Borders identified a list of "15 worst enemies of the internet" as the countries that "crack down hardest on the internet, censoring independent news sites and opposition publications, monitoring the Web to stifle dissident voices, and harassing, intimidating and sometimes imprisoning internet users and bloggers who deviate from the regime's official line" (http://www.rsf.org/print.php3?id_article=15613). The list (in alphabetical order) is Belarus, Burma, China (discussed in detailed below), Cuba, Iran, Libya, the Maldives, Nepal, North Korea, Saudi Arabia, Syria, Tunisia, Turkmenistan, Uzbekistan, and Vietnam. The international media freedom organization identified a range of controls in these countries, including pricing the internet out of reach of the population, blocking of a broad range of websites from within the country, and prison sentences for those who posted politically dissident material. This study reported that China has the largest number of "cyber dissidents," with 62 people in prison for what they posted online. At the same time as Reporters Without Borders identified repressive internet regimes, they warned that more "civic" countries also can challenge the freedom of the online sphere. Among its list of "countries to watch" was the U.S.. The organization noted concern that the U.S., in many ways the dominant internet influence, has laws about the interception of online traffic that do not provide enough privacy guarantees for users. However, this is a minor concern when compared with overt, repressive policies toward the internet.

China is an important case study in internet control and repression. In particular, its "Great Chinese Firewall" of the internet has received a relatively large amount of attention from internet scholars. This Communist country provides an important conundrum: not only is China the most populous country on earth and a rising economic force, but it is relying on a wide spread of the business internet without a fundamental change in its intolerance for political dissent from the Chinese Communist Party line. Can a country simultaneously harness the economic potential of the internet without the political communication aspect of the new technology challenging the political repression of the state? Scholars are somewhat divided on how successful China has been in this endeavor. Some analysts, such as Polumbaum, see the internet as one factor in the changing media landscape in China, a shift that includes greater diversity, economic pressures to attract audiences, and relative freedom from central control that all contribute to the "idea of a monolithic state control of the media" becoming "outdated" (2001: 271). Harwit and Clark (2001) suggest evidence to show that the internet can serve as conduit to greater openness, particularly given projections that the number of Chinese internet users will continue to increase exponentially. In addition, these analysts argue (in an echo of the idea of political "gladiators" from Chapter 8) that those who use the internet are the traditional dissident voices of China, notably students and scientists who live in major cities. As such, the internet can reinforce their intellectual and organizational capacity.

Other scholars, however, are not as convinced of a capacity of the internet to bring change to China. As Hartford (2000) argues, neither internet growth nor its ability to provide political openness is *inevitable* in China. In addition, as Polumbaum notes, the outlook for journalistic freedom remains relatively grim in China, a point underlined by the 62 cyber-dissidents in prison reported by Reporters Without Borders. While Russian journalists often face violence and even murder, Chinese journalists are more likely than those in any other country to go to prison over freedom of speech issues, according to the New York-based Committee to Protect Journalists (www.cpj.org). Indeed, self-censorship could remain one of the most pervasive barriers to change (Abbott, 2001). Scholars disagree about the degree to which the Chinese government can control the Web, with Harwit and Clark (2001) seeing possible gaps in control and Taubman (1998) arguing that the government has the ability to effectively control the democratizing elements of the Web while retaining it as a tool for economic growth. While Taubman wrote this ten years ago, it would appear that the Chinese government remains effective at controlling the democratizing potential of the internet.

The Chinese government has recognized the commercial need for the internet, particularly to be able to compete effectively in a globalized, online economy. At the same time, the Chinese government does not believe in a free exchange of ideas; rather that information and ideas should reflect the policy and ideology of the Chinese Communist Party. The Chinese government, however, has resolved this seeming paradox by strict control on the internet at several levels or "choke points." According to the Open Net Initiative's 2004–5 report, the country "operates the most extensive, technologically sophisticated, and broad-reaching system of internet filtering in the world." The initiative found the "implications of this distorted online information environment for China's users are profound and disturbing" (see www.open-netinitiative.net/ studies/china/).The Chinese government is particularly concerned about specific issues that challenge its ideology, including Taiwanese and Tibetan independence, the Falun Gong movement, the Dalai Lama, the Tiananmen Square protests of 1989, opposition political parties, and anti-Communist movements. It is also concerned about both domestic political activism and international groups who wish to influence public opinion in China. As a result, the country has developed its "Great Firewall," which is a multi-level set of controls of the online sphere within the country.

According to a report by the OpenNet Initiative, there isn't one statute or law that regulates the Chinese internet. Rather, the restrictions include media regulation, protection of state secrets, controls on internet service providers, restrictions for internet content providers, and laws that govern the use of cyber cafés, according to the OpenNet Initiative. This creates a "patchwork series of rationales and legal support for internet filtering by the state" in China. At the same time, these regulations are not balanced by strong rights to privacy in China. This leaves open the important question of what Chinese citizens can possibly consume or produce in terms of information online. According to the OpenNet initiative, access to information fluctuates. The Chinese government blocks some website addresses from regular access within the country (although reports suggest that some sophisticated computer users can circumvent these blockages). While the websites of human rights organizations and most major media outlets are available, there are some key omissions. For example, tests have shown that the BBC website has been blocked in China. The OpenNet Initiative found it difficult to see a consistent pattern in the internet control in China, although finding "strong controls on citizens' ability to view and publish internet content."

Internet filtering takes place primarily at the higher level of China's network, though individual internet service providers also implement their own blocking, according to the OpenNet Initiative. Their research found that major Chinese search engines filter content by keywords and remove certain search results from their lists. In January 2006, Google decided to offer Chinese users a self-censored service (www.google.cn) in order to allow users access to the main search engine. Google's China search engine had previously been blocked by Chinese censors. When the BBC tried to search for the banned Falun Gong spiritual movement on the new Google.cn site, users were directed to articles condemning the movement instead of the most popular sites worldwide.[3] The decision to offer the censored service was a pragmatic business move, as the number of internet search customers in China rivals the number in the U.S.. Aside from filtering, other Chinese controls on the internet include the practice by major Chinese blogs service providers of preventing posts with certain keywords. In addition, some keyword searches are blocked by China's gateway filtering and not the search engines themselves.

China's intricate technical filtering regime is buttressed by an equally complex series of laws and regulations that control both access to material online and publication of material online. This in turn is supported by highly publicized arrests, trials, and prison sentences for those convicted of speaking out on forbidden subjects in China. Chinese officials have created an apparently effective climate of fear and apprehension that breeds online self-censorship. Cyber cafés, which provide an important source of access to the internet for many Chinese, are required by law to track internet usage by customers and to keep correlated information on file for 60 days. Although young Chinese students studying in the U.K. report that there are always ways around most of the restrictions, there is also almost always a risk. In cases publicized by Reporters Without Borders, the search engine company Yahoo! has co-operated with the Chinese police in identifying people who used email accounts to share secret political documents. According to a report from the media freedom organization, Jiang Lijun was sentenced to four years in prison for "subversion" in November 2003, accused of seeking to use "violent means" to impose democracy. The verdict indicated that Lijun wrote that the Chinese regime was "autocratic," that he favored a "so-called western-style democracy," and planned to set up a political party.[4] The internet can do little to foster political opposition and protest in this environment, as the Chinese government is taking great pains to guarantee. Although it clearly takes a great deal of security and administrative resources, the Chinese great "firewall" on the internet is a model that could be deployed in other non-free regimes around the world.

As with social action, protest action online benefits greatly from synergy with the traditional media. A recent example of how this synergy can work is the story of the "Baghdad blogger." During the second Gulf War in the spring of 2003, Baghdad resident Salam Pax posted daily reports on his Dear_Raed blog. As one of the few voices from the inside of the conflict, his blogs soon attracted attention. Eventually, his work was syndicated in the liberal British newspaper, the *Guardian*. While it would be tempting to view this experience as proof that the internet can always provide alternative voices, there were key factors in the ability of Pax to translate his daily experience into a respected media voice.[5] Pax is well educated, with some experience in journalism as a translator. He is clearly fluent in English, which is important in terms of communicating online in the West. Pax was providing information and a point of view that was absent, in a time of war in which many Western citizens were concerned about alternative viewpoints (particularly in Britain). His partnership with the *Guardian* allowed him to make the leap from the internet to a respected print medium. His talent, situation, and the partnership with the newspaper created a particularly strong synergy to translate a personal blog into political journalism. Without the internet, it is unlikely – although not impossible – that Pax's views would have been heard. The question remains about how many individuals and groups have the critical elements – writing talent, online access, a newsworthy situation, an interested audience, and a partnership with an existing media outlet – to make the same impact.

Key points about the internet and domestic protest

- If there is little interest or trust in the internet, it cannot serve as an effective catalyst for protest or political change in a country such as Russia.
- The history and role of the internet in Ukrainian politics suggest that context matters in terms of the ability of the internet to become an effective political communication tool.
- China's "Great Firewall" of internet controls shows that government can devise effective means to control the political content and inculcate online self-censorship, even with massive internet uptake in the population.
- Significant skills such as education, ability to write in English, and a compelling situation contribute to internet voices becoming mainstream internationally.

The internet and international protest

9.3 It is clear from the discussion above that domestic use of the internet for protest is both constrained and informed by a range of political issues and attitudes within specific countries. However, these relationships change a great deal when analyzing the role of the internet in international protest. Is the notion of the internet as a catalyst for social change applicable to global issues? One of the earliest movements to test the internet's capacity for international political influence was the Zapatista movement in the Chiapas region of Mexico in the mid-1990s. The National Zapatista Liberation (ELZN) movement was formed by Indian peasants living in Mexico to combat what they saw as their continuing economic and cultural oppression by the Mexican government. On an international level, they linked this protest and their situation to the new free trade agreement with the U.S.. The group used the burgeoning online world extensively to transmit their message to the outside world. The ELZN used the help of sympathetic friends in the U.S., particularly academics based at the University of Texas,[6] to circumvent the unsympathetic Mexican state media. The internet successfully publicized the struggles of the Chiapas people to the wider world. This, in turn, stimulated far greater traditional media coverage as well as a meeting of more than 3,000 global activists in Lacandon forest to formulate a new worldwide network of resistance to neo-liberal forces (Cleaver, 1995; Ronfeldt et al., 1998; Jefferies, 2001).

There are many elements to the Zapatista movement that made it a prime candidate for online and offline political synergy. First, although the movement centered on the grievances of one ethnic group in a region of Mexico, their cause had global resonance. The Zapatista movement spoke to concerns of a wide range of minority groups in agrarian areas – throughout the Americas and further afield – who had reason to fear being marginalized by a globalizing economy. Although the agrarian people themselves did not have regular access to the internet, academics who sympathized with their cause had the online access, a network of interested people, and the time to devote to promoting the cause. In addition, the Zapatista had articulate leadership in the enigmatic form of a man known only as "Subcomandante Marcos." Finally, the Zapatista movement benefited from being one of the first "causes" on cyberspace, drawing interest in what was then a relatively novel political use of the internet. It should be remembered that this campaign was essentially based on text messages, an older technology but one that served the Zapatista movement (which still continues) well.

Since the era of the first Chiapas online movement, international internet protest has become a regular part of the political landscape. Some examples of this activism are the "Carnival Against Capitalism" on June 18, 1999, in which hundreds of thousands of protestors demonstrated simultaneously in dozens of cities around the world (Chadwick, 2006: 127). Much of the protest was organized through a website (j18.org). Another major event that has been credited to cyber-organization was the protest at the 1999 meeting of the World Trade Organization in Seattle, which also was coordinated online. In a show of technological adaptability, protestors used mobile devices to make live feeds to the internet as well as warnings about the police. When their initial network was disrupted by the FBI and police, protestors bought new mobile phones and rebuilt the communications network (Chadwick, 2006: 127). While greater online mobilization may mean that it is harder for any individual case to garner attention, regular online activism should be able to attract, maintain, and deploy an international group of activists in support of particular causes. In studying this phenomenon, it is important to try to isolate the way in which the internet may have changed – if at all – the fundamental nature of the protest. In general, it is recognized that the internet can mobilize groups that are geographically dispersed to protest causes. It is most evident when groups are mobilized for particular events, such as the protest against the G8 summit in the U.K. in July 2005. However, it is perhaps more relevant to consider the relative dearth of international protest rallies and marches, rather than those that are sparked by internet connections. What is far more difficult to measure is how the internet supports day-to-day resistance and protest, particularly in terms of changing attitudes and opinions into forms of protest. While the Pew Internet and American Life Project provides one of the most advanced studies on how the internet impacts daily activity and attitudes, more research is needed on how the "drip feed" of information on the internet changes political attitudes and political behavior.

Key points about the internet and international protest

- The Chiapas revolt showed that online protest can mobilize international support for those who consider themselves oppressed in their own country.
- There is relatively little evidence of the internet sparking regular, sustained international protests.
- The role of the internet in stimulating protest may be slow and steady rather than manifested in demonstrations and other protest events.

The internet and terrorism

9.4 Chadwick labels much of the work about the internet as "hype and speculation" rather than an attempt to understand the internet as a social actor and a political institution (2006: 1). Much of the research about the internet has been more descriptive than analytical, challenged by both the fast pace of online change as well as a lack of useful models in understanding the role of communication in social change (Oates et al., 2006). At the same time, concerns about the ability of the internet to provide a "force multiplier" to terrorists have increased. For example, in testimony before the U.S. House of Representatives in September 2006, an FBI director reported that the internet was a prime "venue" for Islamic radicalization, with protest activity migrating online in the wake of increased offline scrutiny. He said that

> radicalization via the internet is participatory, and individuals are actively engaged in exchanging extremist propaganda and rhetoric online which may facilitate the violent Islamic extremist causes ... [to] further their indoctrination, create links between extremists located around the world, and may serve as a springboard for future terrorist activities.[7]

These concerns are nothing new to social scientists, security experts, or the general public. Overall, there is widespread concern about the internet as a way to spread anti-civil messages and organize terrorist attacks that are "below the radar" of national or international security forces because of the particularly disaggregated and relatively anarchic structure of the internet. This has fostered the passage of legislation that allows for broader surveillance of the internet in countries such as the U.S. and the U.K., but this is coupled with the frustration that the huge, international sprawl of the online world is vastly difficult to police. In addition, it calls into question whether massive internet surveillance is appropriate in terms of supporting a civil society.

One of the critical questions for nations and their security is when the internet can translate discontent into anti-state violence. Despite fears often reported in the traditional mass media, there have been relatively few "cyberterrorist" attacks via the internet. The more relevant question is not about the internet as a terrorist *target*, but about the online world as a useful terrorist *tool*. It is clear that there are particular features of the internet that terrorists could potentially find attractive. In terms of organizational capability, it offers a relatively secure method of communication. In addition, the internet gives easy access to a great deal of information that would aid in the perpetration of terrorist acts, including instructions for making bombs, detailed maps of areas, public transport schedules, and even places to buy weapons.[8] Perhaps even more worryingly, the internet offers terrorist groups a channel for propaganda that is relatively free from censorship and monitoring, which is a way to aggregate and organize people with grievances across many societies. Can the internet's ability to offer aggregation across broad territories, information relatively free from state control, and anti-state propaganda destabilize societies?

Scholars have come to slightly different conclusions about the power of the internet for terrorist groups. Conway (2006) argues that the internet allows groups such as Hizbollah in Palestine to carry out important "cybercortical" warfare on its website. By reporting information on dead and wounded Israeli soldiers, the Palestinian group also has been able to attract Israeli readers. Conway argues that terrorists are not limiting themselves to the traditional means of communication and increasingly employ the new media to pursue their goals. In order to understand the internet presence of Hizbollah, however, it is important to think about the role the group plays in society. Despite its appearance on the U.S. terrorist list, Hizbollah is a political force with support in Lebanon. As such, it is not universally regarded as "criminal," particularly in parts of the Middle East. Thus, much of the audience in the Middle East would regard it more as a legitimate political player than a "terrorist" group. This makes the case of Hizbollah.org more about political persuasion on the internet and closer to the case of political party websites. The tolerance for the message and the acceptance of the internet presence has perhaps more to do with Middle East politics than with the success of a "terrorist" group in exploiting new technology. It is important to point out that Hizbollah also has a television station. Is this "cybercortical" warfare or just politics as usual in the Middle East? After all, Hizbollah existed long before the internet.

In a study of terrorist groups in Northern Ireland, Paul Reilly (2006) found that the internet offered no particular new weapon of propaganda or organization. Terrorist groups are constrained by the relative visibility of the internet from inciting violence online. Rather, the web pages of terrorist groups on the internet became places in which Catholic Republicans and Protestant Unionists can each give their views of history and attempt to establish moral rights to claim the disputed territory (for more on this topic, see Chapter 7 on Media and Terrorism). While there are some mentions of violence or reference to weapons, they tend to be rare and fleeting. The web pages remain relatively unsophisticated, with little use of modern techniques such as podcasting. Reilly argues that it is not terrorists who are using the internet, but the government that is using the fear of the online presence of terrorists to justify internet restrictions. According to Reilly, the threat of cyber-terrorism is exaggerated by nation-states as a means of justifying internet restrictions. Terrorists are not free to act with impunity on the internet. For example, legislation such as the U.K. Regulation of Investigatory Powers Act in 2000 has limited the ability of the terrorist to use the internet as an offensive weapon (as has the Patriot Act of 2001 in the U.S.). Meanwhile, nation-states manipulate public distrust of the internet to implement policies that restrict internet freedoms. This is because nation-states do not want arguments counter to their conception of civil society to be readily available on the internet (Reilly, 2006).

With the exception of religiously motivated groups in the Middle East, terrorist groups are likely to merely use the internet as a supplementary tool of covert communication. Reilly argues this is because terrorists still primarily need "big spectaculars" in the physical world, such as bombings and murder, for effective publicity for terrorists. Psychological warfare, a necessary component of terrorism, is effectively conducted through coverage of these events on the television news and the front pages of newspapers. In Reilly's view, the internet cannot replicate the shared experience of the mass media, as it is a private viewing box rather than a public medium. As with Hizbollah, terrorist organizations such as the Provisional Irish Republican Army were in existence long before the internet. They have survived decades as terrorist groups, in no small part due to the ability of their terrorist acts to manipulate the conventional mass media – as well as support from some segments of society from a political perspective. As their cause is more complex than one just of disputed territory, the role of the internet is more important for international terrorist groups. Hizbollah and Northern Irish terrorist groups could be described as essentially national terrorist groups. They are primarily concerned with asserting the rights of particular ethno-national groups to distinct territories. This is distinct from international terrorist movements, such as Al-Qaeda, that clearly have much broader goals that stretch globally. Al-Qaeda's objectives are listed as the elimination of foreign influence in Muslim countries, eradication of those deemed to be "infidels," elimination of Israel, and the creation of Islamic cross-national rule.[9] While people in places such as Beirut or Northern Ireland would be socialized into the issues taken up by "local" terrorist groups, groups such as Al-Qaeda need to reach across national boundaries to build a constituency of support for their terrorist activities. As with other terrorist groups, Al-Qaeda draws much of its support from people who are angry or fearful about the U.S. role in foreign policy. Al-Qaeda also has a strong religious element (although its interpretation of Islam is fiercely challenged by many Muslims).

It is clear, however, that Al-Qaeda did not draw worldwide attention to itself merely via a clever internet campaign strategy. Al-Qaeda came to public prominence in the world's largest "big spectacular" in terrorism through the World Trade Center bombings on September 11, 2001. There was then a "spill-over" effect that was based on the internet, including footage of Al-Qaeda statements and access to documents that were available online. Arguably, the internet gives Al-Qaeda the ability to spread information directly, recruit members, and perhaps even organize terrorist attacks online. It provides a focal point in the online world. It certainly gives the organization the ability to issue threats on a regular basis. However, there seems to be little evidence that the internet has fundamentally changed the relationship among the terrorist group, the mass media, and the audience. While the internet gives the terrorists the ability to have an unmediated presence, it also gives the authorities a way to track both the leaders and the followers.

It is more useful to think of the internet as *one factor* within a model of radicalization rather than simply as the *sole agent* for radicalization. In conceptualizing the internet as one factor (or independent variable) that has an impact on the radicalization of an individual (the dependent variable in social-science terms), we can build better and more robust hypotheses for understanding the relative role of the internet in radicalization in general. For example, social scientists and security experts have developed many useful markers of terrorist potential over the years, particularly from experiences in geographically distinct areas such as Northern Ireland. National identity, social class, education, gender, and other factors have played a useful predictive role. The same logic in the offline world of terrorism should be applied to the online world. What significant religious, national, ideological, and other socio-political factors seem to be aligned with terrorist groups online? It is only within this broader model that it is possible to theorize usefully about the role of the internet in fostering terrorism. Which particular elements of the internet – ranging from email to websites to podcasting – seem to be most effective at recruiting an online community? In the case of Al-Qaeda and other groups that use Islam to justify violence, in what ways is Islam cited, discussed, and used as a justification for terrorist activity? What sorts of offline activities, such as lectures, religious services, and training activities, seem to complement the online terrorism recruitment efforts? Without a thorough understanding of the broader forces, it is hard to pinpoint precisely what the internet's role in radicalization – from motivating people to attend protest meetings, stand up to a repressive state, or even turn to terrorist tactics – might be.

Key points about terrorism and the internet

- There is relatively little evidence that special features of the internet provide a unique advantage to terrorists.
- Terrorist groups can use the internet to publicize their political agenda, but there is little evidence that they are influencing a broad audience this way.

- The study of international terrorism and the internet calls for a more complex approach than understanding the relative role of the internet for domestic terrorist groups.
- Al-Qaeda gained worldwide attention via the world's largest act of mass terrorism, not by its presence on the internet.
- The internet does not on its own cause terrorism; rather, it is one factor in potential radicalization.

Chapter summary

It may be tempting to view the internet as a powerful catalyst for protest, but the evidence of its ability to radicalize individuals is rather mixed. In some countries, such as Russia, it would appear that little attention is paid to the internet, even when the traditional mass media show scant information diversity. On the other hand, the internet appears to be an important tool of political communication in Ukraine, perhaps explaining in part the ability of protest to oust a president after a rigged election in 2004. The case of China shows that governments can harness the economic power of the internet while continuing to control the democratizing potential of the new technology. There are some clear cases of online mobilization for international causes, such as the Chiapas revolt and the 1999 WTO protests. On the other hand, there is not an overwhelming amount of international protest to challenge the status quo. This suggests that the internet can broadcast alternative political messages, but relatively few may listen. In terms of terrorism, studies of domestic terrorist groups suggest that the internet does not offer a particular enhancement to their activities. It is more difficult to gauge the role of online mobilization for international terrorist groups, such as Al-Qaeda, but studies that provide more evidence and insight would be most useful.

Study questions

1 Can nations afford to ignore the potential for protest provided by the internet?
2 Is it possible for a country to effectively control the internet? Discuss, in relation to the internet "Great Firewall" in China.
3 Analyze the evidence for the internet to organize international protest events or movements.
4 Does the internet offer special tools for terrorists?

Reading guide

This reading guide is almost the same as for Chapter 8, in that the general principles of the internet are the same for radicalization as they are for mobilization. Again, one of the best books for an overview of the field of internet and politics is Chadwick's *Internet Politics* (2006). This volume outlines key texts and examples to give students and researchers a thorough overview of the field. For particular case studies and research design in internet studies (including two chapters on terrorism), see Oates et al. (2006). The online journal *First Monday* at www.firstmonday.org provides scholarly articles on the internet. In the past few years, more useful studies of the internet and politics have been appearing in journals relating to media and politics (including *Political Communication*, *European Journal of Communication*, and *Media, Culture and Society*).

Internet resources

(Also see Chapter 8 Internet Resources)

www.opennetinitiative.net   The OpenNet Initiative is a collaborative partnership of four academic institutions: the Citizen Lab (www.citizenlab.org) at the Munk Center for International Studies, University of Toronto; the Berkman Center for Internet and Society (cyberlaw.harvard.edu) at Harvard Law School; the Advanced Network Research Group at the Cambridge Security Program (www.cambridge-security.net), University of Cambridge; and the Oxford Internet Institute (www.oii.ac.uk), Oxford University. All of these groups provide detailed updates of analysis of the internet on their websites.

www.rsf.org   Reporters Without Borders [Reporters Sans Frontières] defends imprisoned journalists and press freedom globally. It has nine national sections (Austria, Belgium, Canada, France, Germany, Italy, Spain, Sweden, and Switzerland). In particular, see its report on the 15 worst enemies of the internet from 2005 at http://www.rsf.org/print.php3?id_article=15613.

http://www.pewinternet.org/   The Pew Internet & American Life Project is a non-profit organization that produces reports exploring the impact of the internet on families, communities, work and home, daily life, education, health care, and civic and political life. The reports, often based on extensive surveys, are available for free download.

http://www.eco.utexas.edu/faculty/Cleaver/chiapas95.html   Archival website of the Chiapas protest in Mexico.

Notes

1   For ethical and national security reasons, this chapter will not list the website address of any groups that are defined as "terrorist" by a segment of society. Researchers also should be aware that national security laws in most countries give the government the right to track who is searching and accessing terrorist-related web pages.

2   According to a BBC report on September 9, 1999, referenced by Thomas. For the report, see http://news.bbc.co.uk/1/hi/world/europe/442502.stm.

3   "Google Censors Itself for China," BBC News Website, January 25, 2006, http://news.bbc.co.uk/1/hi/technology/4645596.stm. In an experiment in March 2007, the author searched for the

phrase "Falun Gong" on www.google.com and again on www.google.cn. The results are markedly different, with highly negative stories calling Falun Gong a "cult" appearing on the search page for www.google.cn.

4 "Yahoo! implicated in third cyberdissident trial U.S. company's collaboration with Chinese courts highlighted in Jiang Lijun case," report on Reporters Sans Frontières website, April 19, 2006, available at http://www.rsf.org/article.php3?id_article=17180, last accessed February 16, 2007.

5 His blog was printed as a book: Pax, S. (2003) *Salam Pax: The Baghdad Blog*, London: Guardian Books. A more recent publication of the same type is *Baghdad Burning: Girl Blog from Iraq*, by a blogger known only as Riverbend (2006, London: Marion Boyars).

6 See Acción Zapatista de Austin, "Zapatismo in Cyberspace" at http://studentorgs.utexas.edu/nave/cyber.html.

7 Statement of Donald Van Duyn, Deputy Assistant Director, Counterterrorism Division, Federal Bureau of Investigation, before the U.S. House of Representatives Homeland Security Committee Subcommittee on Intelligence, Information Sharing, and Terrorism Risk Assessment on September 20, 2006. His full comments can be viewed at: http://www.fbi.gov/congress/congress06/vanduyn092006.htm.

8 One university instructor who teaches an internet class in Romania even uses a class exercise in which the first student in the computer lab to find out how to make a bomb over the internet wins a prize (author's research).

9 This information comes from a letter from an Al-Qaeda leader that was obtained and published online by the U.S. Office of the Director of National Intelligence at http://www.dni.gov/press_releases/letter_in_english.pdf. The letter is summarized and referenced in the Wikipedia entry for Al-Qaeda as of April 29, 2007.

References

Abbott, J.P. (2001) "Democracy@internet.asia? The Challenges to the Emancipatory Potential of the Net: Lessons from China and Malaysia." *Third World Quarterly* 22 (1): 99–114.

Bennett, W.L. (2003) "Communicating Global Activism: Strengths and Vulnerability of Networked Politics." *Information, Communication & Society* 6 (2): 143–68.

Chadwick, A. (2006) *Internet Politics: States, Citizens, and New Communication Technologies.* Oxford: Oxford University Press.

Conway, M. (2006) "Cybercortical Warfare: Hizbollah's Internet Strategy." In Oates, S., Owen, D., and Gibson, R.K. (eds.) *The Internet and Politics: Citizens, Activists and Voters* (pp. 100–17). London: Routledge.

Cleaver, H. (1995) The Zapatistas and the Electronic Fabric of Struggle. Online. Available http://www.eco.utexas.edu./faculty/Cleaver/zaps.html.

Hartford, K. (2000) "Cyberspace with Chinese Characteristics." *Current History* (September).

Harwit, E. and Clark, D. (2001) "Shaping the Internet in China: Evolution of Political Control over Network Infrastructure and Content." *Asian Survey* 41 (3): 377–408.

Jeffries, F. (2001) "Zapatismo and Intergalactic Age," in Burbach, R. (ed.) *Globalization and Postmodern Politics: From Zapatistas to High-Tech Robber Barons*, London: Pluto Press: 129–44.

Kahn, R. and Kellner, D. (2005) "Oppositional Politics and the Internet: A Critical/Reconstructive Approach." *Cultural Politics* 1 (1): 75–100.

Krasnoboka, N. and Semetko, H. (2006) "Murder, Journalism and the Web: How the Gongadze Case Launched the Internet News Era in Ukraine." In Oates, S., Owen, D., and Gibson, R.K. (eds.) *The Internet and Politics: Citizens, Activists and Voters* (pp. 183–206). London: Routledge.

Lievrouw, L. (2006) "Oppositional and Activist New Media: Remediation, Reconfiguration, Participation." *Participatory Design Archive. Proceedings of the Ninth Conference on Participatory Design: Expanding Boundaries in Design*, 1: 115–24. Trento, Italy.

Lusoli, W. and Ward, S. (2006) "Hunting Protestors: Mobilisation, Participation and Protest Online in the Countryside Alliance." In Oates, S., Owen, D., and Gibson, R.K. (eds.) *The Internet and Politics: Citizens, Activists and Voters* (pp. 59–79). London: Routledge.

March, L. (2006) "Virtual Parties in a Virtual World: the Use of the Internet by Russian Political Parties." In Oates, S., Owen, D. and Gibson, R.K. (eds.) *The Internet and Politics: Citizens, Activists and Voters* (pp. 136–62). London: Routledge.

Norris, P. (2001) *Digital Divide*. Cambridge: Cambridge University Press.

Oates, S. (2006) *Television, Democracy and Elections in Russia*. London: Routledge.

Oates, S., Owen, D., and Gibson, R.K. (eds.) (2006) *The Internet and Politics: Citizens, Activists and Voters*. London: Routledge.

OpenNet Initiative (2005). *Internet Filtering in China in 2004–2005: A Country Study*. Available online at http://www.opennetinitiative.net/studies/china/.

Polumbaum, J. (2001) "China's Media: Between Politics and the Market." *Current History* (September): 269–77.

Reilly, P. (2006) "Civil Society, the Internet and Terrorism: Case Studies from Northern Ireland." In Oates, S., Owen, D., and Gibson, R.K. (eds.) *The Internet and Politics: Citizens, Activists and Voters* (pp. 118–35). London: Routledge.

Reporters Without Borders [Reporters Sans Frontières] (2005) *The 15 Enemies of the Internet and Countries to Watch*, available online at http://www.rsf.org/print.php3?id_article=15613.

Ronfeldt, D., Arquilla, J., Fuller, G.E., and Fuller, M. (1998) *The Zapatista Social Netwar in Mexico*, Santa Monica: Rand Corporation.

Taubman, G. (1998) "A Not-So World Wide Web: The Internet, China, and the Challenges to Nondemocratic Rule." *Political Communication* 15 (2): 255–72.

Thomas, T.L. (n.d.) "Manipulating the Mass Consciousness: Russian and Chechen 'Information War' Tactics in the 2nd Chechen–Russian Conflict." Fort Leavenworth, Kansas: Foreign Military Studies Office/Joint Reserve Intelligence Center. Available online at http://leav-www.army.mil/fmso/documents/chechiw.htm.

Tucker, D. (2001) "What's New about the New Terrorism and How Dangerous Is It?," *Terrorism and Political Violence* 13: 1–14.

Weinmann, G. (2004) *www.terror.net: How Modern Terrorists Use the Internet*. Washington, DC: United States Institute for Peace.

Research Methods for Media and Politics

10

Central points

- A knowledge of research methods will allow you to design and carry out appropriate projects to address intriguing questions about media and politics.
- It is important to structure your research question in a hypothesis with clearly defined dependent and independent variables.
- In-depth interviews can provide much interesting description about the media and politics, but can be difficult to integrate into a good research design.
- Focus groups allow researchers to gather qualitative information to illuminate subtle points about the relationship between media and politics.
- Content analysis gives researchers the ability to provide convincing data for political communication theories.
- Survey data is particularly useful in understanding the media audience.

Introduction

10.1 Many students of media and politics show a lot of enthusiasm for the idea of being investigative reporters, but they are often markedly less interested in becoming investigative social scientists. In fact, the roles are not that different. Despite their somewhat glamorous reputation, investigative journalists spent a great deal of time in the mundane work of researching their stories, digging through archives, checking background facts, and conducting interviews. They develop and hone a wide range of skills in order to collect data. Just as investigative reporters need to develop skills for collecting information, social scientists also need to hone their own investigative powers. The first thing a social scientist needs to do is to identify the central question that he or she wishes to investigate. This is known as *hypothesis formation*. A hypothesis is the informed speculation, which is set up to be tested, about the possible relationship between one or more elements of a scientific inquiry. Here are some examples of hypotheses discussed in earlier chapters of this book:

- Owners of media outlets have a strong influence on the coverage of the news.
- Negative advertising in political campaigns alienates voters, causing turnout to decline and people to become disengaged with politics.
- Modern military management of war coverage leads to sanitized reporting of conflict.
- The internet can contribute to political protest, but is more effective when used as a catalyst with offline events and causes.

In the case of each hypothesis, researchers need to consider how to define their dependent and independent variables. A dependent variable is an element that is casually influenced by another variable. Independent variables are elements that have causal impacts on another variable. This may sound a bit tangled, but it is important to try – as much as possible – to isolate different elements of the research project. Essentially, you need to be clear whether you are looking at an aspect of the political sphere (the dependent variable) that is affected by elements in society or the very things (the independent variables) that are affecting this factor. For example, many researchers are interested in the link between political advertising and success in elections. They are aware, however, that the presence of political advertising is just one of many factors that influence how people vote. Thus, if they were going to state their research plan in terms of variables, one way to do this would be a define "voter choice" as a dependent variable, with the independent variables of political ads, party affiliation, concern over electoral issues, and attractiveness of individual candidates. In this way, the relevant factors in the hypothesis under study are defined and clarified. This makes it possible for researchers then to gather the appropriate information to measure the variables and, eventually, to try to understand the relative influence of the independent variables (ads, party affiliation, issues, and personality of candidates) on the dependent variable of voter choice.

If you do not have a central hypothesis and clearly defined variables, it becomes difficult to carry out meaningful research. All of your research should be aimed at investigating either your dependent or independent variables. As the research process progresses, you may find you need to refine, modify, or even discard particular variables. You also may find that you have missed a very important element that helps to shed light on the relationship between media and politics. You can add variables later in the process, but it is important to try to stick to your research design as much as possible.

When you are gathering information about your variables – and some central methods of data gathering are listed below – you need to take care that your measurements are both valid and reliable. Making sure your data are valid means that you really are measuring what you are attempting to measure. For example, if you are interested in investigating regular media use of British citizens, the question of "which newspaper did you read today?" will not generate a valid response. Rather, you need to ask "which newspaper do you read regularly?" Otherwise, you will have answers that reflect a particular day that could well be atypical (such as a Sunday or a day in which a major event occurred and the individual questioned quite unusually chose to buy a different newspaper). In addition, the way you gather data needs to be reliable in the sense that if you ask the question a number of times, you will get pretty much the same answer. For example, the question "What do you think of our leaders?" is too vague. The respondent might refer to the local government, the national government, or even business leaders to answer the question. The question will not generate a reliable response. Researchers must develop questions that are as clear and precise as possible, such as "How would you evaluate the performance of President Bush in the aftermath of 9/11 on a scale of 1 to 10, in which 1 is very poor and 10 is very good?" This would generate much more reliable data for a researcher.

Social science researchers have an array of methods that allow them to refine their variables and investigate their hypotheses (see Table 10.1). These are broadly divided into qualitative and quantitative research. Quantitative refers to data that are numerical, while qualitative refers to data that are non-numeric, such as words, images, sounds, etc. In reality, there is not always such a strict division between qualitative and quantitative data. For example, content-analysis coders typically identify the existence of various themes, key words, or images. If the sample is large enough, these findings can be coded as numbers and entered into a statistical analysis program – turning qualitative data into quantitative data. In general, though, qualitative data is often considered less "scientific" and more "descriptive," so care must be taken to show how it fits into a scientific inquiry.

The sections below will discuss in more detail the role of some of the central methods used for the study of political communication from a social-science perspective. The methods discussed below are in-depth interviews, focus groups, content analysis, and a brief look at the role of public opinion data. This is not a comprehensive review; rather, it is designed to give a quick

Table 10.1 Central qualitative and quantitative methods

Method name	Type	Example
In-depth interviews	Qualitative	Transcriptions of one-hour discussions with a dozen BBC reporters and editors discussing how TV news stories are selected, produced, and edited.
Focus groups	Qualitative	Groups of eight Russian citizens talking about their attitudes toward television news and the framing of terrorist threat in the media.
Content analysis	Qualitative/Quantitative	A categorization of items on the U.S. nightly news in the two months before the presidential campaign to see which issues are mentioned most frequently – and in what context.
Public opinion surveys	Quantitative	A Pew survey on use and attitudes toward the mass media. Generally has at least 100 respondents.

and useful introduction to some of the central tools in political science analysis. In addition to reflecting on the value of each method for researching a particular hypothesis, researchers should develop their specific research tools with care. In particular, pilot studies are very valuable. Although researchers craft interview questions, focus group guides, and content-analysis coding sheets with as much care as possible, experimentation is very important. Thus, a small "pilot" in which researchers try out the interview questions on one person, the focus-group guide with one group, and the content-analysis scheme on a small set of news output is crucial. This will allow for important adjustments in the questions or the coding scheme before a large amount of time is invested in the research. Researchers also should think about the "generalizability" of their research, which is how authoritative the study will be in drawing broad conclusions about trends in media and politics. The qualitative methods outlined below are not designed to automatically reflect a broad point of view. Rather, they are designed for in-depth investigation of particular aspects of the relationship of the media to the political sphere. Thus, focus groups of students discussing their use of the internet cannot be factored to the population at large. They can, however, shed important light on the relationship between students and the internet.

A final key point is about the ethical relationship between the researcher and the subjects. A researcher has an obligation to both inform and protect his or her subjects in experiments. The subjects in research projects have the right to be informed about why you are gathering the data and how it will be used (to the extent that it does not unduly influence their opinions). Unless explicitly stated and agreed to in advance, the subjects have the right to anonymity and the researcher must present the findings in such a way as to protect that anonymity. In repressive political situations in which there could be harassment or even arrest for the expression of opinions counter to the government, a researcher must take particular care.

In-depth interviews

10.2 One of the most common research methods suggested by students for their projects is the in-depth interview. Whether they are testing the idea that media owners influence editorial coverage or how people decide to vote, students are attracted to the idea of getting in touch with the people involved and asking them questions directly. Unfortunately, however, in-depth interviews are often not the best approach to gathering data for media and politics research projects. In many cases, the information the students are seeking from elites already exists in published interviews. In addition, busy media professionals and political leaders will not have the time for student interviews. Finally, students often don't realize the amount of time needed for meticulous interview preparation, transcription, and analysis of the findings.

Interviews for research fall into two broad categories. First, there is the structured interview, in which the researcher creates a set of relatively narrow questions for the respondent to answer. The second category type is the unstructured interview, in which the researcher gives the respondent the topic and a few questions, but generally encourages the subject to talk freely in a general way. In practice, even the best-organized "structured" interviews tend to have some unstructured elements, as people answer questions quite differently, may refuse to answer others, and often go off on tangents. By the same token, the interviewer might decide to follow up on certain statements, ideas, or themes instead of sticking to a particular script.

The key to a good interview is careful preparation. You should not set up an interview to ask a busy person basic factual questions. The researcher needs to read all the relevant background material. For example, if a researcher wanted to interview Ted Turner about his reasons for founding CNN, he or she would need to read a wide range of published information (including Turner's autobiography) about the establishment of CNN. With easy internet access to a wide range of information, researchers are able to become informed on virtually all subjects. The people you interview, particularly those with busy careers, will not respond well to uninformed or naïve questions. On the other hand, they will typically appreciate well-informed and knowledgeable questions that show the interviewer has taken the time to prepare properly.

Given the existence of archival material on the internet and in print, researchers should consider quite seriously the value of in-depth interviews for their research. In the case of any public figure, it is likely that there are several interviews already in print and easy to access. Many people have auto-biographies or biographies that provide a wealth of detail. It is likely that the questions have been asked and answered, which will save you time. If you review the material and believe there are additional questions that are key to your research – and that you have a chance at truthful answers from your interview subject – then you can craft a good set of interview questions to fill in these blanks. There are times when an interview with a key individual can provide a critical piece of information in a research project, but this is rela-tively rare. While students should be commended for their desire to gather original data, interviews are often not the best way to obtain useful informa-tion for a research project. The central pitfalls with using interviews as a research method tool are the following:

- *Access to respondents.* For much research – particularly about news production – researchers need access to key editorial personnel at news organizations. Not only are these people extremely busy, often they are not comfortable being interviewed by researchers about their decision-making processes or other issues.
- *Obtaining reliable and valid information.* Getting appropriate answers from interview respondents is quite difficult. It is almost impossible to have a series of individuals who will respond to questions in the same way. Other people cannot or will not tell you the truth, for reasons ranging from business confidentiality to fear for their safety in some authoritarian regimes. For example, when asked about receiving bribes from candidates in Russia, journalists and news producers generally claimed that they were not even offered (much less accepted) money in exchange for favorable coverage. However, it was widely known among both candidates and reporters in Russia that this is a common practice (European Institute for the Media, 2000). This calls into question the value of interviews in many contexts.
- *Establishing and maintaining rapport.* Both structured and unstructured interviews cre-ate challenges for the researchers and respondents. The interviewer must be a sym-pathetic listener, yet remain in control of the interview process. This is a difficult balancing act, as you must know when to encourage a respondent to elaborate – and how to get them to stop talking too much about the wrong things as well! The interviewer must keep his or her distance while at the same time maintaining a relatively friendly environment. This is particularly difficult if you are seeking information that the respon-dent might view as "negative," i.e., that newspaper owners influence news coverage or that reporters are biased toward a particular group.
- *Time.* In-depth interviews are surprisingly time-consuming. Although it is possible to con-duct brief interviews over the phone or even via an exchange of email, these are not par-ticularly satisfying. As a result, you will need to schedule the time to make the interview arrangements, prepare all the background material, develop a set of questions, travel to the interview location, conduct the interview, and analyze the results. Many researchers find it important to transcribe the interview, which is time-consuming if you don't have the funds to pay someone to do it. All of this work must be done before the analysis of the information or the results are written up.

Upon completion of the interview, it is time to analyze and write up the results. The key point is to examine the interview proceedings to see how the information contributes to your research. Did the interview reveal any additional information about your dependent or independent variables? Does it contradict or confirm what you had earlier learned about the subject? Do you feel that the interview respondent was candid with you? If not, what does that suggest about your topic? Even when attempting structured interviews, it can be quite difficult to compare the results of different in-depth interviews because of the variation in individuals and responses. You may have had excellent rapport with one respondent, but barely managed to get another person to respond at all to the same set of questions.

Interviews are hard work, but sometimes they provide critical insight into a particularly puzzling situation. In 1999, I was assigned to interview journalists, editors, and news producers for a report on media performance in the 1999 Russian elections (European Institute for the Media, 2000). While working on the report, I interviewed a journalist who wrote about television for a Moscow newspaper. One of the things she said to me was that it seemed to her that political parties were nothing more than "broadcast parties" (*yeferniyie partii*), created for television but with no roots in the electorate. From that conversation grew an entire theory about these parties that are only "screen-deep," called "broadcast" parties. Thus, sometimes one comment in a series of interviews or comments that are threaded throughout several interviews will add unique – and irreplaceable – illumination to a research project.

Key points about using interviews for researching media and politics

- The prospect of conducting interviews might seem exciting and interesting, but you must consider carefully if you are really adding to your knowledge.
- The central challenges of interviewing include access to respondents; obtaining valid and reliable information from interview subjects; establishing and maintaining rapport during the interview; and the significant amount of time invested in organizing, conducting, and analyzing each interview.
- Interviews can add color and insight, but you must do background research carefully to make sure you are asking relevant, fresh, and useful questions.

Focus groups

10.3 In focus groups, a researcher brings together a group of people for an organized discussion about ideas and issues. There is no particular "magic number" for the number of focus groups participants. This varies from discipline to discipline and country to country. Practically speaking, however, it is hard to have a meaningful discussion with more than a dozen people in the room. The optimal size for a focus group is between six and ten people, which allows for a range of voices and still retains a degree of cogency.

Projects try to have as many groups as time and budgets will allow. As focus groups are not designed to create a "critical mass" in terms of numbers, there is no hard and fast rule about the minimum or maximum number of groups. However, you would probably need a total of about 100 respondents in eight or more groups to be able to reach any general conclusions. By the same token, more than about 30 focus groups would start to become quite difficult to analyze (unless you were examining a range of different groups that were deliberately divided into certain characteristics such as age, gender, level of education, ethnicity, etc.).

The idea behind a focus group is that in a relatively intense, guided discussion of an hour or more, people will find the interaction stimulating and provide a range of open opinions. In addition, they will interact with both the moderator and the other members of the group to provide insights on a dynamic range of expressions regarding their thoughts and feelings. Focus groups are particularly useful when researchers are trying to:

- Examine a range of ideas or feelings;
- Understand differences in perspectives between groups or categories of people;
- Uncover factors that influence opinions, behavior, or motivation;
- Deliberately look for ideas that will emerge from the group interaction;
- Test ideas in a pilot situation;
- Ascertain the key issues in a broad subject area in order to figure out the right questions to ask in a large public opinion survey;
- Capture the nuance of the language and the ways people talk about certain issues.

For example, older researchers might convene focus groups of young internet users to find out more about the social conventions of online chat rooms. In addition, focus groups can give researchers from one culture relatively quick insight into another culture. This is why I used focus groups in Russia to learn about how Russians felt about their media and how they assessed election campaigns in 1999–2004. This was particularly important to the project because the data from public opinion surveys on Russian media use sometimes seemed quite contradictory, in that Russians reported that they trusted the state-run television although they knew much of the coverage was biased. Focus groups revealed that the notion of "trust" in television for Russians was not the same thing as expecting a station to be balanced or objective. Rather, Russians "trusted" their main state channel to try to put the best face on the many difficulties confronting the young Russian state, which often means omitting or ignoring bad news (Oates, 2006).

Organizing and conducting focus groups is a difficult but rewarding process. Focus groups are even more complicated to organize than a series of interviews. You will need to make decisions about who you want to recruit to take part in the groups – and who you can reasonably persuade to take part in the groups. Unlike public opinion surveys, focus groups are not meant to generate opinions that can then be projected onto an entire population. Rather, they are useful for guiding researchers in the right direction toward developing theories to explain some of the puzzles in media and politics. The first thing the researcher must consider for focus groups is the set of questions to ask. He or she must write a moderator's guide that will be used with all of the groups. It is best to start with a round of quick introductions and relatively easy, non-controversial questions. For example, in our research on election campaigns in Russia, the U.S., and the U.K., we generally started by asking people which media they used daily – and then asked them which media outlets they used in the campaign. The guide then moved on to more thought-provoking questions, such as how the focus-group participants felt about the fairness of the election coverage and why they chose to vote for certain candidates. The focus groups were not asked about more sensitive issues, such as reactions to the Iraq War and terrorist acts, until toward the end of the group.

It is surprisingly difficult to predict how useful questions will be in the focus groups. For example, in a series of focus groups just after the U.S. presidential election of 2004, people in a pilot group were asked to talk about political advertising. However, most of the group members claimed they couldn't remember any particular advertisements (which was quite surprising for the researchers, particularly given the hundreds of millions spent on television ads by George W. Bush and John Kerry). In subsequent groups, the respondents were shown a set of election advertisements (both pro-Bush and pro-Kerry) and asked to comment on them. In addition, original plans to talk about the role of the terrorist threat in the U.S. election campaign had to be modified because the respondents did not see overt links. However, once a set of questions got them to talk about how they felt about 9/11, it was clear that many of those emotions spilled into their assessment of the two candidates in the 2004 elections.

As a result, you need to think quite hard about which group to target for focus group research. For example, if you are puzzled about why young people do not vote in as large numbers as older citizens, you should organize groups of young people. Preferably, the groups should include both those who vote and those who do not, in order to get a cross-section of the behavioral patterns. If you are interested in how much attention people pay to election campaigns, you might want to formulate groups that span a range of ages. It is important to consider, however, whether the group will feel comfortable enough together to have a reasonable discussion. In Russia, researchers tend to divide groups by age, as younger people have traditionally deferred to older people in groups. In my recent project in the U.K. on the framing of terrorist threat in election campaigns, groups were recruited through clubs and places of employment in order to find individuals who had some existing links and could engage more readily with one another. We also divided the U.S. groups by age, but we weren't as concerned about whether strangers would be ready to talk in the U.S. The knowledge of the cultures made us confident that Americans will talk readily in a group of strangers while British participants will be more reticent. In all three of the countries, we had to "pre-screen" focus-group participants to make sure that they used major media sources on a regular basis. In a pilot group, it turned out that some people hadn't seen the news in months, which meant they didn't have much to say about news coverage in general.

Recruiting a group is one thing; controlling the people in it is something else again. It takes a talented, experienced, and rather strong-willed moderator to manage to engage the group in the question set, elicit honest responses from all of the participants, and strike a balance between a lively conversation and sticking to the topic. Sometimes participants genuinely disagree and it is down to the moderator to keep the atmosphere peaceful and productive. It is difficult to keep the more talkative people with relatively strong opinions from overwhelming the quieter participants. If you let the dominant individuals take over the groups, however, you have little chance of getting a useful and genuine range of opinions. The ability to control focus groups and move individuals usefully (and tactfully) through a set of questions definitely improves with practice. This is why experienced moderators are typically quite well paid.

Once you have completed your focus groups, it is time to analyze the findings. As with in-depth interviews, interpreting the findings is both art and science. Although it is expensive and time-consuming, it is difficult to analyze focus groups without a written transcript. Researchers typically film the focus groups (and also use a back-up voice recorder) so that accurate transcripts can be made. It is surprisingly difficult to tell most speakers apart just on audio tape. Watching the film can be very illuminating for the researcher as well, in particular as people's body language and facial expression can be quite revealing. The significant data for most projects, however, lie in the words spoken by the focus-group participants. A researcher can glean impressions and ideas from reading the transcripts, but this data will have to be organized in a more accessible way for research reports. There are a range of different approaches to the reporting of focus group data, including:

- *A general written overview and impressions.* Researchers write a narrative of what they perceive to be the important central ideas and themes. This can make interesting reading, but often leaves the reader unconvinced of the scientific nature of the exercise.
- *Identifying particular themes and keywords.* For example, if you conducted ten focus groups on internet use among 16- to 18-year-olds and asked about personal blogs, you would probably focus in on every mention of "blog" in the transcript. This would no doubt appear fairly frequently, so you would need to devise additional keywords or themes for further work on the data. For example, you could further break it into categories of "flirting and blogs," "schoolwork and blogs," and "politics and blogs." A coding scheme such as this would allow you to

organize and analyze the statements of the focus-group participants across a number of groups. At the end of the analysis, you could produce a general statement about blog usage in these particular areas.

- *Highlighting quotations.* One of the best things about focus group research is the interesting, enlightening, or sometimes downright strange things that people say. It can be quite powerful to include some of the direct quotations from people in the focus groups (while maintaining anonymity). However, be aware that these quotations should be introduced properly, they should illustrate a point, and should be kept relatively short.
- *Software for content analysis.* There are well-established software programs (such as NVivo) that aid content analysis. Qualitative analysis software is designed to help researchers organize the data found in documents. Although qualitative software analysis can be a useful tool, it cannot replace careful research design as well as the identification of the central themes, keywords, and interactions among your participants. On a positive note, qualitative research software has become much more affordable and easier to learn in the past few years.[1]

Key points about using focus groups to research media and politics

- Focus groups can provide quick and useful insight into the nuances of how people think about media and politics but they do *not* provide findings that can be generalized to an entire population.
- You need to decide in advance which questions to ask, which groups you plan to use for focus groups, and how to structure them to get a good rapport.
- Moderating focus groups is a delicate and tricky task.
- You will need to carry out careful content analysis to get the most out of your focus-group research.

Content analysis

10.4 Media content is one of the central three areas in the study of media and politics. In the media research model used throughout this volume, media content is located between news production and audience consumption of the media. Without a thorough examination of actual media content, analysis of the role of the media in the political sphere would be mostly speculative. Data on media content add enormously to the understanding and analysis of media and politics. That said, content analysis is challenging. It is also very time-consuming, although it is helpful that much media material is now archived in electronic form on the internet. Researchers need to trawl through an enormous amount of printed and/or visual matter to identify key themes and trends in coverage. For example, consider the study of a single U.S. presidential election. The relevant content for this would include election news for the hectic finale between Labor Day and Election Day; almost two years of primary elections and campaigning before Election Day; tens of thousands of commercials; websites of parties, candidates, and support groups; political blogs; and typically now debates as well. Trying to collect – much less code and analyze – this volume of information would be a monumental task. It's important to realize that you will have to pick a significant sample of material rather than try to collect, code, and analyze all relevant content.

The first step in a content analysis exercise is to focus in on the most relevant content for the study. Is it newspapers, television, the internet, or radio, that are the most important for your study? However, it is not simply a question of deciding what would be best for the study – it is also a question of what is available. While newspaper archives are relatively easy to access (although earlier ones often are not in electronic, searchable form), the other three categories are more complex. There are organizations that collect and archive television news, but it can be costly to get access and they do not record every channel at all times. The most prominent collection of U.S. television footage is at the Vanderbilt Archive (http://tvnews.vanderbilt.edu/). In the U.K., researchers can use an archive at the British Universities Film and Video Council (http://www.bufvc.ac.uk/) via membership if they are affiliated with an educational institution that has a membership (and subject to certain other conditions). While many researchers receive grants to collect television footage, they are constrained from putting the material in a central archive due to copyright restrictions. As a general rule of thumb in television research, consider a research project in which you can record the programs yourself (which is acceptable if you use the material only for research).

Radio coverage is even more ephemeral, although transcripts for some programs may be available. In addition, the internet can be particularly frustrating. Projects that have been launched to archive the internet are far from encyclopedic or easy to access. Attempting to download websites over a period of time can be frustrating as well, even with automated computer "spiders" that will save entire websites. Any student or researcher working on a particular site should be sure to download as much as possible and store it, as sites can change or disappear overnight.

The issues involved in content collection mean that researchers need to be very disciplined about which content to study. There are logical ways to narrow the choice. For example, if you are interested in change over time – such as the way that the spouses of candidates are covered in the news or how journalists talk about the environment – the printed media will provide the most accessible record over time. However, if you would like to look at how female candidates are framed on television in elections, you can arrange to tape a month or two of the evening news during an election campaign. The evening news is a small part of the daily coverage, but it is a significant and important element of news production. Sometimes you can contact individual news outlets for content, but be aware that most of them do not keep archives for any length of time and most are not obligated to share them with researchers.

Once you have decided on a sample, you need to devise a coding frame. While an analytical framework is important for in-depth interviews and focus groups, it is particularly key in coding media content. If there is no coding frame, the research becomes more a description of content rather than a scientific attempt to qualify the coverage. As a result, for most content analysis projects of any size, it is important to have both well-developed coding instruments and a team of coders trained to implement that frame. A coding instrument is essentially a "fill-in-the-blank" sheet for content coders. It is developed and written by researchers in order to mine the appropriate data from the content. It should be designed in such a way that it is both reliable (different coders almost always arrive at the same interpretation of a coding category) and valid (it is a reflection of what the researcher is attempting to measure). Some of the information is quite straightforward, such as date of publication or broadcast, which newspaper or news show the item appeared in, the headline of the piece, etc. Typically, coders will look for the mention of a particular word, issue, or individual. They will note the overall length of the piece.

At the end of the coding, the researcher should have a data base with the information. The coders should be coding in the same way. This is tested by having the coders all code the same material in a blind test. The results of this "intercoder reliability" test should show that the coders are coding the same thing at least 80 percent of the time (although well-trained and experienced coders should achieve an even better rate). If coders cannot agree and there is little inter-coder reliability, it usually means that the coding instrument is faulty. For example, in my research we could never achieve reasonable inter-coder reliability as to whether a televised news item was "positive" or "negative" about a candidate or party in Russia. Eventually, we dropped the category, although coders made notations about anything they suspected was biased either for or against a particular candidate or political party.

Each type of media has different requirements in coding. In newspapers, it is important to note where the article was played; the headline size and style; whether there were any graphics with the article; and, in some cases, who wrote the article. The analysis of radio broadcasts can include tone and expression of the announcers (sometimes regional accent is relevant as well). For television coverage, the demands on coders increase substantially, as the expression, voice, and appearance of the announcer can be relevant. In addition, coders have to consider the use of images, the appearance of subjects in news stories, as well as the use of music and other background sounds. Researchers will need to make decisions, usually after reviewing some material and trying out a pilot scheme, on which elements can be reasonably captured in a reliable and valid way in a coding scheme.

The internet provides a whole new generation of challenges for content analysis, not least of which because of the dynamic and expanding nature of the online world. A researcher needs to consider which element of the internet he or she plans to study (i.e., blogs, podcasts, web pages, email, forums, etc., as discussed in Chapters 8 and 9). There is audio, graphic, video, and text on the internet. The way in which web pages – and their hyperlinks – are organized and displayed is also relevant.

One of the key studies of the internet has been to consider how political parties use the Web. In 2000, Rachel Gibson and Stephen Ward published an article about coding web page content that became an important standard tool in internet analysis. Under the Gibson and Ward scheme, coders identify the presence of various features from a list of internet tools that represent information provision, resource generation, openness, participation, networking, and campaigning. Gibson and Ward, as well as many others, have used this scheme to compare and contrast how effectively political actors appear to be using the internet (for example, see Gibson et al., 2004). In particular, Gibson and Ward have used this scheme to make comparisons of how political parties use the internet. As internet features expand with the rapid technological capability, this scheme is now being augmented and refined by other social scientists. The Gibson and Ward scheme, however, remains a good place to start when attempting to compare different websites.

Below are some examples of research using content analysis:

- *Kaid and Johnston (2000)* examined paid advertising in U.S. election campaigns and identified several key elements of advertising to determine which candidates were more likely to use negative ads. This allows for a discussion and analysis of why candidates use more negative ads and how this impacts the political system.
- *Iyengar (1991)* found that television news frames issues of crime in episodic ways that fail to take into account broader social problems related to crime in the U.S.
- *European Institute for the Media*. Over the course of five election campaigns from 1993 to 2000, the European Institute for the Media collected and coded the television coverage of candidates and political parties in five Russian elections. The researchers found that, in every election, state-run television devoted an unfairly large amount of time to candidates and parties favored by the Russian president. This provides convincing evidence that, despite laws that are supposed to guarantee fair and equal coverage, state-run television in Russia acted unfairly in all Russian national elections. (See European Institute for the Media reports, archived online at http://www.media-politics.com/eimreports.htm).

Key points about using content analysis

- Content analysis can provide some of the most convincing data for the study of media and politics.
- Researchers need to tailor their projects to perform content analysis on a sample that is neither too large nor too hard to find in archives.
- Television content is both more difficult to analyze and harder to find in archives.
- Content analysis demands the construction of coding frames and the training of coders to achieve good inter-coder reliability.

Public opinion surveys

10.5 Quantitative data in the field of media and politics can take many forms. For example, there are data on spending on political advertising, investment in media outlets, and the number of times a particular theme or individual is covered on television. However, the type of data that is the focus of this chapter is the result of public opinion surveys. Sometimes referred to as a poll, public opinion surveys seek to interview enough people to get a representative sample of a population. Typically using a list of specific questions (a closed-end survey instrument), researchers can get information from a large enough sample of people to then generalize those findings to a much bigger group. For example, the Pew Research Center regularly holds surveys of more than 1,000 respondents for its study of how Americans use the mass media in their political life. The construction of surveys, how to carry them out, and how to use the data properly is an entire subfield in the social sciences. That being said, knowing the basics about survey design, implementation, and data can allow a wide range of people to glean quite useful information from surveys. In addition, there is now a great deal of survey data available to researchers, particularly as the Pew Research Center makes its survey data available for free via its website. Countries such as the U.S. and the U.K. have central depositories of social science data sets and much of this information is freely available to researchers as well (details on the websites for access to these data sources are listed in Internet Resources, below). An entrepreneurial researcher can find a great deal of existing data on media and politics through these data archives.

The statistics that are generated from public opinion surveys can provide useful evidence in the study of media and politics. For example, it is particularly helpful to know the percentage of people who watch television regularly in a given country. In addition, surveys ask a variety of interesting and insightful questions about attitudes toward media and politics. However, there are a few important guidelines when using public opinion data:

- *Correlation is not causality*. This means that just because survey respondents say they use media with a particular political persuasion, it does not necessarily mean that the media outlet "caused" them to hold these views. This is best explained via example. For example, Pew surveys regularly find that a majority of people who watch Fox News are Republican. However, it is unlikely that the influence of Fox News alone is "turning" people Republican. Rather, people who were Republican to start with were likely to find Fox News to have the coverage and tone that best fit with their political outlook. Research has shown that people tend to pick media outlets that best parallel their own political views, rather than seek out media outlets that challenge their attitudes. This is a key point, because students of media and politics are particularly attracted to the "propaganda theory" of the media, i.e., that the media has immense power to mold political opinion. However, a large amount of research in democracies suggests that the power of the media is far more complex and subtle.

- *Are the data timely and relevant?* In particular, it is difficult to find data about media and politics that stretch over a span of time. Major exceptions to this are the National Election Survey in the U.S. and the British Election Survey in the U.K. These surveys have been conducted for decades (around election campaigns) and the data are available via the data archives listed below. However, particularly in the case of the British survey, there aren't that many detailed questions relating to media use. In addition, they aren't that helpful to researchers who are not interested in media and elections. The Pew Research Center provides a wide range of datasets on various issues in the media, but comparable data in other countries is harder to find.
- *The data are not fully available.* The open policy of sharing data over the internet at the Pew Center is still more the exception than the rule. Many times you can find references to a survey on media and politics in the press or another academic source. However, most authors don't release the full details of the survey, so you must rely only on their description. This can be frustrating, particularly if you suspect that the description is incomplete.

Chapter summary

This chapter has explored a range of research methods used in the study of media and politics. It has discussed how to formulate a useful hypothesis as well as relevant dependent and independent variables. In the social sciences, research typically is organized around a central hypothesis that allows researchers to create, augment, or even challenge central theories in the discipline. It is key for researchers to understand their central hypothesis, as the development of their dependent and independent variables will evolve from this core idea.

In terms of research tools, this chapter took a brief look at in-depth interviewing, focus groups, content analysis, and public opinion data in political communication research. While all of these methods can contribute to a research report, all of them also require a degree of training and caution for implementation. While in-depth interviews are an appealing prospect for research, they require more time for preparation and analysis than most researchers realize. In turn, focus groups offer a relatively quick and exciting way to explore attitudes, but are also somewhat tricky to organize, moderate, and analyze. Neither in-depth interviews nor focus groups can provide opinions that can automatically be assumed to reflect public opinion in general. Rather, interviews and focus groups provide greater insight into the issues surrounding media and politics for particular individuals or groups. Both of these methods provide a way for a researcher to think about how to approach a question or ways to design a large public opinion survey.

Content analysis is a key tool in the study of media and politics. It also requires rigorous preparation and application. In particular, researchers should be aware that merely finding the raw data can be difficult. As content analysis can be quite time-consuming, researchers should consider quite carefully the scope of the project. Coding broadcast content is even more complicated than coding printed material.

Finally, quantitative data can add a key dimension to research. In particular, large public opinion surveys about attitudes toward the media and politics are very useful. However, it is important that a researcher not become unduly focused on large numbers and fail to consider the underlying structure of the survey. Are the questions asked relevant to your research? Can you understand the reporting of the survey? Do the questions and the data appear to be both reliable and valid? As with other research methods in media and politics, quantitative information is useful only if it is carried out professionally and if it is relevant to your central hypothesis.

Study questions

1 Develop a hypothesis about the relationship between media and the political sphere. Define one dependent variable and at least three independent variables.
2 When, and for which reasons, are in-depth interviews more appropriate than public opinion surveys?
3 Give examples and briefly discuss types of research that would be particularly appropriate for focus-group research.
4 Discuss the main challenges of designing and applying content analysis coding schemes for both print and television content. Give some examples.
5 What are the main methodological challenges of doing research on the political impact of the internet?

Reading guide

Students can find a comprehensive overview of research methods in Alan Bryman's *Social Research Methods* (2004). For a guide with more emphasis on political science, see Burnham et al., *Research Methods in Politics* (2004). A useful and very readable guide to focus groups is Krueger and Casey's *Focus Groups: A Practical Guide for Applied Research* (2000). A useful, general guide with examples of coding frames is Hansen et al., *Mass Communication Research Methods* (1998). An important introductory text for content analysis is Krippendorf (2004). In addition, *Media Research Methods* by Bertrand and Hughes (2005) provides an overview of analysis of audiences, institutions, and texts for media studies.

Internet resources

http://tvnews.vanderbilt.edu/   The Vanderbilt Television News Archive collection at Vanderbilt University near Nashville, Tennessee, holds the world's most extensive and complete archive of television news. Material is available for a fee, although the cost is lower for those affiliated with institutions holding membership in the archive.

http://www.bufvc.ac.uk/ The British Universities Film and Video Council holds an archive of video footage (including news) available to researchers who are affiliated with educational institutions that are members.

http://people-press.org/ The Pew Research Center for the People and the Press provides information on U.S. elections, attitudes, and the media in detailed, but comprehensible reports (free access).

http://www.icpsr.umich.edu/ Located at the University of Michigan, the Inter-University Consortium for Political and Social Research is the world's largest archive of digital social science data. Access to the data is via universities who are members in the ICPSR scheme.

http://www.data-archive.ac.uk/ The U.K. Data Archive, hosted by the University of Essex, provides a gateway to data and studies about British politics, including research on political communication. The data is available via universities who are members of the archive.

Note

1 For example, see the QSR International website (http://www.qsrinternational.com/) for a discussion and demonstration of NVivo qualitative analysis software.

References

Bertrand, I. and Hughes, P. (2005) *Media Research Methods: Audiences, Institutions, Texts.* Basingstoke: Palgrave Macmillan.

Bryman, A. (2004) *Social Research Methods.* 2nd edn. Oxford: Oxford University Press.

Burnham, P., Gilland, K., Grant, W., and Layton-Henry, Z. (2004) *Research Methods in Politics (Political Analysis).* Basingstoke: Palgrave Macmillan.

European Institute for the Media (2000) *Monitoring the Media Coverage of the December 1999 Parliamentary Elections in Russia: Final Report.* Düsseldorf: European Institute for the Media. Available online at http://www.media-politics.com/eimreports.htm.

Gibson, R.K. and Ward, S. (2000) "A Proposed Methodology for Studying the Function and Effectiveness of Party and Candidate Websites." *Social Science Computer Review* 18 (3): 301–19.

Gibson, R.K., Römmele, A., and Ward, S.J. (eds.) (2004) *Electronic Democracy: Mobilisation, Organisation and Participation via New ICTs.* London: Routledge.

Hansen, A., Cottle, S., Negrine, R., and Newbold, C. (1998) *Mass Communication Research Methods.* Basingstoke: Palgrave Macmillan.

Iyengar, S. (1991) *How Television Frames Political Issues.* Chicago: University of Chicago Press.

Kaid, L.L. and Johnston, A. (2000) *Videostyle in Presidential Campaigns: Style and Content of Televised Political Advertising.* New York: Praeger.

Krippendorff, K. (2004) *Content Analysis: An Introduction to Its Methodology.* London: Sage.

Krueger, R. and Casey, M.A. (2000) *Focus Groups: A Practical Guide for Applied Research.* 3rd edn. London: Sage.

Oates, S. (2006) *Television, Democracy and Elections in Russia.* London: Routledge.

Conclusions

This book has introduced some of the key concepts in analyzing the role of the media in the political sphere. One of the main themes is that this is a complex relationship that requires careful analysis. When we think about the interaction between the media and the political sphere, we have to consider a number of different dynamic elements that are constantly influencing one another. That is why this book has stressed the need to try to separate various elements in order to consider them in relative isolation. Part of this in done through dividing the media into three basic components – the production of news and the political environment in which it is formed; the actual content of the news; and the audience reaction to the news. While the book has discussed overarching models that strive to show how the media function within political systems, it has also emphasized the need to "think outside the box" of a single country. For example, if one suspects that ownership of the mass media matters in terms of politics, than it is important to consider various situations in which different ownership structures exist. This allows us to free ourselves from merely describing a media system within a certain political structure to actually analyzing the interaction. In this way, students and researchers have new tools for insights into the complex and fascinating relationship between media and politics.

The first chapter of the book was dedicated to some of the "big ideas" about media and politics, particularly media models. It introduced the classic four models of the press: libertarian, social responsibility, authoritarian, and Soviet. In particular, the libertarian and social responsibility models have been key to the discussion throughout the book. The U.S. conforms to the libertarian, or commercial, model quite well. It is a system that is essentially consumer-driven, in which news is generally produced by commercial media outlets in ways to appeal to particular audiences. In many cases, this is the broadest audience possible, leading to fears that media outlets ignore complex issues and "dumb down" the news into entertainment that does not adequately inform citizens. The social responsibility model, exemplified by the British broadcasting sphere, encourages journalists to mold coverage into useful information to foster an informed, civic society. While this assigns more power to the media to lead society, it also discourages the tactics of scaremongering or failing to cover critical (albeit dull or unpopular) issues in the media. However, the British media sphere is schizophrenic, with newspapers coming closer to the libertarian model with more audience-driven news production. Although these media models and others introduced in the chapter help us to think about the links between the media and political spheres, models also have their drawbacks. In particular, models can blur or obscure important issues of how news is produced and sometimes have trouble "traveling" across country boundaries.

Chapters 2 and 3 focused on the idea of the News Production Model, to try to reach beyond the central media models and think about the influences on news production – particular in the three key case studies of the US, the U.K., and Russia. Chapter 4 discussed the audience reaction to news. The News Production Model allows us to analyze the relative influence of the political environment, media norms, media regulation, ownership, as well as the impact of the journalistic and public relations professions on the production of news. By comparing these elements in different countries, it is clear that influences on shaping the news are vastly different long before the journalist in the newsroom turns on his or her computer to start writing a story. In the U.S., there is a democratic regime with a long tradition of freedom of speech, which is found in the Constitution and supported by the legal system. However, there are still tensions between the limits on freedom of speech and national security, especially in the wake of 9/11. The U.S. media system fits well into the libertarian media model and the notion of "objectivity" is still central to the journalistic ethos in the country. However, this has been challenged by both the overt bias and the nationalistic tone of the popular Fox News Network. The U.K. is also a democracy with a tradition of freedom of speech, albeit with no "balance of power" in the American sense and with more controls on the media industry. The norm in the British media is "balance," but this is adhered to far more in the socially responsible broadcast sector than in the more commercialized, libertarian elements of the British press. The British Broadcasting Corporation (BBC), as an organization funded directly by fees from the public, is a major influence on journalistic norms for broadcasters. However, evidence shows that while the BBC is supposed to be accountable to the public, the government itself does have influence over this major media outlet.

It is clear there are flaws in the democratic model of the news production in both the U.S. and the U.K. In particular, there are legitimate questions about whether a commercial system can truly serve the best needs of a society in the U.S. American journalists report that they do not feel independent as a profession, with the ability to challenge their media organizations or to have political power as a group (see Chapter 3). This is echoed by their British peers, who are more tightly controlled via the Lobby system of government information briefings. On the other hand, the U.S. public shows enthusiasm for its media system, seeing flaws and making complaints, but generally remaining "switched on" to the political information from television and the internet. In the U.K., there is widespread support for the BBC and the notion of socially responsible broadcast media. In addition, there is relatively high (albeit dropping) newspaper consumption. In Britain, this shows that some citizens will happily consume high-brow BBC shows alongside sensationalistic tabloid offerings. While the public relations sphere grows increasingly large and pervasive, there is no widespread evidence that it has fundamentally changed the news production system in the U.S. or the U.K.

The case of Russia throws into relief the issues of media freedom suggested by the News Production Model. The Russian media could be said to operate in a "neo-Soviet" media system, in which restraint on the part of media organizations and self-censorship on the part of journalists has led to the narrowing of information available to Russian citizens. There is great interest and attention to the central television stations in Russia, more so than in other countries with a broader use of cable, satellite, and internet outlets. Both state and commercial media outlets in Russia toe the Kremlin line. They are aware that if they challenge the presidential administration on sensitive issues such as the war in Chechnya or the fairness of election campaigns, they may be forced out of business by the selective application of media, financial, tax, or other legislation. Although freedom of speech is promised in the 1993 Russian Constitution, this is empty rhetoric. As the Russian system is based on oligarchic power rather than democratic principles, the promises in its Constitution and via a vast array of laws are not relevant. Rather, the narrow terms of political debate are defined by the Kremlin as part of the process of maintaining power for the elites. As a result, Russian citizens do not have adequate information to make informed political choices. Research into citizen attitudes suggests that Russians are pragmatic about the flaws in their media system. They see a frank and free debate as destabilizing and dangerous to their fragile new nation and have strongly supported the Putin administration. Although the public is generally aware that they are not fully informed by their media, they continue to watch, trust, and approve of their central media outlets. Russians overwhelmingly reject the notion that journalists could be "objective" or "balanced," perceiving them as political players rather than political observers. Meanwhile, journalists operate primarily as political pawns in an atmosphere of physical menace and even assassination by those they challenge in their reporting. It is unsurprising that Russia has developed rather sophisticated and aggressive methods of "PR," which include smear campaigns to blacken political opponents of the Kremlin on the heavily biased state news programs.

How do media systems function under the stress of important political or violent events, such as elections, wars, or terrorist acts? Chapters 5, 6, and 7 addressed these particular issues in terms of media and politics. Elections highlight important differences that result in varying media roles even between democracies. In both the U.S. and the U.K., the role of the media in elections needs to be considered within the overall model of voting behavior. Party identification – although lower than it was decades ago – is still very important in determining vote choice, reducing the role of the mass media to influence election results. This means that the function of the media in elections is far more important when there are closely contested battles (such as in 2000 and 2004 in the U.S. and 1997 in the U.K.). There is concern with the possible "Americanization" of campaigns. This is the idea that elections have become increasingly negative, based on image rather than issues, and that getting elected is more about how well you campaign rather than how well you can govern. While there is evidence in the U.S. that campaigns have become more negative at the same time they have become much more expensive, the media do not have a strong "propaganda" effect. The media cannot sway millions of voters overnight through a few clever ads or a handful of negative news reports. However, the campaign (and hence the media) do matter when only a small number of voters are needed to change the outcome. The same is true in British elections, which are marked by a greater degree of communications strategy than in the past. However, as political parties hold significantly more power in the British system, arguably they are able to counter any of the creeping trends toward "Americanization." In addition, as paid political advertising is not allowed on British television, there is significantly less concern about mud-slinging or negative advertising turning off the public to the campaign in general.

Again, the Russian case shows that problems of American or British elections turning into "beauty contests" or "horse races" are relatively small evils when compared with the lack of the genuine will to accept the mandate of the masses. As the Russian political system was started from scratch in the first post-Soviet election in 1993, there is virtually no enduring partisan identification in Russia. At any rate, most parties do not last more than a single election. Successful presidential candidates have eschewed party affiliation, which has undermined the development of political parties as the Russian president holds most of the political party in the country. When elections are held, it is clear that Kremlin-backed parties appropriate state resources to run expensive election campaigns. Instead of making a serious attempt to cover elections as news, most Russian media show clear bias in support of their favored candidates. This is particularly true on the most influential media outlet in the country, state-run Channel 1 television. Although both American and British voters complain about the lack of substance in election campaigns, image has essentially replaced policy statements or even ideology in Russian election battles. Media-driven "broadcast" parties that rely on media image over political substance for votes have subverted the development of parties with grass roots. While the internet has developed into a deeper, broader source of information for concerned voters in the U.S. and the U.K., the Russian internet has not evolved to challenge the biased media in Russia. Russian elections have been notable for mud-slinging and dirty tricks. These elections now serve to translate power from one group of elites to another, with the bulk of the Russian media complicit in this appearance of electoral democracy. The Russian media do this by exaggerating the benefits of the Kremlin-based parties while ignoring or vilifying genuine political opponents such as the Communist Party of the Russian Federation.

War coverage is best understood not by examining how different countries handle conflict coverage, but by how this coverage has evolved since the mid-twentieth century. In particular, the perceived impact of media coverage in Southeast Asia and the "Vietnam Syndrome" has shaped the development of modern military media management across country boundaries. In Vietnam, reporters had relatively free access to the battlefield as well as newer technology that allowed them to send back moving images much more quickly than in previous wars. While this made Vietnam the first "television war" as the long conflict paralleled the rise of television as a central medium, analysis suggests that it was not negative war coverage that "lost" the war for the U.S. military. Rather, the news coverage was not particularly negative until divisions began to arise in the elites about both the conduct and legitimacy of the war. These divisions were then reflected in the media coverage to an audience that was experiencing a radical realignment toward authority and power in general in the turbulent late 1960s. However, the notion that "negative" war coverage was the significant factor in the ultimate defeat of U.S. forces in Vietnam was a powerful influence in the military's approach to information management in subsequent conflicts.

The short Falklands War between the U.K. and Argentina in 1982 introduced a new relationship between the military and the media. During the three-month war, British journalists were given only very limited access to the battlefield, operational information, or to communications equipment to transmit their stories back to Britain. In Britain itself, the government attacked and criticized news outlets, particularly the BBC, that voiced opposition to the conflict. The fact that the Falklands War was a short, very faraway, and very one-sided conflict made it relatively easy for the British Ministry of Defense to give a positive and nationalistic "spin" to the war. Although the circumstances were quite different from the long, multilateral conflict in Vietnam, the brief Falklands War demonstrated how a government could use media coverage of a conflict to support, rather than challenge, its authority and legitimacy. This media management strategy was expanded and refined very successfully by the U.S. military in the first Gulf War (1991). In this war, the U.S. military deployed two central communication strategies by allowing only a few chosen reporters access to the front via a pool system as well as by distributing compelling details and video footage via its briefings. The conflict was framed as "video war," remote from battlefield carnage, with almost no coverage of opposition to the war. The media moved from being perceived to challenge the government to becoming a positive part of the government's information strategy in maintaining public support for the war.

The role of journalists as an element of military media strategy has been further developed in the second Gulf War by the policy of allowing journalists to "embed" with the troops. This provides compelling coverage of the front lines, which supports the invasion without delving into civil and international issues that could question the legitimacy of the conflict. In addition, the patriotic mood in the wake of 9/11 makes questioning either the war – from the tactics to the justification for the U.S. invasion – unacceptable to much of the American audience. This is made particularly clear by the popularity of Fox News, which employs a patriotic coverage of the war that has clearly found broad resonance with the U.S. audience. It is noteworthy that the Russian military have not adopted the same sort of media management strategy, instead essentially imposing censorship on Chechen reporting by making it too dangerous to visit the area and releasing little meaningful information on the conflict. On the other hand, Russian citizens report that they are not particularly interested in the details of the Chechen war and are unsympathetic to the Chechen point of view. However, a propaganda war between Russia and its breakaway region of Chechnya does exist on the internet.

While the American and British governments seem to have found successful ways to manage the media during wars, the issue of terrorism coverage is far more problematic. At the heart of the problem is the knowledge that the media themselves are part of the terrorist equation: they can provide the critical "oxygen of publicity" that allows terrorists to translate relatively small acts of violence into widespread campaigns of fear. However, the notion that all terrorism can be stopped if the media cease reporting on their atrocities is too simplistic. In part, this is because the definition of who is a terrorist and who is a freedom fighter depends very much on political points of view. In fact, it is difficult to find a single model to describe the interaction between the media and terrorists because the political situations that spawn terrorism are so different. Like war coverage, coverage of terrorism tends to focus on the immediate news rather than delve into the causes of political violence. At times, this can lead to considerable concerns about terrorism, with few reasonable ideas for ways to stop the violence. For example, although the vast majority of Americans are very unlikely to be personally affected by terrorism, focus groups held in 2004 suggested that fears about terrorism and national security played an important role in the re-election of President George W. Bush. Thus, the media cannot ignore terrorist acts because they are important news.

At the same time, media can exacerbate the potential for violence by either demonizing particular political forces or failing to include them in civic dialogue. Evidence from the U.K. suggests that terrorism can be alleviated, to a degree, by the encouragement of dialogue between entrenched enemies via the media. In fact, newspaper columns were used to open a dialogue between Catholic and Protestant groups to help broker a peace agreement in Northern Ireland in the 1990s. In addition, focus groups in Britain in 2005 suggest that even in the immediate aftermath of the July 7, London terrorist bombings, British citizens are more pragmatic about terrorism and its relative threat than their American counterparts.

As with military coverage, the Russian government does not appear to have a media management plan for terrorist attacks, although there have been several high-profile attacks linked to Chechen terrorists. As coverage of these events fits into the Russian government strategy of demonizing the Chechens, no real media management is necessary. Russia is not the only country in which "demonizing" enemies is useful in terms of pursuing a particular political agenda. Many analysts argue that the aftermath of 9/11 and the fears of terrorism have allowed the Bush administration to control the news agenda. In the emotional wake of the attacks, it has been impossible to mount a serious challenge to the security "frame" of the need to invade Iraq and Afghanistan to decrease the risk of terrorist attacks on the U.S. The lack of introspection and analysis of terrorist attacks – and the role that U.S. foreign policy plays in inculcating hatred of Americans – has an eerie parallel to the lack of civic dialogue in the Russian media regarding terrorism. Findings from focus groups and content analysis of the news in both countries suggest that superpowers may have much in common in terms of demonizing their enemies, even when they share little else in terms of their media and political systems.

Chapters 8 and 9 discuss two distinct elements of the internet – its potential to build democracy as well as its ability to support protest. The conclusions in Chapter 8 on the internet and democracy suggest that the online world has not radically changed the fundamental relationship between rulers and citizens. However, this new communication medium does provide useful tools for activists to mobilize for specific political causes. It blurs the traditional distinctions between news production and news consumption. While this gives people the ability to reach a mass audience directly, it is hard to realize this potential. While it is difficult to prove that the internet has really change politics, studies of specific events suggest that the internet has the ability to act as a catalyst in certain political situations. This is particularly true when there is online and offline synergy, with the internet using its particular communication capability to build support for a specific cause or event. While the internet has not replaced the traditional media, the relationship between the traditional mass media and the online world is increasingly synergetic and symbiotic.

If the internet can sometimes act as a beacon of democracy, how effective is it at fostering protest? It is clear that the diffuse and decentralized nature of the internet offers opportunities for protestors in countries that lack freedom of speech. There is evidence that the internet can help protestors within countries disseminate information. In addition, the internet provides distinct advantages to protestors attempting to organize internationally. While this has been effective for social movements such as the Chiapas resistance in Mexico, the internet itself is not generally powerful enough to create change when faced with organized state repression. In particular, the effective management of the internet by the Chinese government shows that a determined, multi-level effort at control can effectively shut down the democratizing potential of the internet, even in a society with rapid online growth. Although there have been fears that the internet can provide particular aid to terrorist groups, there is still relatively little evidence that the internet empowers terrorists in a special way. Overall, while the internet does not appear currently to have the power to change the fundamental relationship between the political elites and the masses, it could provide access to information to contribute to challenges to repression within countries over a long period of time.

Chapter 10 presented some suggested research methods to apply to the study of media and politics. In particular, the chapter stressed that is important to structure research questions with hypotheses that clearly define the key elements under study. There is a range of methods, each with advantages and disadvantages. In-depth interviews can provide much interesting description about the media and politics, but are often difficult to integrate into a good research design. On the other hand, focus groups allow researchers to gather qualitative information to illuminate subtle points about the relationship between media and politics. However, focus groups can be difficult to organize and run effectively until you have some experience as a moderator. As the actual study of media output, content analysis gives researchers the ability to provide convincing data for theories about media and politics. At the same time, content analysis – especially of television broadcasts – can be time-consuming and somewhat complex. There is a wealth of quantitative data available via organizations that study the media, information that students and researchers can often take advantage of just by downloading over the internet. However, statistics should always be used with some caution, particularly in trying to "prove" that certain media use has a direct political effect.

Overall, this text has made an attempt to empower students and researchers in media and politics by encouraging the use of models, method, and case studies. People are often passionate about the media. The media can engage, enrage, enlighten, or merely entertain. The lines between all of these feelings evoked by the media can be quite thin or even overlap. At the same time, the media are embedded into complex and distinct political systems. Making the effort to isolate and study this fascinating relationship between the media and politics can help us to better understand our contemporary society. It's a tough job, but worth it.

Index